Travellers' guide to Southern Africa

A concise guide to the wildlife and tourist facilities of
South Africa, Botswana, Lesotho, Namibia, Swaziland
and Zimbabwe

Third edition

GEOGRAPHIA

Thornton Cox Travellers' Guides
Southern Africa

The publishers gratefully acknowledge the help in checking
this book of the Botswana, Lesotho and Swaziland government information services, of SATOUR and CAPTOUR, and
of the Zimbabwe National Tourist Board.

Originally compiled by Richard Cox

Revisions by Clive Wilson and Mike Nicol

Drawings of animals by David Cook

Line drawings by Philip Bawcombe, F.R.S.A.

Maps by Tom Stalker-Miller, M.S.I.A.

Edited by Richard Cox

© Geographia Ltd, 1981
First published by Thornton Cox Ltd, 1967
Second Revised Edition by Thornton Cox Ltd, 1974
Third Revised Edition by Geographia Ltd, 1981

Geographia Ltd
17–21 Conway St
London W1P 5HL

Set in 9/10pt Univers by
Rowland Phototypesetting Ltd, Bury St Edmunds, Suffolk
Printed in Great Britain by
The Anchor Press Ltd, Tiptree, Essex

ISBN 0 09 208200 9

Contents

Useful Facts sections follow each country's chapter

Foreword

AN INTRODUCTION TO THE GREAT
WILDLIFE RESERVES, CITIES AND BEACHES
OF SOUTHERN AFRICA

Lions and gold, ancient forts and native dancing, elephants on the wide horizons of the veld, long empty beaches, the cool white grace of Cape Dutch homesteads – Southern Africa is as many faceted as the celebrated diamonds it produces.

When Sir Francis Drake, the Elizabethan navigator, saw the Cape of Good Hope in 1580 he called it 'a most stately thing and the fairest cape we saw in the whole circumference of the earth'. Since then Cape Town has grown into one of the world's most beautiful cities, and the interior has revealed its riches of both minerals and wildlife. In this book we describe six countries of Southern Africa, each of which offers the traveller contrasts and experiences to be found in no other continent, like the Zambezi river plunging down the mile-long arc of the Victoria Falls, watched by elephants and crocodiles.

5

Zimbabwe   The wide upland country of Zimbabwe has fine game reserves, mysterious ruins, a splendid climate and excellent facilities and hotels. Zambia (mentioned but not fully described in this book) lies on the other side of the Zambezi river with plenty to see.

Botswana   West of the Falls are the up and coming game parks of Botswana, a country the size of France and teeming with wildlife, which has become the kind of promised land to international safari-goers that East Africa was in the 1900s and 1920s.

Up in the misty hills between Mozambique and the Republic of *Swaziland* South Africa sits a tiny African State, Swaziland. Its legends, its scenery and its people inspired both Rider Haggard and John Buchan in some of their best known books. While further south, *Lesotho* completely encompassed by the Republic, is Lesotho, a mountain kingdom of proudly cloaked African horsemen, that was known as Basutoland before it became independent in 1966.

South Africa   The giant of Southern Africa is, of course, the Republic of South Africa, incorporating a vast variety of landscape, of people, and of opportunities for both enjoying oneself and making a fortune. As roughly half the book is devoted to the Republic there is no need to dilate on its attractions now.

Namibia   Finally there is the UN mandated territory of Namibia (South West Africa), nearing independence at the time of writing: a country with magnificent game reserves and full of curiosities, human, geological and botanical, a place you tell stories about for the rest of your life.

Together these six countries occupy the whole southern end of the African continent. They are as varied politically as they are physically, from white-run governments to wholly African governments. This makes no difference to the traveller – indeed the reason for grouping these countries together in one book is that from a tourist's point of view they are complementary. You can pass freely and easily from any one into any other, just as you can in Western Europe. In our experience, politics seldom bother the visitor.

The editorial form of the Guide is simple. The General Information gives overall advice on the area. There are guides to wildlife and to safaris. Each country has its own chapter, subdivided where necessary, followed by Useful Facts on such things as customs regulations. Finally there are maps, travel tips and an index. Our recommendations are based on the personal experience of our South African editor and five contributing authors.

6

General Information

How to get to Southern Africa – Airlines

South African Airways (SAA) is the biggest airline on the African continent and operates nine flights a week from London (seven to Johannesburg, one each to Cape Town and Durban), five per week from New York, two from Sydney and Perth and others from Frankfurt and European cities, as well as direct links to South America and the Far East. Other international carriers serving Jan Smuts airport, Johannesburg, the main South African terminal, are Alitalia, British Airways, KLM, Lufthansa, El Al, Alberia, Olympic, Qantas, Swissair, TAP, and Aerolineas Argentinas. *South Africa*

SAA run a weekly flight both ways between Frankfurt and Windhoek, and daily flights Windhoek–Johannesburg. *Namibia*

Harare (formerly Salisbury) is served by Air Zimbabwe, British Airways, Kenya Airways and Lufthansa coming from Europe or East Africa and by SAA from Johannesburg. There are also connecting flights in from Botswana and Zambia. *Zimbabwe*

Botswana, Lesotho and Swaziland can all be reached via Johannesburg, as well as via Harare. The north of Botswana is more easily accessible from Harare and Lusaka.

The only direct cheap flights from Europe to South Africa are operated by Luxavia Airways from Luxembourg to Johannesburg. SAA and British Airways both offer APEX fares from London. There is a cheap coach air service operated by Air Zimbabwe from Harare to Johannesburg, which may provide a link to cheaper flights from Europe to Harare in the future. Consult a travel agent on this. *Cheap Flights*

For further information on domestic southern African services and excursion fares see page 166. *Excursions*

How to get to Southern Africa – Shipping

The leisurely days of sailing to South Africa are all but over. Although there are no longer passenger services it is still possible, with some difficulty however, to book a berth on a freight ship.

Altitude and Climate

The climate in the countries described varies from sub-tropical in Botswana and Natal through desert in Namibia to Mediterranean at the Cape. It is warm and sunny throughout this area, and rains usually come in short, sharp downpours. The biggest single climatic influence is that inland from the coasts the land rises to a vast plateau. A large proportion of Southern Africa, including all

Zimbabwe, Botswana and 40 percent of the Republic of South Africa, is on this plateau and lies 900–1,220 m (3–4,000 ft) or more above sea level. This means that though the sun is hot, it is less humid than at the coast, and colder at night. The second major influence, which affects South Africa and Namibia most, is the cool air brought by south east winds from the Antarctic. Equally the Benguela current keeps the sea cool along the west coast.

Obviously the variations in climate cannot all be described here, so we have detailed them in chapters on each country. See also under Health below. The further south you go, being south of the Equator, the colder it will be in winter – in Johannesburg it can snow.

Currencies

See under each country's Useful Facts section.

Dress and Cosmetics

Comfortable clothes matter a lot, as the remarks above on climate will have indicated. The local standards of female fashion are not high. For women a jumper is essential and a light woollen suit useful. At the coast during the day light cottons and linens are the thing, preferably washable, and trousers and shirts for safaris. Sandals can be bought locally. Swimsuits and beachwear are useful. You will need one pair of flattish shoes, and a raincoat, preferably a lightweight one. Sunglasses and a sunhat (obtainable locally) are all but vital. Take some lightweight clothes hangers.

For men a lightweight suit is useful in the cities. Bring plenty of shirts – incidentally in our experience synthetic fabrics can become very sticky in tropical areas and there is no substitute for cotton if you want to stay cool. A pair of washable trousers will be useful and so will both long and short sleeved sweaters. Down in South Africa you need normal weight suits in winter, and sweaters in the mountains.

Anyone going on safari will need neutral coloured clothes so as not to alert animals to their presence. Jungle green or khaki bush shirts, trousers and skirts can be made locally, or bought off the peg. You will look right in them and they will be cheaper both in tailoring charges and airfreight than any similar clothes you bring with you.

The degree of formality varies. In South Africa many hotels insist on a suit, collar and tie being worn in the evening even if it is sweltering hot. But you do not often need a dinner jacket (tuxedo), a dark suit is normally enough, unless you are on an official visit. The other countries are less formal.

Virtually all the internationally known beauty preparations are sold in South African cities, but are less available in the smaller countries. Sun lotions and moisturising creams are essential in the sun. Take lip salve on safari. Many hotels have sockets for men's electric razors – the usual current is 220 volts AC.

Driving and roads

Roads vary. A vast programme of road building has made most of South Africa's main highways as good as you find in many European countries, and with far less traffic. Side roads are gravelled. In Zimbabwe roads are mostly fully tarmacked, but a few minor roads still exist with two strips of tarmac each 60–90 cm (2–3 ft) wide, down to gravel. In Botswana there is very little tarmac. Take two tips from us about driving on gravel. First check on the road's condition if it has rained, otherwise you may get stuck, especially if you are unused to this kind of driving. Secondly insure your windscreen and headlights glass against breakage. Most insurance companies now give this cover for R 2 or so a year, and claims do not affect your no-claims bonus.

It is well worth joining the Automobile Association, or a similar body, like Rondalia in South Africa. You get help, free maps, and many other facilities. The A.A. *Guide to Southern Africa* is first class.

Throughout Southern Africa you drive on the left. An International Driving Licence is necessary in South Africa if your home country's licence does not have your photograph in it. Traffic lights are called 'robots' in South Africa.

There is a 90 kph (55 mph) speed limit in South Africa on country roads and a 60 kph (37 mph) limit in urban areas. Petrol is not available in South Africa from midday Saturday to 0700 Monday, though tourist visitors can legally buy fuel at weekends: the local police will advise in emergency.

Car Hire firms are listed under the cities, and there is more about local road conditions in the text. If in doubt – ask for advice.

Etiquette

In general the welcome you get in Africa is refreshing. Both Europeans and Africans like to talk to the foreign visitor. In the newly independent States, like Botswana and Lesotho, as in Zambia or in East Africa, you may find some sensitivity on the subject of colonialism. Throughout Southern Africa you must also be tactful on two other points when dealing with Africans (who in South Africa are officially referred to as Africans or blacks and whose homelands you cannot wander about in without a permit, though you can drive through them). Firstly there is religion. If you visit an African or Asian Moslem mosque, you must remove your shoes before going inside. It is also best to ask the guardian of the mosque for permission to enter. Secondly there is the question of

Africans

9

photography. Some tribes regard cameras as 'the evil eye', others resent private dances being photographed merely because they are held in the open air. This applies whatever your own race or colour.

Europeans With Europeans, if you are white yourself, you will find that etiquette and manners are very much as they are in Britain. In South Africa the policy of separate development means that there are separate hotels, restaurants and facilities for non-white people, though South Africa now has some 'international' hotels and restaurants which are open to all races. The other countries described are multi-racial.

Gratuities

Usually 10 percent is added to hotel and restaurant bills. When tipping it is perhaps more general to give 10 percent than 15 percent. Hotel porters, train attendants and others should be happy with 50c–R 1.00.

Health

You need international certificates of vaccination against cholera and smallpox to enter Southern Africa, and you may have to get a Yellow Fever certificate, so check before you leave. In a number of areas in South Africa, Zimbabwe and Botswana, malaria occurs and it is wise to take anti-malarial pills, like Daraprim or Daraclor. Tap water is drinkable in South Africa and Zimbabwe.

Do not swim in the inland lakes or rivers unless you are told it's safe, since they are often infested with bilharzia (a disease carried by water snails). Beware of overexposure to the sun, and heat exhaustion, which can be seriously injurious.

Hotels, Restaurants and Bars

South Africa Nearly all hotels in South Africa are classified from five star downwards and registered with the Hotel Board. The Board controls the standard of hotels and makes sure they maintain their ratings. A five star hotel is comparable with the best in the world, while a one star hotel is an unpretentious establishment without the luxuries of either television or air-conditioning in the rooms.

Hotels in Namibia and Zimbabwe have a grading up to five stars. In Botswana there is no grading system, nor is there in Lesotho or Swaziland, though establishments are subjected to government inspection and lists of approved hotels are printed. We recommend only those hotels that keep a reasonably high standard. These naturally tend to be the more expensive but we have included some reliable cheaper ones. With care you can explore Southern Africa on R 25 a day, at the cost only of occasional discomfort. The local Publicity Associations and hotel guides will help you.

In South Africa ladies used not to be admitted to bars, and *Bars* although this is gradually changing, there are still 'Ladies Bars'. Men are admitted to them – after all someone has to pay for the drinks. Generally speaking the average bar is pretty rough. There are no such restrictions in the other countries.

South Africa's cities have restaurants to suit all tastes. The *Restaurants* Johannesburg *Yellow Pages* alone list 185 establishments, including ones specialising in South African, Austrian, Chinese, German, French, Italian, Greek, Spanish, Indian and even Polynesian dishes. Both Cape Town and Durban have fine seafood. Prices are low compared to Europe. Outside the cities there is less variety, though most South African towns have a snack bar or roadhouse where you will get coffee and a hamburger for about R 3.50. However many such places are not licensed.

In the other countries there are small English-style restaurants and they are usually licensed to sell liquor.

Language

English is spoken throughout Southern Africa.

Photography

The sunlight here can be intense and you should allow a slightly faster exposure than you would in Europe. The DIN, ASA and Weston meter settings recommended by film manufacturers are now for the minimum exposure, not the average, and so are just about right for African conditions. However, where there is a lot of refracted light, as on the dazzling white sands of the coast or some of the open plains, you will need a still shorter exposure. A lens hood is invaluable, while an ultra violet filter cuts down the effect of glare.

Photographing game you are obviously unlikely to get close enough to take a meter reading off the animal itself, which will need a greater exposure than the landscape it is in. A good way to check is by taking a reading off a dull-coloured piece of clothing, remembering to take a reading in shade if the animal you are about to photograph is lying in the shade. When using a telephoto lens, especially one you have not used before, it is wise to open the aperture an extra half stop.

Photographing Africans, whose dark skins reflect very little light, you need to open the aperture by at least one stop (e.g. f8 to f5·6). Or you can halve the shutter speed (e.g. from 1/250th to 1/125th sec.).

There are hundreds of photographic shops in Southern Africa. Many will develop black and white film properly in from one to four days. Colour work usually takes a week. Photographic equipment carries customs duty, but only at a low rate. But both colour and black and white film is more expensive than in Europe.

Public Transport

Trains

Train services are good. They have a prestige here that they are losing in Europe. If you are not in a violent hurry it's well worth consulting South African Railways and Zimbabwe Railways about their schedules. The main expresses are mentioned in the text; among them is a train which leaves Johannesburg for Harare every Thursday at 1230 and takes 21 hours. The return fare is R 80.95 first class or R 56.45 second class. The trains from Johannesburg to Cape Town are also substantially cheaper than air travel.

Buses

South African Railways run long distance coach services, but these are mainly for Africans. However there are local buses for Europeans in the cities and elsewhere – where there is no colour segregation – there are invariably bus services. Do not believe travel agents who tell you that cheap bus services do not exist in Southern Africa.

Sport

The facilities for sport are practically endless. Golf, bowls, rugger, cricket, tennis, squash, swimming and surfing are favourites. The surfing along South Africa's coastline is among the best in the world. You can count on finding sporting facilities in the smallest places. There are many flying clubs, also a few parachuting clubs.

Time

South African standard time is two hours ahead of GMT and the other countries follow suit.

Tourist Offices

The South African Tourist Corporation (SATOUR) has offices in Europe in London, Frankfurt, Amsterdam, Paris, Milan and Zurich and in the Americas in New York, Chicago, Los Angeles, Toronto, Rio de Janeiro and Buenos Aires. There are also offices in Sydney, Tokyo, Tel Aviv and Harare (Zimbabwe). The London office is in Regency House, 1–4 Warwick Street, London W1R 5WB (telephone (01) 439 9661). The New York office is in the Rockefeller Centre, 610 Fifth Avenue, New York, NY 10020 (telephone (212) 245 3720).

Tourist Information can be obtained from the High Commissions of Botswana, Lesotho, Swaziland and Zimbabwe in London. At the time of writing Namibia (South West Africa) was represented by South Africa.

Hunting and Photographic Safaris

The mystique of the hunter – his searching knowledge of living in the wild, his uncanny ability to locate game – this is the key to the true safari. The countless books that have been written about big game hunting, like Hemingway's *Green Hills of Africa*, all carry the same message of the fascination of the hunter's craft, and the easy companionship of life on safari. The word 'safari' is Swahili, from East Africa. In that language it just means a journey. But internationally it stands for an expedition into the wild after game, whether to shoot or to photograph; pitching camp where it best suits your purpose; rising at first light to hunt before breakfast, when it is best; swapping stories over a sundowner in the evenings.

The absolute minimum time for a safari is five days – too little in our opinion. If you want to shoot first-class specimens you should allow yourself four to six weeks. A major photographic safari can be done comfortably in thirty days. During this time you are excellently looked after. Game trackers, gunbearers, skinners, cooks, personal servants and porters are at your beck and call. When they set up camp for the night it includes spring mattresses, refrigerators, hot baths, luxurious insect-proof tents, dining tables, and a two-way radio link with the outside world. You get good food and have the appetite to appreciate it.

The standards of professional hunters who take clients out (customers are always known as clients) are high. Remember that the hunter is your guide, philosopher and friend and even though you are paying him, you are in a real sense his guest. The bush is his country and without him you would be pretty helpless in it.

In the interests of game conservation the regulations in Southern African countries are fairly strict, though the various licences for different types of animal enable you to shoot enough to satisfy any true sportsman. There are no restrictions on photography, of course. Broadly speaking, all big game are protected in the Republic of South Africa, though you can shoot antelope and other species on hunting reserves. At the moment South Africa is trying to standardise its hunting laws, since the four provinces have differing ordinances on hunting. Remember that since South Africa is a signatory to CITES (the international convention for trade in endangered species) certain animal products, such as spotted cat skins, may not be exported.

In Namibia there are more opportunities, especially for gemsbok and greater kudu. But for the big five – elephant, lion, leopard, buffalo and rhino – you must go to Zimbabwe or Botswana, where there is some of the best hunting in the whole continent.

A safari needs detailed planning. The hunting firms will start this long before you arrive, though not all safari companies will clear your guns or cameras through customs. To import your arms into South Africa, a temporary import/export permit is issued at the point of entry. Proof of ownership is necessary, such as an arms licence issued in the country of origin. Between 25 and 33 percent of the fee is payable in advance. Being treated like a Maharajah is never cheap either. A safari for two people will cost around R 175 each day. By yourself it would be proportionately more, with four people it would be less per person. The length of the trip affects the price too, which does not include the price of the animal killed. Licences range from R 800 for a leopard to R 400 for Nyala, R 320 for kudu to R 50 for impala. There are also additional costs from field preparation, disinfecting, packaging, insurance and forwarding of trophies to the operation's taxidermist. The mounted trophy is then exported to its final destination on an Airfreight collect basis. There are special package safaris on offer at an average price including airfare of about R 3,500 for one person for 14 days. The price is based on two clients hunting together. Generally alcohol, ammunition, film, hunting licences and hotel accommodation off safari are all extra expenses. Don't forget that tips can set you back R 300 by the time you have rewarded the whole retinue, plus any present you feel the professional hunter deserves. For obvious reasons photographic safaris work out noticeably cheaper than hunting safaris.

The main safari companies operating in Southern Africa, are listed under this heading in the country chapters. If you feel you cannot afford a full safari then some of these also run tours, while there are many other companies listed who offer everything from day trips round the game parks onwards. One last word – you pay what is seemingly a lot for a safari, but you get good value for money. It is an unforgettable experience.

**Here are twenty-five of the animals
you are most likely to see on safari or
in National Parks and Game Reserves**

Southern Africa's Wildlife

The **African** or **Black Buffalo** basically
eats grass, though often civilisation
has driven it into the forests. Buffalo
stay in herds and though shy are
among the most dangerous big game
animals. A grown bull weighs 680
kilos (1,500 lbs), and the span of its
horns may be 1,270 mm (50 ins).

The **African Elephant** is larger than
the Indian Elephant, particularly its
ears. A bull weighs up to 6,096 kilos
(6 tons) and stands 3·35 m (11 ft) high
at the shoulder. Its tusks can weigh
over 45 kilos (100 lbs) each. Elephants
are intelligent, live in herds and are
vegetarians, consuming half a ton of
food a day. Their life span is about 60
years.

The **Hippopotamus,** whose name is
Latin for 'water horse', is really of the
pig family. Hippos congregate in
'schools' and being amphibious
spend much of their day submerged
in water up to their nostrils. A grown
hippo weighs 2,535 kilos (2½ tons) or
more and can outrun a man. Male
hippos fight each other to the death.

The **Crocodile** lives by rivers, lakes
and swamps. It is not as slow moving
as it looks and can swing its tail like a
whip to hit an adversary. An average
length is 3·66 m (12 ft) though it can
be 4·57 m (15 ft) long. Its diet is
mainly fish.

The **Black Rhinoceros,** smaller and more aggressive than the white rhino, still weighs over 1,000 kilos (1 ton). It is a solitary animal, fond of thorn scrub. It has poor sight but good smell and hearing. Although a vegetarian it is not pacific and will charge anything, even a car or a train.

The **White Rhinoceros** is larger and better tempered than its cousin. However it is not white. Its name derives from the Dutch 'weit' meaning wide, which refers to its distinctive square jaw. It is fairly rare and animals from the famous herd at Umfolozi in Natal have been resettled in Zimbabwe. The horns of both species are composed of tightly packed hair, not real horn.

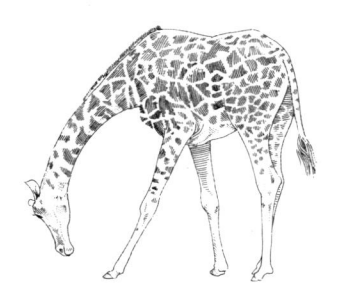

The **Giraffe,** the tallest mammal, was first discovered in Namaqualand. It grows to 5·49 m (18 ft) and can weigh a ton. It eats leaves, likes open country and is unaggressive. It can move surprisingly fast. The **Reticulated Giraffe** is so called because its markings are square, within a network of whitish lines, instead of star shaped. It is not found in Southern Africa.

The **Zebra** is in fact the only remaining wild horse in Southern Africa. Burchell's Zebra feed on grass, leaves and shrubs, and usually move in herds, often with other species. A male zebra stands 1·52 m (5 ft) high at the shoulder and weighs 318 kilos (700 lbs). The other main type of zebra down here is the **Cape Mountain Zebra,** which has a small dewlap and on which the stripes go right down the legs instead of stopping at the knees.

The **Lion** lives in open country, like the Kruger Park. A full grown male weighs 180–227 kilos (400–500 lbs). The lioness has no mane. 'Prides', or families, of lion doze in the shade during the day and hunt at dusk. They can charge at 80 kph (50 mph) and kill by springing on the back of the zebra, wildebeest, or whatever else they have stalked. They kill only when hungry, once in three or four days.

The **Leopard** hunts by night, is wary and dangerous when wounded or cornered. Unlike the cheetah its spots are arranged in rosette pattern. A male weighs under 68 kilos (150 lbs) and measures about 2·30 m (7½ ft) from nose to tail. Leopards make their lairs among rocks in thick bush. Their favourite food is baboon, though they will descend to rodents and even insects if hungry.

The **Cheetah** has relatively longer legs and a smaller head than a leopard, while its spots are isolated, not arranged in a pattern. It hunts by day and is the fastest mammal – it has been timed at 96 kph (60 mph). Cheetahs stand ·91 m (3 ft) high at the shoulder and are about 2·13 m (7 ft) long. They are easily tamed and have been raced against greyhounds in Europe.

The **Spotted Hyena** is a night time scavenger, though it can be seen by day in the Kruger Park, the Kalahari Gemsbok Park and elsewhere. Though its powerful jaws can crush bones it is a coward and only attacks weak or aged live animals. Its colour is yellowish, it weighs about 68 kilos (150 lbs), and has a characteristic, unpleasant, howl. Hyenas 'laugh' when lions are around.

17

The **Warthog** is named after the warts on its grotesque head. It lives in families, or 'sounders', and breeds in holes. When running it holds its tail stiffly erect. During the day it crops grass, or digs for roots with its tusks, whilst kneeling on its forelegs.

The **Baboon** is a large dog faced monkey, noted for its cunning. It may live to 45 years old. Baboons usually move in troops under the leadership of a big old male, and sleep under trees at night. They will eat almost anything, animal or vegetable. The babies ride on their mothers' backs.

The **Vervet Monkey** is one of the only two true monkeys in South Africa, the other being the Samango. The Vervet is the more common. Its distinctive face is black, with an outline of white. It is extremely cunning.

The **Wildebeest,** or **Gnu,** is one of the commonest antelopes in Africa. It stands about 1·52 m (5 ft) high at the shoulder, weighs up to 227 kilos (500 lbs), and its horns look slightly like a buffalo's. Its body is dark grey, with a shaggy mane, and it moves with a clumsy gait. Wildebeest live in herds. When alarmed they will gallop off, then suddenly turn in unison and face the danger.

The Reedbuck, generally buff-greyish in colour, with a white underside, inhabits most parts of Southern Africa. It stays by itself or in family parties, and rests in the heat of the day. It eats grass and when disturbed runs off with a 'rocking horse' motion, its white tail flashing. Like most buck the female has no horns. The **Mountain Reedbuck** is smaller and more gregarious.

The **Waterbuck** is a large antelope that usually lives near water. Its coat is shaggy, greyish brown, and with a white ring on the rump. One bull may lead a herd of up to thirty cows, who have no horns. Waterbuck are numerous in the Kruger Park, and on the lowveld.

The **Duiker** is one of the smallest of the antelopes, though it is stronger than it looks. There are three species – Blue, Red and Grey, which rather overstates the variation in colouring. They stand about ·61 m (2 ft) high.

The **Eland,** the largest of the antelope, is so placid that it was almost shot out in South Africa. It is now being reintroduced to the National Parks. Both sexes carry twisted horns. They are found in open country, like the Kalahari and the Kruger Park. Their colour is greyish brown with light stripes and a grown bull can weigh 1,000 kilos (1 ton) and stand 1·83 m (6 ft) high at the shoulder.

19

The **Sable Antelope** is a particularly splendid animal, standing nearly 1·52 m (5 ft) high, almost black, and bearing great scimitar shaped horns. It is white on the underparts, rump and face. It stays in small herds and is relatively rare, preferring to live in wooded country.

The **Roan Antelope** is a close relative of the Sable, though more heavily built. It stands about 1·37 m (4½ ft) high at the shoulder and is aggressive. Its colour is a light reddish brown, with the underparts white, and its tufted ears are often more noticeable than its horns. It prefers rolling upland country, but will take to living in forests, and tends to stay in troops of up to a dozen.

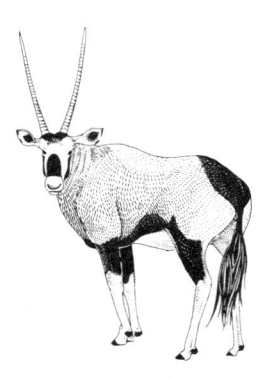

The **Gemsbok,** or **Cape Oryx,** a noble looking, savage and powerful animal, is found only north of the Orange river. It is generally fawn grey in colour. Both sexes have straight horns up to 1,117 mm (44 ins) long. A typical plains animal, it also exists in the Kalahari and Namib deserts, finding moisture from tsama melons and wild cucumbers if there is no water. It is wary and not easily approached.

The **Oribi,** a graceful smallish antelope, inhabits the grassveld roughly between the Zambezi river and Cape Province of South Africa. Oribi are a rufous yellow in colour, with a white underside. They tend to stay in pairs, rather than herds, and prefer country between about 457 and 1,066 m (1,500–3,500 ft) above sea level.

The **Impala** is a timid, graceful, medium sized antelope, famous for leaping in the air when alarmed. It can jump 9 m (30 ft), rising 3 m (10 ft) above the ground. Impala move in herds. They have smooth chestnut coloured coats. The females do not carry horns and are fought for by the males in the rutting season.

The **Springbok,** in English, Spring-buck, gets its name from its almost vertical leaps in the air. It is South Africa's national animal. Its colouring is fawn, with a distinctive broad band of dark reddish brown on its flank, and a white underside. The females' horns are thinner and less curved. It is a species of antelope.

The animals of Southern Africa have suffered considerably at the hands of mankind. The veld used to teem with vast herds of springbok and other game. Hunting, both for trophies and for the pot, sadly reduced some species, and completely destroyed others, like the magnificent black-maned Cape lion, the Blue Antelope and that curious relative of the zebra, the Quagga. These three are now extinct. However since President Kruger started the present Kruger Park, the preservation of game has taken enormous strides forward. Today all the countries described in this book devote time, money, and more important, enthusiasm, to improving game reserves and protecting species. Some excellent reference books on animals are *Wild Life in Southern Africa* by Stevenson-Hamilton, *The Mammals of South Africa* by Austin Roberts, *Focus on Fauna* by James Clarke, *The Wildlife of South Africa* by Paul Rose and *Mammals of Southern Africa* by John Hanks. *African Wildlife* is the journal of the S.A. Wildlife Society, while the magazine *Custos* is published by the S.A. National Parks Board. Both these magazines are available in bookshops. The authoritative reference work on birds, of which Southern Africa enjoys a breathtaking profusion, is Robert's *Birds of South Africa*, published by McLachlan and Liversidge.

Table Mountain from gardens in Cape Town

The Republic of
South Africa

The Country South Africa is a country of breathtaking diversity. Watching the game in the vast Kruger Park, you are in the wild Africa that fascinated John Buchan and stirred the spirit of the hunter in Hemingway. To the east the sub-tropical valleys of Natal once sheltered the kraals of those bloodthirsty Zulu kings, Chaka and Dingaan. Seventeen hundred and sixty km (1,100 miles) of unspoilt beaches run from Durban to the Mediterranean climate of the Cape resorts, with magnificent surfing and big game fishing. Inland you can find everything from the quiet vineyards and wine presses of Paarl and Stellenbosch, to ostrich farming in the Little Karoo and the roaring development of Johannesburg and the Rand gold-fields.

What it all adds up to is a big country, with a long tradition of outdoor living, and energy to match. Physically its 472,675 sq miles make it the size of half Europe. Its potential and opportunities have spawned fantastic characters like Rhodes and Barney Barnato, its gold and diamonds have become legendary, its legislators have created great nature reserves. More prosaically, a lot of effort has lately been put into improving its facilities for visitors, though the

22

major attraction of a sun-drenched climate could hardly be improved upon.

The first European settlement in South Africa was established in History 1652 when Jan van Riebeeck, whose head you see reproduced on the Republic's coinage, landed near the Cape of Good Hope. He was an employee of the Dutch East India Company and his mission was to secure this halfway house on the trade route between Europe and the Far East and to establish gardens that could provision the Company's ships. From this tiny start grew a Dutch colony, which fell into British hands in 1806 and, as the Cape Province, became part of the Union of South Africa in 1910.

Altogether four provinces made up the Union. Natal was a British colony from its beginnings. But the Transvaal and the Orange Free State had been independent Boer republics. Boer is the Dutch for farmer, and the republics were founded by farmers who trekked away to the interior from the restrictions of colonial life at the Cape. The Voortrekkers, as they were called, first moved off at much the same time as American settlers began their historic opening up of the West. The climax was the Great Trek of 1835, which is now part of South Africa's folklore.

The end of the nineteenth century brought the discovery of gold on the Rand and the Boer War between Britain and the Boer republics. During the struggle the Boer farmer-soldiers added camouflage and trenches to military tactics, and the word 'commando' to military language. In the end it took 200,000 British troops to subdue 180,000 Boers – men, women and children. That was in 1902.

Happily a reconciliation followed and eight years later, on 31st May The Union 1910, the Union was formed as a sovereign State. Pretoria was made the capital and Cape Town the seat of Parliament. Every year officials and diplomats move down to the Cape for the six month Parliamentary session.

On 31st May 1961, South Africa became a Republic and left the British Commonwealth. Soon afterwards a new decimal currency was introduced, in which the basic unit of one Rand is worth approximately 55p sterling, US $1.28 (1981).

When the Cape Colony was founded, the only indigenous The People inhabitants in this southern tip of Africa were Hottentots and Bushmen. Much of the land was completely unpeopled. Over the years the Hottentots became absorbed into the Cape population, whilst the Bushmen moved away north into South West Africa and the Kalahari Desert. The Cape's expansion and the founding of Natal also brought the settlers into conflict with the Bantu tribes of Central Africa, who were inexorably spreading south. As a result there are substantial areas of South Africa in African occupation today, including one completely independent African kingdom,

Lesotho (Basutoland) (see page 127), within the Republic's borders, and another, Swaziland (see page 135), between the Republic and Mozambique.

Over the years the Boer and British settlers were joined by Huguenots, Germans and other Europeans, whilst the racial composition of the country was further complicated by the immigration of Indians to work in the sugar fields of Natal, and Malays who were brought to the Cape originally as slaves.

Broadly South Africa's 26 million people can be divided into four groups: Africans 17 million, whites five million, coloureds three million and Asians one million. There is an official policy of separate racial development, formerly called Apartheid. Under this the Government is establishing self-governing African states. The first to receive independence was the 16,000 sq mile Transkei in October 1976, which now has its own passport controls at the frontier. This was followed by Bophuthatswana in December 1977 and Venda in September 1979. There is no racial segregation in these states. In the rest of South Africa you will notice that public facilities such as lavatories, railway carriages and hotels are reserved for either whites or non-whites. This practice is slowly being abandoned and some hotels have 'international' status which means they are open to all races.

Transport

Transport facilities in the Republic have already been mentioned in the General Information and are first class – well up to Europe's standards. See also the regional travel section later in the book.

Caravanning

South Africa's climate encouraging an open air life, caravanning has become very popular. There are caravan parks with toilet, washing and cooking facilities all over the Republic, too many to list. If you want more information write to SATOUR or to the Automobile Association, PO Box 596, Johannesburg 2000, or to the Caravan Club of South Africa, PO Box 50580, Randburg 2125.

Hiking

Since 1973 South Africa has been developing a series of hiking trails and it is now possible to walk along a hiking way that extends from the Limpopo in the north to the tip of the Cape Peninsula. In addition to the trails there are various walks: the Elephant Walk through the Knysna forest, the Bushbuck Walk near Port Elizabeth, and two in the Eastern Transvaal – the Lourie and Forest Falls walks. Like the trails these walks are routed through beautiful well-wooded country and each provides a leisurely stroll. For details about the trails contact the State Department of Forestry, Private Bag X93, Pretoria 0001 (telephone 48 2911). The tariff for the trails is R 1.50 per night. There is no charge for the walks.

Fishing

Fishing is a national sport. Licences are cheap and easily obtained locally, although there are bag limits in most areas. There is an enormous variety of species from shark and barracuda, to brown trout and barbel. There are frequent references to fishing in the text

24

and we recommend SATOUR's booklet *Fresh and seawater fishing in South Africa.*

As already mentioned SATOUR handles overseas inquiries with its *Information* headquarters in Pretoria, and offices abroad. The Railways have travel bureaux in the main towns and cities. The National Tourist Bureau has an office in virtually every major town in the Republic, with a mass of leaflets available, while the petrol companies print useful road maps.

Since South Africa is so large we shall describe it province by province, starting with the Transvaal and Johannesburg, where most air travellers arrive initially.

A land of wild, untamed beauty.
A land that never fails to excite and stimulate your senses.
Gametrackers, pathfinders of old Africa, are waiting to welcome you on their leisurely and widely comprehensive safaris.
Comfortable, but rugged, fully equipped safari vehicles. Small and intimate groups of passengers – and luxury at beautiful lodges or under canvas. Experienced rangers to share their knowledge and pride in the land they know so well.
Lions hunting in the night. Flaming African dawns silhouetting morning giraffe – and unbelievable splendour!
It never fails to excite us, so what will it do for you!
Write to GAMETRACKERS, Box 41017, Craighall 2024, Transvaal, Republic of South Africa for our brochure on safaris in the real Africa.
Botswana's Okavango Delta – Namibia's Etosha Pan – Timbavati.

Game Reserve Rest Camp

The Transvaal

The Transvaal – a name which simply means the country across the Vaal River – was opened up by the Voortrekkers only a century and a quarter ago. Subsequently the discovery of gold on the Rand changed the course of its history. But wealth only added another dimension to the Transvaal, which was already blessed with three great assets. These are the colour and variety of its wide and inspiring landscape; big game living in vast tracts of unchanged Africa; and an excellent climate. No travel agent could ask more than this for his clients, and certainly not when gold has added to it a great city, Johannesburg, with all the facilities and aids to travellers that a metropolis offers.

Geographically the province's 110,000 sq miles make it twice the size of England. They extend from the Vaal River north to the Limpopo, a distance by road of 643 km (400 miles). In the south and west, on the highveld plateau, the altitude is 1,660 to 2,000 m (5,000 to 6,000 ft). The transition from this highveld to the lowveld in the north and east, close to Mozambique, is made by a part of the Drakensberg Mountains, the same range that is such a feature of Natal (see page 80 onwards). It is a most dramatic transition with breathtaking passes and a mile-deep canyon at Blyde River.

26

On the lowveld, especially in the north end of the Kruger Park, the *Climate* daytime temperature can be over 38°C (100°F) in the shade in January and February, though it cools off in the evening. As you get higher, the heat and humidity lessen. Up on the highveld you find a healthy, invigorating climate. Summers are warm with an average temperature of 22°C (70°F), and frequent afternoon thunderstorms that last for half an hour or so. Autumn and spring are pronounced seasons, like Europe has, and emphatically unlike most of Africa. In winter it can be cold. Johannesburg occasionally has snow, and the average temperature is 10°C (50°F). But the sunshine averages nine hours a day.

Historically there is still much to discover in the Transvaal. The *History* Boer trekkers who found this land largely empty, except for teeming herds of game which they unfortunately shot to the point of extinction in places, thought they were pioneers here. Research has now revealed that in fact hominids, those creatures of mankind's dawn who evolved between apes and the first men, first hunted the golden savannah and tested their prehistoric weapons in the highveld depression that drains into the Vaal River. A thread of continuity can be traced in the fact that the uranium used in the first atomic bombs came from this same area.

Again, before the European came, the movement of Bantu tribes down from Central Africa led to bloody battles. There were some pastoral African clans living here, with whom the renegade Zulu, Mzilikatze, clashed after his hordes crossed the Vaal from Zululand, now part of Natal. Battered and leaderless Africans roamed the veld as the Zulus rounded up their cattle. Finally the white man clashed with the Zulus, chased Mzilikatze into Zimbabwe, and established peace. Today there are still a few Zulus in the province. But the main tribes are Vendas in the north, Shangaans and Sothos.

In 1857 the Boer farmers declared the Transvaal an independent *President* republic. Its indomitable President, Paul Kruger, led his people in *Kruger* the Boer War that flared up as a result of the discovery in 1896 of the fantastic goldfields of the Witwatersrand, which we shall describe in a moment. You can hardly be in South Africa five minutes without realising that Kruger is a legend. Every town has a street named after him, his statue dominates Church Square in Pretoria and many other lesser places. He stands there in top hat and frock coat, a portly, stumpy man, with a huge strong bewhiskered face. He was not always like this. In his youth he was an athlete, hunter and soldier. But the overriding image is of 'Oom Paul' (Uncle Paul), puritanical, knowing the Old Testament by heart, leading his people against the British and finally carrying the insignia of state with him in an ox-wagon so that wherever he stopped became the Transvaal's capital. He died in exile in Switzerland in 1904, sadly before the Union and final independence of 1910. But his determined spirit still guides the Republic in many ways.

Johannesburg being the Republic's commercial capital, and Pretoria the official capital, communications from them to the rest of the country and the outside world are excellent. Jan Smuts airport, almost equidistant from the two cities, is now being rebuilt in a literally massive redevelopment plan that will make it one of the world's most modern airports – not that it was inefficient before. Over the years we have found its staff, including immigration and customs officers, notably helpful. Daily air services link Jan Smuts with Europe, Zimbabwe, including direct flights to the Victoria Falls, and Bulawayo, Mozambique, Durban 502 km (312 miles), Cape Town 1,271 km (790 miles), Port Elizabeth, Bloemfontein and Kimberley.

Express trains link Johannesburg and Pretoria with Cape Town, including the new luxurious Blue Train. The 1,526 km (949 mile) journey takes 25 hours. The basic first class single fare is R 72.70. The Trans Karoo Express does the same route in 28 hours. The Trans Natal Night Express reaches Durban in 15 hours at R 37.55 first class single. Within the Transvaal Province trains run to Nelspruit, near the Kruger Park (page 40) and through Pietersburg and Louis Trichardt and Beit Bridge on the way to Zimbabwe. Frequent Durban trains link Johannesburg, Pretoria, Germiston and Witwatersrand towns. Most of the roads in the province are tarred. There are regular coach and bus services. For information contact South African Railways Travel Bureaux in the cities, or ask for the local bus terminus. Meals and bedding are always extra.

National Parks and Game Reserves

THE KRUGER PARK NATIONAL PARK

The best known of South Africa's Parks. In the NE Transvaal, it is described fully on page 41. There are 11 rest camps in this 8,000 sq mile Park and each offers thatched huts and camping facilities. Kruger Park's animals include elephant, buffalo, lion, hippo, rhino, leopard, cheetah and hundreds of smaller species.

LOSKOP DAM NATURE RESERVE

This is a favourite fishing spot and has a modern camp at the water's edge. There is a well-stocked game reserve which includes rhino, leopard and several kinds of buck.

BARBERSPAN RESERVE

This reserve, five sq miles in extent, centres around an ancient pan possibly carved out of the remarkably flat veld by feet of millions of springbok over the course of centuries. It is a favourite spot for many species of birds.

SUIKERBOSRAND RESERVE

At 51 sq miles this new reserve is one of the largest in the Transvaal. It is situated in a chain of low mountains 40 minutes drive from Johannesburg. It is not fully open to the public as it is being restocked with a variety of game. It already has 1,500 blesbok, a number of white rhinoceros, and a breeding population of cheetah.

PILANESBERG GAME RESERVE

Situated around an extinct volcanic crater, this 193 sq miles reserve in Bophuthatswana is gradually being restocked with all the species that used to occur in the region. To date eland, rhino, cheetah, hartebeest and zebra have been introduced. The translocation of animals to this reserve has been called 'Operation Genesis' as it is the largest programme for game movement in the world.

In addition to these government run reserves, there are various private reserves in the Transvaal, notably: Mala Mala, Londolozi, Motswari, Inyati, Tanda Tula, and Thornybush, all situated near the Kruger National Park. Altogether there are almost 500 proclaimed reserves.

As well as animals, the Transvaal has magnificent birds and butterflies, while new varieties of plants are often discovered. It has been known for 1,600 species to be identified in one area in one day – as many as are known in the entire British Isles.

The Witwatersrand and the Gold Mines

'The ridge of white waters', on which Johannesburg stands, has seen one of the fastest developments of this century anywhere. The place names you see along it emphasise what it was like less than a century ago. Elandsfontein, and Olifantsfontein, so called because they were the springs at which eland and elephant used to drink, are now suburbs. The thing that changed the landscape, and made 'The Rand' an international symbol of wealth and furious development, was of course gold.

Although pockets of gold had been found in the deep forests of the Drakensberg escarpment in the 1870s, causing a minor gold rush, the discovery that really made world news came in 1886. An Australian digger, George Harrison, chanced on a rocky outcrop of a gold-bearing reef on a farm between Potchefstroom and Pretoria. This main reef is now thought to go down eight km (five miles) at an angle of forty-five degrees. In places it is three m (12 ft.) thick and the gold mines of the Rand now stretch in an unbroken line for 96 km (60 miles) along it, though three miles is the deepest mine so far planned. The 55 mines produce nearly 70 percent of the free world's gold, but four tons of rock have to be mined to extract a single ounce of the precious metal.

Visiting goldmines It is possible to visit some of the mines by contacting the Public Relations Adviser, Chamber of Mines, PO Box 809, Johannesburg 2000. (Telephone 838 8211.) These half day tours of surface workings are conducted on Wednesday and Friday mornings. Bookings should be made at least two weeks in advance.

Mine Museum It is also worthwhile touring the historic Simmer and Jack gold mine in Johannesburg. The three-and-a-half-hour tours begin daily at 0830 from Monday to Saturday. They include surface and underground workings, a museum, an Ndebele village, and end with refreshments. There is a cover charge of about R 10. Reservations should be made at least two days in advance to Simmer and Jack Gold Mine, PO Box 192, Germiston 1400. (Telephone 51 8571.)

The Chamber of Mines makes bookings to see the celebrated mine dances on Sunday mornings. These are inter-tribal competitions by the African mineworkers, robust, energetic and including both war dances and more modern variants of them, like the Gumboot Dance. Most car hire firms and travel agents can arrange visits for you. Sadly, however, the spontaneity of the dancing is becoming affected by its tourist attraction.

Johannesburg

Nobody is sure after which Johannes the city was named. What is certain is that whoever he was, he started an amazing transformation. 1986 will be Johannesburg's 100th anniversary. In this short century it has grown from a mining camp of shacks dotted about the place indiscriminately to a roaring metropolis, the financial and industrial hub of Southern Africa. The gold rush did it. Within a year the population was 10,000, within eight years 100,000, now it is 1,700,000. About the only thing you will not find in it is 'African atmosphere'. Johannesburg is a European city. Although many Africans work there, the street markets and bustle of Africa are missing. Instead there are budding skyscrapers, like the R 90 million Carlton Centre complex; and attractive suburbs, like Parktown where Mr Harry Oppenheimer, the millionaire mining financier, lives and Houghton and Morningside, with their great mansions. More and more business offices are moving out to suburbs like Rosebank and Sandton, where huge shopping centres have been built in recent years. This is having a considerable effect on the city centre, which is less lively in the evenings than it used to be. Hillbrow, ten minutes by taxi from the centre, is the cosmopolitan, active place to go in the evening, where bookshops stay open until 2230 and there is a host of small restaurants, bars and discos.

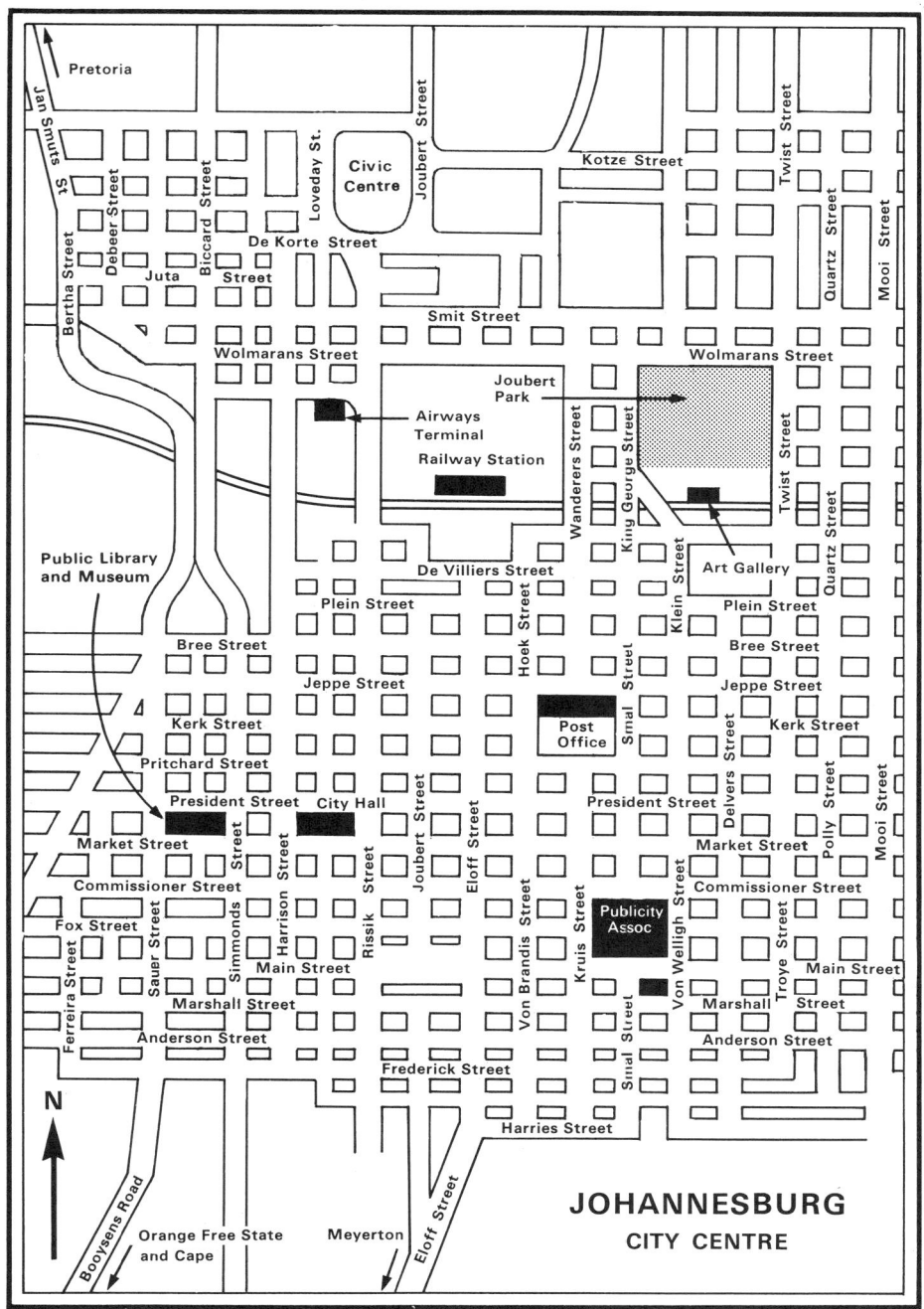

JOHANNESBURG
CITY CENTRE

31

This warning given, we can assure you that during the week Johannesburg is a fairly lively place, not least artistically, and has its own moments of beauty, like the sunset on the incredible golden sand mountains of mine tailings outside the city. And you will find people work very hard, starting at 0815 and finishing at 1700.

City Centre　　The central area has a gridiron plan of streets, most of them one way only for traffic and cursed with a formidable array of parking meters. There are, however, some pedestrian malls, such as the one in Smal Street near the Station. Pavement hawkers give this mall an atmosphere of bustle. Eloff Street, the main shopping street has wide pavements and a busway snakes down the middle. This golden street is known for its jewellers and a variety of shops including department stores such as OK Bazaars and John Orr. A major attraction in downtown Johannesburg is the Carlton Centre, a vast underground shopping centre with curio and photographic shops, hairdressing salons and restaurants.

Hotels　　Johannesburg has built some fine hotels in recent years including the skyscraper five star Carlton Hotel in the Carlton Centre (charges from R 46, room only). The five star Llandrost Hotel in Plein Street and the four star Rand International in Bree Street. Charges run from R 46 (room only) down to R 36. For the more budget conscious there is the New Library (two stars) in Commissioner Street charging R 10.50 bed and breakfast. About 20 miles out of town at the Grand Prix circuit of Kyalami is the Kyalami Ranch (three stars) at R 17, room only. This has a swimming pool. All these hotels are licensed but there are a number of cheap, clean non-licensed hotels in Hillbrow and Berea a few minutes from Johannesburg city centre. If you want to rent a serviced apartment (no meals served) then we recommend the Statesman Executive Apartments, 16 Joel Road, Berea, which charges R 80 approximately per week.

Restaurants　　Most four and five star hotels have restaurants, notably the Barnato in the Llandrost and the excellent Prospect Room at the Sunnyside Park Hotel, the latter being Lord Milner's former home, set in its own gardens in Parktown. Others are The Carvery in Claim Street, Dentons in Fox Street and the Villa Borghese on Claim and de Villiers Streets. One problem in central Johannesburg is finding a place to eat after the theatre. Rugantino's, an Italian restaurant at 6 Twist Street, stays open late. In general dinner for two including wine will cost from R 15 to R 20, but there are plenty of steak houses where you can eat for less and a variety of small restaurants up in Hillbrow.

Nightclubs　　The best of the night spots are Tiffanys on Henri Street in Braamfontein, Annabel's in the Llandrost Hotel, the Top of the Carlton in the Carlton Centre, Spangles and the Kyalami Ranch. A night out for two, including floorshow, would cost R 40 to R 50. A few discos are open all night in Hillbrow. Like any big city, Johannesburg also has its clip joints.

The city has generated 13 theatres and a very active cultural life. *Theatres*
The Academy and the Andre Huguenet theatres in Hillbrow often
stage light comedies, the Intimate offers revues and The Company
at the Market theatre performs both local and international drama.
Productions are advertised daily in the *Star* newspaper. Many stars
and plays have emerged from South Africa to hit London and New
York: actresses like Moira Lister and Glynis Johns, the African
actor Winston Ntshona. The playwright Athol Fugard too. The
musical *Ipi Tombi* is only one of several to achieve international
fame. Ordinary Africans are very musical and you should watch
out for the groups of singers who gather on Johannesburg's street
corners in the evenings.

There is also an energetic South African film industry, though most   *Films*
films shown are from abroad. Cinema seats, like theatre seats, are
bookable in advance, except at the drive-in cinemas. See the local
press for details. The newspapers here, incidentally, maintain high
standards. The best known English language papers are the *Rand
Daily Mail* and the *Star*. As in America, the size of the country has
prevented the creation of a nation-wide daily newspaper.

Johannesburg is not a place to spend the weekend without friends.   *Weekends*
At weekends people stay in the suburbs or the country, play games
of all kinds, cook traditional braaivleis (barbecues) and entertain in
their homes. Or they leave for weekend resorts. This is fine if you
have introductions, or if you belong to a European or American
club that reciprocates with a South African country club. If not,
then you risk a dull Saturday and Sunday. It is best to fix yourself a
weekend tour through a travel agent, or through the information
bureau in the South Station Building, on Eloff and de Villiers
Streets.

Some of the best places to go are the Kruger Park, the Mala Mala
Game Reserve, Londolozi, Sun City in Bophuthatswana with its
casino and the adjacent Pilanesberg Game Reserve, the Swaziland
Spa and casino or the casinos at Maseru or Gaberone. All can be
reached by air charter. Some more local drives are mentioned
later. For more details of places to drive to than we can list, buy the
Transvaal Weekender (R 1.50). This is strongly factual. The snag
about many local South African publications is that they enthuse
wildly about places that are unlikely to make much impact on
sophisticated overseas visitors.

Far and away the cheapest coach tours are run by South African   *Tours*
Railways, notably to the Kruger Park and to Durban via the Kruger
Park going on to Cape Town. Their office is in the Central Station
and they have branch travel bureaux throughout the country. The
Visitors Bureau, on the corner of Eloff and de Villiers Streets, is
helpful and can arrange various local tours, including ones to the
diamond cutting factories, and to the African townships outside
the city. There are numerous travel agents, including an American
Express office.

Car Hire	Car hire is not as expensive as in Britain or Europe. A two-door Golf costs R 10 a day and 10c a km. Reliable firms are Avis, Main Street (telephone 28 2515), Hertz, 2 De Villiers Street (telephone 37 4260), Budget Rent-a-Car, Carlton Centre (telephone 213631). Budget also arrange tours.
Safaris	Two companies which organise safaris both in the Republic and neighbouring countries are Gametrackers Ltd, 279 Kent Avenue, Ferndale Randburg (telephone 48 0408) and Afro-Ventures, PO Box 10848, Johannesburg 2000 (telephone 836 6421).
Air charter	Two companies are Comair, telephone Johannesburg 34 9311 and National Airways Corporation, telephone Johannesburg 34 9333. Both are at Rand Airport, Germiston. A Cessna 182 taking three passengers, cruising at 240 km (150 miles) an hour, costs R 80 an hour including pilot. Self-fly is available.
Sport	South Africans are great sporting enthusiasts. Horse racing takes place on Saturdays at Turffontein, a high class course in an otherwise low class southern part of the city, with smaller meetings on Wednesdays at Newmarket. There are also courses at Germiston, Benoni and Vereeniging. Racing of the motorised variety goes on at Kyalami, where the circuit is host to Grand Prix races. Vereeniging is famous for waterskiing too.

Rugby, the Republic's national game, is played every Saturday afternoon during the winter at the new Ellis Park Stadium. For soccer go to the Rand Stadium and for cricket to the New Wanderers Ground, in summer. The South African national teams, the Springboks, have an international reputation, especially in rugby. For a list of all the other sporting clubs and facilities ask at the Visitors Bureau, or consult the newspapers.

Zoo	Even when people live close to wildlife, zoos remain popular. Johannesburg has one in Jan Smuts Avenue (admission 30c, children free). At the Zoo Lake you can go picnicking or boating. There is a bird sanctuary at Melrose Road, Birdhaven, reached by the No 1 bus to Rosebank and a pleasant walk of a mile. Finally there is Africa's largest snake park, the Transvaal Snake Park, at Halfway House, 24 km (15 miles) along the bus route to Pretoria. Admission 50c (children half) and you can see snakes being milked for their venom, used in making snake bite serum. It is open on Sundays but closed Tuesdays. To see typical South African flora, including proteas, the national flower, go to the 45-acre Wilds on Houghton Drive. September to December is the best time.

Other places worth a visit are the Art Gallery in Joubert Park, near the city centre, which has paintings by Renoir, Cézanne, Picasso and others; the Africana Museum in the Public Library; the 214-metre-high (700 ft) radio tower at Brixton – its observation roof gives you a panoramic view of the city; and the Planetarium in Braamfontein. Finally you can watch trading on the Stock

34

Exchange on working days from 0930 to 1530. The Hall of South African Achievement is next to the Visitors Gallery.

Once a year, around Easter, the Rand Show is held at Milner Park. It *Rand Show* is a parade of industrial, commercial and agricultural achievement. All the big exporting countries have stands.

Frankly the neighbourhood of Johannesburg and the Rand is not *Outside* exciting, save for the gold mines already described. It is after all *Johannesburg* primarily an industrial complex. One of the best excursions is down to the Vaal Dam, near Vereeniging, a drive of 96 km (60 miles) or so, or to Parys in the Free State. See page 49 for description. At Germiston, 12 km (7½ miles) from Johannesburg, there are weekend recreations and swimming in Germiston Lake. At Krugersdorp, 32 km (20 miles) north-west of the city, there is a small game reserve, from which you can conveniently drive on the 11 km (seven miles) to the Sterkfontein caves and then to the scenic spots of the Magaliesburg mountains. The waters of the Hartbeespoort Dam are in this range, 54 km (34 miles) from Pretoria, and pleasant for camping, fishing and boating.

Pretoria

Pretoria's life revolves around politicians, diplomats, and the 11 faculties of Pretoria University, one of the largest in South Africa, while UNISA is the largest correspondence college in the world. Where Johannesburg hustles, Pretoria walks at a dignified pace, consonant with being the Republic's administrative capital. It has several really notable buildings, and 480 km (300 miles) of its streets are planted with mauve flowering jacaranda trees, that bloom in October.

Founded in 1855 by M. W. Pretorius, first president of the Transvaal Republic, and named after his father, who was the victor of Blood River, the city started at the Fountains Valley. This is now a favourite picnic spot, while the city has spread out to cover 518 sq km (220 sq miles), including suburbs, and now has a population of 600,000. Frequent but slow train services connect it with Johannesburg, 56 km (35 miles) to the south. The Putco buses leave from Bosman Street and are slightly cheaper. A map is on page 37.

The focal point of the city is Church Square, with its statue of President Kruger, the Raadsaal and the main Post Office. From Church Square Paul Kruger Street runs up to the railway station, while there are shopping streets and new arcades close to the *Shopping* square. The National Tourist Bureau office is in Frans du Toit Building, Schoeman Street (telephone 286531).

Pretoria has plenty of hotels. Among the best are the Burgerspark, *Hotels* on the corner of Minnaar and Van der Walt streets, the Boulevard at 186 Struben Street, the Palms in Pretoria Road, the Continental at 152 Visagie Street and the Culemborg in Pretorius Street. Prices run from R 16 to R 40 per night for bed and breakfast. For cheaper hotels consult the SATOUR accommodation guide.

Restaurants The restaurant at the Burgerspark hotel and the Flamingo restaurant at the Boulevard Hotel have excellent reputations. Two other good places are Janina at 333 Andries Street and the Elite in Du Toit Arcade, Paul Kruger Street. There are coffee bars and several nightclubs. Generally, however, Pretoria people tend to entertain at home.

The city is the headquarters of SATOUR (Arcadia Centre, Arcadia) who are very well equipped to give every kind of assistance to **Travel Agents** overseas visitors. Travel agents include American Express and Cook's. There are three car hire firms: Avis, Bosman Street (telephone 30871), Budget Rent-a-Car, 405 Pretoria Street (telephone 26 3314), Hertz, on the corner of Paul Kruger and Vermeulen streets (telephone 28 7357). The Railways Travel Bureau is located in the Merino Building, 239 Pretorius Street. National Airways Corporation are at Wonderboom Airport, a few miles out (telephone 5 3529).

Historic Among Pretoria's historic buildings are Paul Kruger's small
buildings unpretentious house, and Melrose House which Lord Kitchener used as his headquarters in the Boer War. Also open are the State Model Schools, where Winston Churchill was kept prisoner and from which he made his celebrated escape the day before he was due to be handed back to the British anyway. But the only truly magnificent edifice is the Union Buildings, the seat of the Government on the Meintjieskop Ridge overlooking the city. They were completed in 1913 by Sir Herbert Baker who, sent to Europe to study as a young architect by Cecil Rhodes, designed many splendid South African buildings, and became justifiably famous.

Other places to visit are the Geological Museum in Paul Kruger Street; the Zoo, whose collection of 'cats' is remarkably complete **Wonderboom** and includes a Bengal tiger; and the Wonderboom Nature Reserve, just beyond the Zoo, 13 km (eight miles) from the city. The wonderboom is a fantastic species of fig tree, whose branches sprout when they touch the ground. Over the ages this specimen has formed five concentric circles of growth that can literally shelter a thousand people. The Zoo and Reserve are open daily.

The old Museum next to the Zoo has an unusual exhibition of Bushmen art. Out in the suburb of Gezina is the Janse Entomological Museum's renowned collection of a million moths and butterflies. Visits must be arranged through the Visitors Bureau.

Some of the suburbs, like Waterkloof eight km (five miles) out, are most attractive – they revise one's ideas about 'urban' living. The delightful Country Club, near Waterkloof Ridge, reciprocates with some overseas clubs.

About three km outside the city to the south rears up the somewhat stern Voortrekker Monument, effectively a shrine of the Afrikaner people. A marble frieze depicts the Great Trek story, and on 16th December, the anniversary of the battle of Blood River, a shaft of sunlight falls on the monument's altar.

The Premier Diamond Mine, 40 km (25 miles) east of Pretoria, is the world's biggest diamond mine. Barely three years after it was opened in 1902 it yielded a 3,024-carat white diamond measuring five inches across, the largest diamond yet found anywhere. They named it the Cullinan. It was bought by the Transvaal Government for a nominal £150,000 and presented to King Edward VII, who had it cut into more than 100 stones, all of which are now in the British Crown Jewels. The mine itself is now 884 m (2,900 ft) across in one direction and 426 m (1,400 ft) in another, with an average depth of 152 m (500 ft), and has produced seven tons of diamonds so far. It was closed from 1932 until 1950 as uneconomical. Since reopening it has produced a million carats a year, mainly of industrial diamonds. Visits may be arranged through the PRO, Premier Diamond Mine, Cullinan (telephone 012 312). Booking is essential.

Premier Diamond Mine

You can see the Ndebele tribe, in their traditional dress, living in a kraal of geometrically painted houses at Klipgat, 48 km (29 miles) north-west of Pretoria. Permits are essential and are obtainable from the Bantu Commissioner, Room 6, corner Von Wielligh and Struben Streets, Pretoria (telephone 2 7217). Permits obtainable 0800 to 1245 – 1330 to 1500 but closed Saturday and Sunday. The village is open daily excluding Sundays.

Ndebele Village

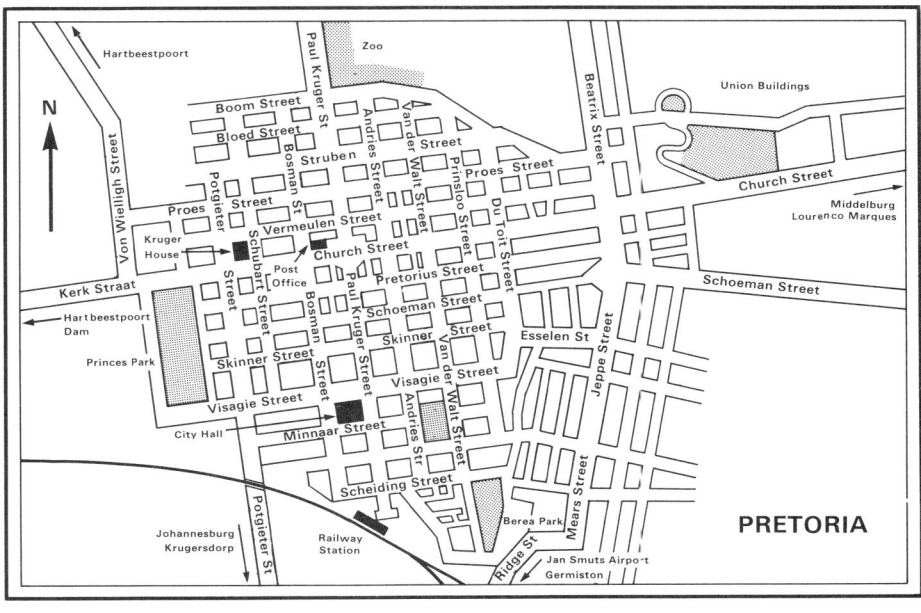

The Northern Transvaal

Apart from providing the Great North Road up to Zimbabwe, the Northern Transvaal is mainly noted for its mineral baths, a complete list of which can be had from SATOUR offices, for mountain scenery, fishing, and game. Being mostly upland country it has an invigorating climate and it is increasingly attracting tourist development, though less well known than the north-eastern Transvaal. It offers interesting side trips and a number of small pleasure resorts. Some of the minor roads are not tarred. For exact routes consult the *AA Guide* or the *Transvaal Weekender*.

Warmbaths

Taking the road north from Pretoria you come to Warmbaths, 112 km (70 miles) on. This is a popular mineral bath area, with golf, tennis, bowling and a caravan park. We recommend the Bronne-hof, 31 Sutter Road and the White Horse Hotel (PO Box 15). Prices are from R 10.50 to R 25 per day. Driving on through the tobacco lands to Potgietersrus, you should visit the huge caves to the north of the town. In one of these, men blasting for lime exposed a rock face upon which could be 'read' the history of the human race from the time of hominids and the world's first firemakers. Fossilised in the strata are relics of sub-human forms of life. In the last century Makapan and his tribe were cornered in one cave by a Boer commando after they had murdered a party of Voortrekkers at Moorddrif (Murder Drift).

East of Potgietersrus, an agricultural centre, are extensive citrus estates where 'Outspan' oranges are grown. The Great North Road continues up on to the Pietersburg Plateau, 1,220 m (4,000 ft) above sea level. Pietersburg itself is the largest town in the Northern Transvaal, and has three hotels including a Holiday Inn. The Ranch Motel has first-class food and its own air strip. An interesting side trip from here is to Haenertsburg and the Magoebaskloof, a huge cleft in the Drakensberg Mountains, which runs from Natal.

The modern Magoebaskloof Hotel is 1,433 m (4,700 ft) up with spectacular views down the Letaba Valley to the lowveld. By going down the Kloof road, dropping 609 m (2,000 ft) in a few miles, you reach Tzaneen, from where it is 115 km (72 miles) tarred to the central Kruger Park entrance at Phalaborwa (see Kruger Park, page 41). Phalaborwa itself is a copper mining boom town with a first-class air conditioned hotel. It is pretty hot, but who cares with 315 million tons of copper sulphide there.

Letaba
Reserve

The Rondalia Letaba Game Reserve is 32 km (20 miles) to the north, bordering the Kruger Park. For details write to Rondalia, PO Box 2290, Pretoria, which is a South African touring organisation similar to the Automobile Association.

Merensky
Reserve

North-east of Tzaneen is the Hans Merensky Nature Reserve, a stretch of lowveld with a variety of game. Merensky was a notably

38

successful geologist. Among his many discoveries were the enormous copper deposits at Phalaborwa.

Duiwelskloof, 19 km (12 miles) from Tzaneen, despite its name which means Devil's Valley, is an attractive small town, and has an extraordinary primeval forest of cycads. These are palm-like trees, up to three m (10 ft) high, that flourished in the days of the dinosaurs and are extremely rare. Also near here is the home of Modjadji, legendary Rain Queen of the Bavenda tribe, around whom Rider Haggard devised his novel *She*. The Bavenda, incidentally, have a curious sub-tribe called the Lemba, who guard their holy drums, and are inexplicably Semitic in origin. They observe Kosher rules, eat no pork, are astute businessmen, and have a mixture of Semitic and African facial features. To visit the tribal area and the cycads you need a permit from the Bantu Commissioner in Duiwelskloof.

Cycads

The Rain Queen

You regain the Great North Road at Bandelierkop. Louis Trichardt, 400 km (250 miles) from Pretoria, is a beautiful little town 945 m (3,100 ft) up in the forested Soutpansberg foothills and a good stopping-off point en route to the northern entrance of the Kruger Park, 142 km (89 miles) or the Drakensberg escarpment. Good hotels near the town are the Clouds End (two miles north) and the Mountain Inn, eight km (five miles) north, both charging from R 10 (room only) per night and in glorious mountain scenery with riding, swimming and other sports. North-east of the town is Mapungubwe, a flat-topped holy mountain. The relics of its ancient civilisation are now in the Pretoria Museum.

Louis Trichardt

From Louis Trichardt you cross the Soutpansberg between perpendicular cliffs at Wyllies Poort and reach Messina, 14 km (nine miles) from the Zimbabwe border. This is the place where, during the early stages of the Rhodesian sanctions campaign, a pair of British diplomats sat anxiously counting the petrol lorries passing through to Beit Bridge, until they themselves became headline news. Messina is within easy reach of various historic sites, including the stone forts and prehistoric copper workings of Dlinza, similar to Zimbabwe (see page 143). The area is alive with game, including lion and elephant, and dotted with grotesque stumpy baobab trees, typical of Central Africa. The health-giving Tshipese Springs 40 km (25 miles) south-east of Messina are worth a visit. There is a hotel.

Finally at Beit Bridge you cross the Limpopo River, which Kipling in his *Just So Stories* called 'the great, green, greasy Limpopo River, all set about with fever trees'. Actually it is muddier down in Mozambique, where it reaches the sea. Like All African rivers its banks are a watering place for game.

Eastern Transvaal

This is a part of South Africa best known for its game, down on the lowveld east of the Drakensberg escarpment, where it is decidedly hotter and more humid than on the highveld, though the nights can be cold. Driving east from Pretoria on National Road 4 towards Nelspruit and the Kruger Park you pass first through the farming lands of the highveld. After Witbank, where Sir Winston Churchill hid during his Boer War escape, it is worth turning off north to the *Loskop Reserve* Loskop Game Reserve, created around a dam. You can hire boats to fish, there are rondavels, a restaurant and swimming pool. For reservations write to Loskop Dam Public Resort, Private Bag X1525, Middelburg, Tvl. Or try the Bundu Inn, 43 km (28 miles) off (address PO Box 33, Dennilton). From Loskop you can return south to Middelburg. Continuing on the N4 you come to Belfast, with the Sterkspruit Falls six km (four miles) away, and then to Machadodorp, with nearby radioactive sulphur baths and trout fishing.

Summit Route Here you are almost at the Summit Route, not so much a route as an area which you can drive round in various ways, and which stretches between the Drakensberg, Nelspruit, the Kruger Park, the Sabie River and Lydenburg. It is justifiably renowned for its unrivalled landscapes ranging from mountain waterfalls to lowveld. It is very well provided with hotels, charging between R 12 and R 30 per day, except where we indicate otherwise. In many places you will find old mining camps from the gold rush days. Both the AA and the Rondalia Touring Club print useful maps of it. Remember that in summer heavy rain may make gravel roads impassable.

Although the N4 from Machadodorp towards Nelspruit takes you past a good place to stay, the Bambi Motel, at the point where the road to Lydenburg branches off, there is a more attractive way through the Eland River Valley. The railway also takes this route, through the dramatic Elandsberg Pass. Near Waterval-Bo are a 90 m (295 ft) waterfall and a nature reserve. You rejoin the N4 near the Montrose Falls and the Montrose Hotel.

Nelspruit Nelspruit, the junction for the Sabie and White River railway lines, is the commercial centre of this lowveld citrus fruit area and a stopping place for most coach tours. It has six hotels, about the best being the Drum Rock. The Country Club is open to overseas visitors and has good amenities. From here the N4 goes on past the southern edge of the Kruger Park, where there is an entrance at Crocodile Bridge, to Komatipoort and so to Maputo, the capital of Mozambique.

Barberton South from Nelspruit lies Barberton, born of the 1888 gold rush, and still a mining town, with names like 'Revolver Creek'. There are splendid drives around here, and you can cross the mountains into Swaziland, described on page 135. Barberton's two main hotels are the Impala (PO Box 83) and the Phoenix Hotel in Pilgrim Street.

40

It was about Barberton and its neighbourhood that Sir Percy Fitzpatrick wrote his classic *Jock of the Bushveld*, describing the experiences of his dog and himself when he was a transport rider working on the wagon route to the gold fields there.

However, most people come through Nelspruit en route not for Barberton but for the Kruger Park, five hours' drive from Johannesburg. There is a daily flight to the Park from Jan Smuts airport. The Park is 402 km (250 miles) long and has six main entrances. In the south there are Crocodile Bridge, Malelane, Numbi and Orpen, in the centre Phalaborwa, and in the north Punda Milia. It is a good idea to enter by one and leave by another. Basically it is an enormous tract of flat veld, broken by rivers in which hippo and crocodile laze. The part most visited is the south, mainly as communications are better in the areas around Pretoriuskop, Olifants Camp and Skukuza. The north of the Park, which used to be closed from October to March because of the rains, is now open all year round. Even on a short visit you can expect to see elephant, giraffe, buffalo, zebra, wildebeest, sable, kudu, waterbuck, impala, hippo, crocodile, hyena and possibly lion. In a longer trip, especially one that takes you to the north, you see more game, like rhino, leopard and cheetah. The best elephant country is around Shingwidzi in the north, where the landscape is also wilder and more beautiful.

The Kruger Park

The Park's 2,400 km (1,500 miles) of roads are suitable for ordinary saloon cars. The speed limit is mostly 40 kph (25 mph), although 16 kph (10 mph) is more sensible if you expect to see game. You are not allowed to get out of your car except in a camp area. The animals are quite used to cars, and lions have even learnt to use exhaust fumes to mask their scent when ambushing prey, but to leave your car is dangerous. You must be in a camp by sundown and may not leave again before dawn.

The 11 camps vary. In general they have simple accommodation in thatched rondavels, a restaurant and a shop. Cooking facilities are free for campers, though you should tip the African attendants 50c per meal. Pretoriuskop and Skukuza camps are the more luxurious. Entry fees to the Park are R 2 per adult plus R 2 per vehicle. A bungalow costs from R 10. You must book at least three days before arriving if you are going out of school holidays, or three weeks in advance during school holidays.

Rest Camps

Three wilderness trails are now run in the Park. They are the Wolhuter in the south, Olifants in the central region and Nyala in the north. These trails begin weekly on Mondays and Fridays and offer three nights and four days in the bush. Cost per person is R 67.60. Reservations can be made at the National Parks Board, PO Box 787, Pretoria (telephone 44 1194). Useful leaflets are obtainable about the Park both from the Parks Board and SATOUR.

Wilderness Trails

Having visited the Park, take the Summit Route north from Nelspruit to White River, a pleasant village surrounded by citrus farms, where we recommend the Pine Lake Inn (PO Box 94, White River). The Winkler (telephone 293) R 25 bed and breakfast, is an unusual motel in a striking setting. From here it is a fast run through beautiful country to the Numbi Gate of the Kruger Park, which we shall describe in a moment, past the Bushman's Rock, 11 km (seven miles) from White River, upon which you get wide views over the lowveld. The Bushman's Rock Hotel (PO Box 178, White River) is a pleasant place to stay, while there is a good motel 16 km (10 miles) from Numbi, called the Numbi Motel (PO Box 6, Hazyview). This is by the Numbi turn-off to the Park. If you continue straight on you come to the Sabi River Bungalows, and a hotel of the same name with swimming pool and golf course, delightfully

Sabie River

situated at the end of the Sabie River Valley, where at the turn of the century the transport riders bringing mining equipment from Delagoa Bay (now Maputo) to the Rand used to stop to water their horses. You can still ride, as mounts are available on the 120 acre estate. Equally you can land an aircraft on the golf course. The hotel is three star, is air-conditioned and also offers tennis and fishing. Address PO Box 13, Hazyview, or book through Southern Sun Hotels.

Mala Mala

A number of private game reserves have been established near the Kruger Park to cater for individually minded – and well-heeled – visitors. About the best is Mala Mala, with 100,000 acres to itself, reached by taking the Kruger gate turn-off from Hazyview and then turning left at the Lisbon store, from which it is signposted, the distance from Hazyview being 40 km (25 miles). Mala Mala has 150 staff for 50 guests; European guides and African trackers look after you and it's as good a game lodge as can be found anywhere. We flew in unexpectedly at 0730 one morning – flying is the best way to get here. Within 20 minutes a vast breakfast was ready. Within an hour a game ranger was driving us out to the game-viewing platforms in the bush. South Africans think Mala Mala expensive at R 155 a day, but it's worth the money. Bookings at Suite 4916, Carlton Centre, Johannesburg 2001.

Londolozi

Literally a few kilometres down the road from Mala Mala is Londolozi Game Reserve overlooking the Sand River. It offers chalets or rondavels and excellent food. The reserve, 69 sq miles in extent, offers guided walking tours and game spotting in open landrovers. All-inclusive costs per day for the chalets are R 79, and R 47 for the rondavels. Reservations can be made at 26 Stanley Avenue, Auckland Park, Johannesburg 2092 (telephone 726 6701).

Timbavati Game Reserve

North west of Kruger National Park's Orpen Gate is the 289 sq miles Timbavati Game Reserve where there are two excellent game lodges. One is Motswari Game Lodge which offers luxury accommodation in air conditioned bungalows at R 95 a night per person. Dawn, sunset and midnight drives in open landrovers or trails on foot are conducted by experienced game rangers.

42

Reservations can be made in Johannesburg at PO Box 3234, Johannesburg 2000 (telephone 39 1398). Timbavati became famous a few years ago for its white lions. However they are now in zoos elsewhere. In the north of the Reserve Tanda Tula Game Lodge has six luxury chalets with air-conditioning and offers much the same game viewing opportunities as the other lodges. All inclusive fly-in safaris range from R 297 for one night to R 658 for four nights. Book at Game Trackers, 279 Kent Avenue, Ferndale, Randburg.

Tanda Tula

North of Acornhoek you come to Phalaborwa and the unbroken stretch of thorn bush that runs through Zimbabwe, Malawi, Tanzania, Kenya and finally dies out in Somalia not far short of the Red Sea. As Hemingway succinctly put it, 'just miles and miles of bloody Africa'. Better to turn back and explore more of the Summit Route. Pilgrim's Rest, 1,310 m (4,300 ft) up in the mountains, is a sleepy former gold rush town. Book in advance, as there are only two hotels, the Royal and the Pilgrim's. Both are magnificent examples of gold rush architecture. The 19th century atmosphere has been sensitively preserved. If you want a newer hotel, try the cottage style Mount Sheba Hotel (PO Box 4, Pilgrim's Rest) some 600 m (2,000 ft) above the town. There are breathtaking views too over the lowveld from God's Window, a vantage point 17 km (11 miles) from Graskop. North from Pilgrim's is the Blyde River Canyon, a 600 m (2,000 ft approx) deep and six and a half km (four miles) wide indentation in the black granite wall of the Drakensberg. Many sub-tropical birds haunt the forests and there are some leopards around. The 16 km (10 miles) long canyon is part of the Blyderivierspoort Nature Reserve and accommodation is available.

Blyde River Canyon

Between Pilgrim's Rest and Sabie (46 km/29 miles west of Sabi River Bungalows) are several gorges and waterfalls. The Sabie Falls Hotel is comfortable (PO Box 58, Sabie). The town lies below Mt Anderson and a splendid drive across the 2,133 m (7,000 ft) Long Tom Pass, named after a Boer War gun taken along it, leads you to Lydenburg, known for its trout streams. The Grand Hotel is comfortable. We can hardly say too often that this whole area of the Eastern Transvaal is scenically superb and offers great scope for fishing, walking and riding.

Free State farm

The Orange Free State

The Orange Free State is both geographically and emotionally the heart of the Republic. Its 49,866 sq miles have no coastline. To its basic farming have been added the developments of the largest goldfields in Southern Africa. Although landlocked it has quite a lot of attractions. For many years practically all one saw there was the 'dust' of other people's journeys north or south. But recently the province has been opened up and its tourist facilities greatly improved, though overall it remains a country of farmers to whom the Voortrekkers are very much living ancestors.

History

You cannot hope to understand the Free State without knowing something of its history. The Orange River itself was named after the Royal House of the Netherlands by a professional soldier called Colonel Robert Jacob Gordon in the 1770s. When the Boers, people of Dutch, German and Huguenot origin at the Cape, trekked away from British rule in 1836 they crossed the Orange River and found vast uninhabited tracts of land suitable for stock breeding. Here they outspanned their ox wagons and then built homesteads, ploughed, cultivated, ranched – and soon claimed the whole area between the Orange and Vaal rivers. Technically, they were still subjects of the British colony at the Cape. After 18 years of continual conflict the British decided to cut their losses and in 1854 recognised the Orange Free State by the Bloemfontein Convention.

44

The Boers who crossed the Vaal River in further search of land created the Transvaal (see page 26). During the Boer War much of the fighting took place in the Free State. The highly mobile Boer commandos, mounted on horseback and carrying their food and ammunition in their saddlebags, long outwitted the British infantry. They were only finally defeated by the construction of long lines of forts that divided up the countryside into controllable zones, some still visible today. If you are interested in the Boer War an excellent and impartial account of it is given in *Goodbye Dolly Gray* by Rayne Kruger, the grandson of President Kruger.

In 1910 the Free State, having lost its independence in the war, regained it as part of the Union. In recognition of its importance, Bloemfontein was made the South African judicial centre, and houses the Appeal Court, a classical building with fine stinkwood panelling inside.

The Free State is all on the high inland plateau; in consequence the days are sunny and warm, and the nights cool and crisp. Rain falls mostly in summer. Average temperatures at Bloemfontein 1,422 m (4,665 ft) above sea level are 24°C (74·7°F) in summer and 8°C (47·3°F) in winter.

National Parks

GOLDEN GATE HIGHLANDS NATIONAL PARK

The plum in the Free State's pie, from the visitor's point of view, is the Golden Gate Highlands National Park, a pocket of magnificent scenery in the State's north-eastern corner. It is among the foothills of Lesotho's Maluti mountains, just around the corner from the Drakensberg resorts in Natal (see page 91), and 58 km (36 miles) from Bethlehem. You can reach it as easily from Johannesburg as from Bloemfontein. Scenically the best approach is from the little town of Kestell. Being between 1,828 m (6,000 ft) and 2,743 m (9,000 ft) above sea level, the Park has very different vegetation from South Africa's other National Parks. In autumn the red, green and deep yellow of the indigenous trees – oudehout, protea, mountain sage and wild olive – are unrivalled. So are the sunsets, whose golden light on the huge rocks and sandstone cliffs gave the Park its name. Wind and water erosion have carved some of these cliffs into extraordinary shapes.

Wildlife being re-established here includes eland, black wildebeest, blesbok, red hartebeest, mountain reedbuck, grey rhebuck, duiker, klipsringer and baboon. The Park is also the habitat of the rare black eagle and the lammergeyer and it is worth bringing binoculars. The 26 km (16 mile) Rhebuck hiking trail through the Park takes two days to follow. There is a hotel which charges from R 11.00 per night as well as chalets, rondavels, and a golf course. Camping sites are available. There is a shop, a swimming pool, and petrol is available. Picnicking is allowed and you can hire horses for 25c per hour. Reservations and enquiries can be made through travel agents, to the Director, National Parks Board, PO Box 787, Pretoria (telephone 44 1194).

WILLEM PRETORIUS GAME RESERVE

Near the Allemanskraal dam, this small reserve includes a lake. Animals to be seen include springbok, eland, black wildebeest and impala. Two hundred bird species have been identified. In the hills nearby are prehistoric beehive-shaped stone huts. A resort near the Reserve has swimming, golf, water-sports, and a restaurant. See page 50.

Lesser reserves in the Free State include the Soetdoring Nature Reserve by the Krugerdrif Dam and the Franklin Game Reserve, both near Bloemfontein.

The Eastern Free State

Bethlehem

Most of the Eastern Free State, near the Park, is known for good fishing and spectacular scenery. Bethlehem, situated appropriately on the Jordan River, spent R 500,000 on turning nearby Lake Athlone into a holiday resort. This natural park area now has cottages for rent, a restaurant and a caravan park. Within easy walking distance of Bethlehem's centre is the Pretorius Kloof bird sanctuary, spread along both sides of the river, which winds through a forested mountain gorge. A good hotel in Bethlehem is the Park Hotel (one star) in Muller Street, which charges R 10 bed and breakfast. There are two other one star hotels.

Harrismith

Further east again, on the Natal border, is Harrismith, called after a former Governor, Sir Harry Smith. His wife gave her name to Ladysmith in Natal. Harrismith was originally a military outpost and became a strategic point in the Boer War, and one of the blockhouses is still preserved east of the town by the river. It is an extremely beautiful highland area, and a good place from which to look around the dramatic valleys of Van Reenen's Pass, and to strike out for the Drakensberg resorts of Natal (described on pages 91–95). The Drakensberg Botanic Gardens in the town contain flora representative of the area. The Central Hotel is comfortable, though do not expect too much in small towns like this. There are some Bushman paintings near Harrismith, and next to the town hall is a petrified tree thought to be 150 million years old. Piet Retief's rock, where his daughter wrote his name in 1837 (see also page 140), is at the head of the Oliviershoek Pass. But before taking the lesser road past it and through to Bergville and the Drakensberg, check on its condition. It can be bad after rain.

Ladybrand

At Ladybrand, round the mountains nearer Bloemfontein, there are an interesting gorge and underground cave, both geological oddities, while nearby at Modderpoort there are excellent examples of prehistoric rock paintings. The Modder River itself has been used to make a 'beach' centre, 27 km (17 miles) from Bloemfontein. This is Mazelspoort, known as the playground of the Free State. Trim lawns and cobbled paths lead from an enormous freshwater swimming pool 135 m (444 ft) long, down to the river. Boats can be hired, and in the evening the band at an open air dance floor gets to work, while people make their own *braaivleis* (barbecues, invariably abbreviated to *braai*). There is a good restaurant if you don't want to cook for yourself.

Mazelspoort

Bloemfontein

Bloemfontein is the capital of the Free State, a city of spires, gardens and monuments to a pioneering past of which its citizens are intensely proud. Its central situation in the Republic has made it a popular venue for congresses and conferences, as well as an educational centre. Daily air services connect it with Johannesburg (374 km/233 miles – one hour's flight) and there are frequent flights to other cities. The Orange Express operates twice weekly in both directions between Cape Town and Durban, calling at Bloemfontein and Kimberley. Daily trains call at Bloemfontein on their way from Johannesburg to Cape Town. By road Johannesburg is 425 km (264 miles), and Cape Town 1,901 km (645 miles).

Since its foundation in 1846 the city has grown to a population of over 185,000, with a large and active University. But the hub of the city continues to be Hoffman Square, with its lawns, trees and its notable fountain. At night this is illuminated in ever changing colours as a reminder that the city's name means 'fountain of flowers'. The fountain is a favourite rendezvous.

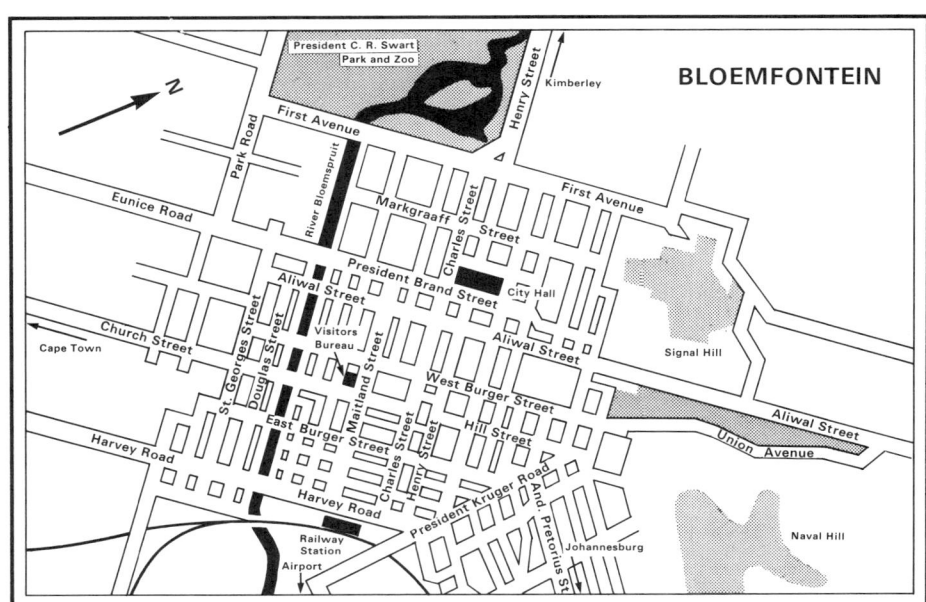

47

Hotels

The Visitors Bureau is on Hoffman Square and the main shopping streets are near it. The offices of the National Tourist Bureau are in the FVB Centre, Maitland Street (telephone 7 1362). You can obtain all the items you would expect in a city. Among the hotels we suggest the Bloemfontein, East Burger Street (four star), President, Union Avenue (three star), the Cecil on St Andrew Street (two star), and the Fontein on Zastron Street (two star). Prices range from R 16.50 for bed only to R 39 for dinner, bed and breakfast. Car hire can be arranged through Avis (telephone 33 2931), Hertz (33 2132), or Budget Rent-a-Car (33 1178). Taxis, as elsewhere in South Africa, can seldom be hailed on the street. Get your hotel to call one. For air charter ring NAC at Tempe airport (78841).

Of the many public gardens Kings Park is the largest, and is a blaze of colour all year round. Its lily ponds are particularly attractive. The Prince's Rose Garden covers eight acres and is one of the biggest anywhere in the world.

The most interesting building is also the least pretentious. This is the Old Raadsaal in St George's Street. It was originally built as a school, then served as a church, as Government offices and as the Free State Parliament. Within its whitewashed mud walls, surmounted by a thatched roof, were held the meetings that led to the signing of the Bloemfontein Convention and the recognition of the Free State in 1854. Naturally the Free Staters hold it in very special affection. The present Raadsaal, with its sandstone pillars, is in President Brand Street and is quite a notable piece of architecture. H. V. Morton in his book *In Search of South Africa* called it 'a little fragment of the clear classical world in blossom upon the highveld'.

Other places of historic interest include the Fort, built in 1848, and the Women's National War Memorial, an obelisk 34 m (113 ft) high, commemorating the women and children who died in the Boer War.

Though many British people do not realise it to this day, the South African War was one in which the Boer families, men, women and children, were totally involved. Many had their houses and farms burnt down by the British as reprisals. Hence the monument, beneath which lie the ashes of a most courageous Englishwoman, Emily Hobhouse, who worked for the welfare of the prisoners, alongside the Boer leaders, President Steyn and General de Wet. Close by is the War Museum which houses a comprehensive collection of relics and antiquities of the war period, both military and domestic, including the first radio ever used in warfare.

Museums

Another museum, the National Museum, is worth visiting to see the fossil remains of the largest known dinosaur of the Triassic period; and the Florisbad skull of a primitive sapient man.

Opposite: Hex River Valley, Cape Province. Photograph SATOUR

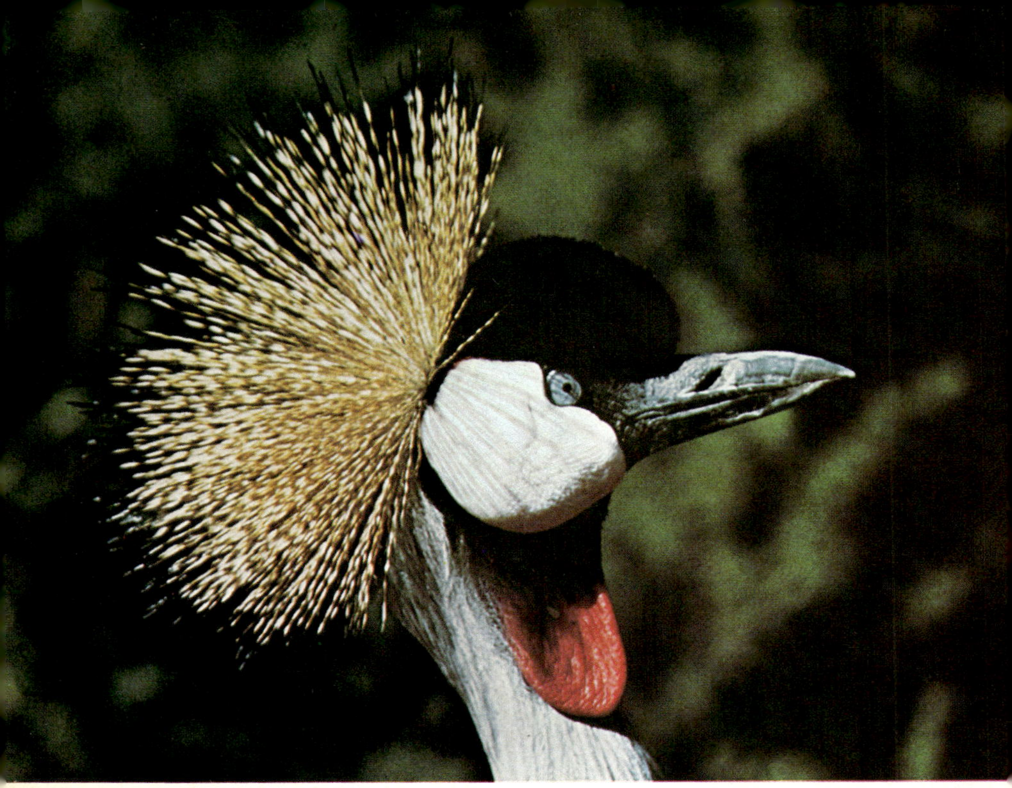

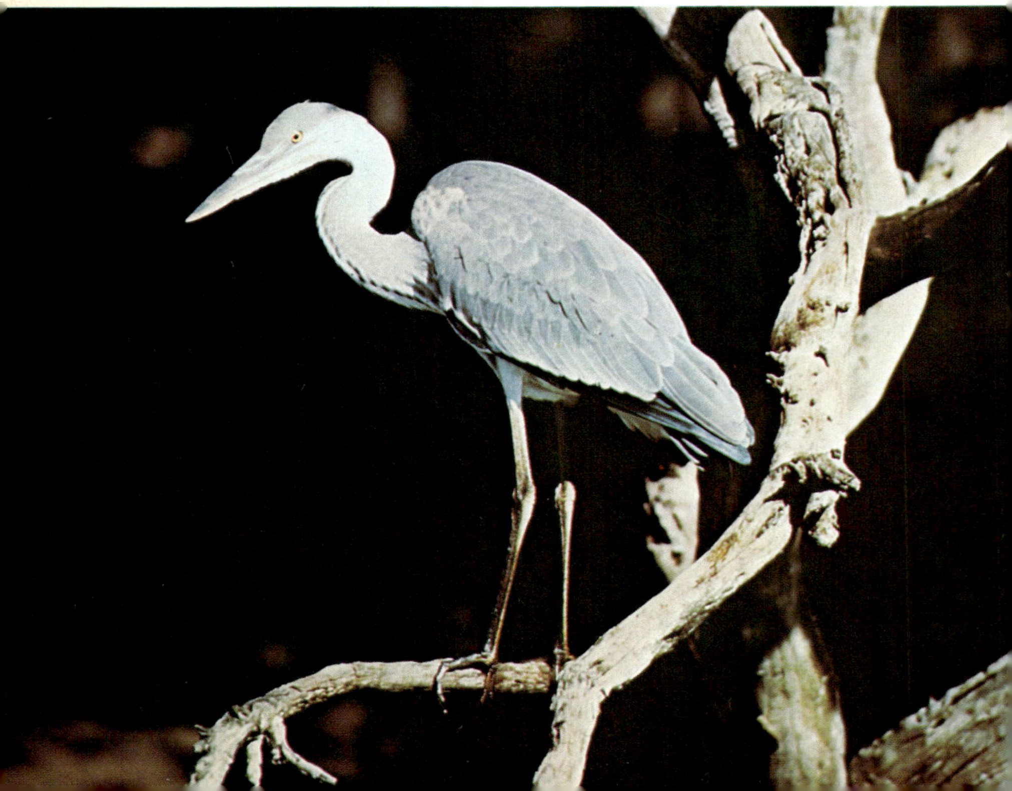

Having a remarkably clear atmosphere, Bloemfontein has become an internationally known centre for astronomical observation. Out at Mazelspoort is the Boyden Station of the Harvard College Observatory of the USA, which moved here from a previous site in the Andes Mountains of Peru. A rival to it is the Lamont-Hussey Observatory of the University of Michigan, established on Naval Hill in 1928. It specialises in the study of double stars, a name given to two suns revolving around a common axis. So far it has discovered 7,300 of these. You can visit the observatory by appointment and, who knows, you might be present when a star is 'born'.

Naval Hill is actually part of the Franklin Game Reserve, very near the city centre and with good views. The Reserve covers 500 acres and contains springbok, blesbok, eland, zebra, ostriches and various species of birds. Incidentally some humorist, commenting on the lack of night life in Bloemfontein, once remarked that Naval Hill was the sexiest thing the city possessed. Indeed for entertainment you are limited to the Civic Theatre and a few cinemas. But in this climate you get more value out of doors, and sporting facilities are first class. The Ramblers Club offers a clubhouse and most sports for both men and women. Visitors can apply for temporary membership. The city has five bowling clubs, two golf clubs, 11 rugby clubs, horseracing, polo, archery, and yachting.

Franklin Game Reserve

Sport

The Southern Free State

The southern part of the Free State has frankly not much to offer, though near Fauresmith the Kalkfontein Dam is a pleasant place to go camping, while another resort has been created near the giant Hendrik Verwoerd dam on the Orange river, the largest water supply scheme in Africa, north east of Colesberg. Kimberley, the legendary diamond city, is of course just inside the Cape Province (see page 66) though closer to Bloemfontein than any other city. Quite a number of Boer War sites lie between the two cities. During the war itself Thomas Cook, the travel agents, sold battlefield tours in Britain, much to the annoyance of the British authorities. Today interest in the subject is reviving, just as in the United States the Civil War battlefields have become tourist attractions, and are signposted.

Aliwal North has a famous mineral spa, where pools and baths draw on a mineral spring delivering two million litres of water a day at a temperature of 35°C (95°F). The town is on the Orange river.

The Northern Free State

As you come south from Johannesburg on the N1 road, your first taste of the Free State is the resort town of Parys, the 'Pride of the

Opposite top: Crowned Crane.
Bottom: Grey Heron. Photographs SATOUR

Vaal River	Vaal River', set in beautiful scenery. It is a bracing and popular place with several hotels, including the Echos Motel in Boom Street (R 10 room only). The Vaal Dam, some 56 km (35 miles) away on the Transvaal border, is developing as an inland resort with fishing for barbel and yellow fish, and golf. There is a good hotel called the Riviera, actually on the Transvaal side. (R 9.20 bed and breakfast. PO Box 128, Vereeniging, Transvaal.) Also on the border is Sasolburg, notable as the place where low grade coal is converted into oil. From Parys 90 km (56 miles) south bring you to
Kroonstad	Kroonstad, a modern town nestling peacefully on the Vaal River and a good base for a fishing holiday. Watch out for the traditional South African game called jukskei, very like pitching horseshoes, except wooden yoke-pins as used on the Great Trek are pitched at a peg, instead of horseshoes.

Although your first impression of the Free State will have been of mile upon mile of golden maize crops – not for nothing is it nicknamed the granary of the Republic – at Kroonstad you begin to see the influence of a different wealth. Suddenly the horizon is dotted with mine dumps as you near the towns of Welkom, Odendaalsrus, Virginia and Allanridge, all built on gold.

Goldfields	The goldfields of the Free State were only discovered in 1946. Yet today they are working up to a production of 350 million fine ounces of gold a year, worth R 175 billion. Welkom turned from barren veld and grass into an imaginative town in under 20 years – in fact if you want to see what a boom town of the 1960s looks like you should stop in Welkom, then compare it with pictures of Kimberley or the Rand in the old pioneering days. They have even achieved a traffic system without any traffic lights. No longer does getting rich quickly involve making a shambles of the environment. Of the hotels at Welkom we recommend the 147, in Stateway, and the Golden Orange, both charging R 18.50 bed and breakfast upwards. One extraordinary sight near Welkom is the water pans of the mines on which thousands of waterbirds, seagulls and flamingoes settle.
Willem Pretorius Game Reserve	A little south-east of the goldfields is the historic small town of Winburg, not far from which is the Willem Pretorius Game Reserve. Although this reserve has no carnivorous animals it does boast a number of white rhinoceros, giraffe and antelope. The scenery is striking, flanked by the rocky ridge of the Dorinberg, and drops from these mountain slopes through wooded gorges to open plains, and the lake formed by the Allemanskraal Dam. You can reach the dam from the road between Winburg and Kroonstad and you will find it to be a small masterpiece of game reserve planning, stocked with indigenous fish and attracting a lot of bird life. Boats can be hired, which provide a good way of obtaining a vantage point for watching the game come down to drink at the lakeside in the late afternoons. There is a swimming pool and a restaurant.

50

Cape Dutch farmhouse

The Cape Province

To most people the name 'The Cape' summons up a vision of Table Mountain towering above the city of Cape Town, of warm beaches and of vineyards in the valleys behind with their whitewashed Cape Dutch homesteads. The magnificent bays, flowers and plants to delight and astound any botanist, pine woods, gardens and superb climate all contribute to giving the Cape Peninsula a drama of contrasts that is all its own. It was first discovered by the Portuguese navigator Bartholomew Diaz in 1488.

What is not realised so immediately is that the Cape Province is in fact substantially larger than France. Its 270,000 sq miles run north to the Orange River and the frontiers of Botswana. They include part of the Kalahari Desert and the famous Big Hole at the diamond mining city of Kimberley.

Naturally the climate varies within this vast area. Basically it is Mediterranean at the coast with low humidity and temperatures between 13°C (55°F) at night and 27°C (80°F) by day in summer (November–February) and 8°C (48°F) and 18°C (65°F) in winter (June–September). In spring the countryside is aflame with wild flowers. All in all the climate is one of the healthiest in the world. Most of the rain falls between May and September. Deep inland, for instance in the Great Karoo, it becomes hotter and dryer.

Climate

51

National Parks and Game Reserves

Comparatively little big game remains in the Province, except of course in the National Parks. For instance the elephant and leopard in the Knysna forests are only rarely observed. But you will most certainly come across smaller animals such as springbok. There are some 75 reserves either under the control of the province or local authorities. These are the National Parks:

THE KALAHARI GEMSBOK NATIONAL PARK

Forming a wedge between the borders of the Cape Province, Namibia and Botswana, some 9,500 sq km (3,800 sq miles) of the Park's million sq miles total lies within South Africa, most of it being in Botswana. The Park is 1,104 km (690 miles) from Cape Town and 320 km (200 miles) from Upington. Lion, wildebeest, gemsbok and others. Prolific bird life. Three rest camps. Open all year, though March to October is best. See page 68.

AUGRABIES FALLS NATIONAL PARK

Mainly known for its interesting rock formations and aloes this small Park also has many baboons, monkeys, klipspringers, and small feline species. Open all year round. Visitors can stay in thatched huts or a camp. Restaurant.

THE ADDO ELEPHANT NATIONAL PARK

72 km (45 miles) from Port Elizabeth, mostly forest, with many other animals besides elephant. Rest camp and restaurant. Open all the year. See page 64.

THE MOUNTAIN ZEBRA NATIONAL PARK

27 km (17 miles) from Cradock in the Great Karoo. Farmhouse accommodation, huts, and camping. Open all year.

KAROO NATIONAL PARK

Situated near Beaufort West. No accommodation, but there is a three day trail and hikers stay overnight in huts. Open all year.

TSITSIKAMA FOREST AND COASTAL NATIONAL PARK

Part forest and part coast on the Garden Route, near Storms River. Rare birds and forest trees. Marine plants and animals. Chalets and restaurant. Open all year. See page 71.

BONTEBOK NATIONAL PARK

Just south of Swellendam. Preserves the bontebok, a rare species of antelope. Open all the year. See page 69.

Cape Town

The classic introduction to Cape Town is to arrive by sea, unhappily seldom possible today, though you get the same view from the Bloubergstrand beaches. There before you rises the 1,164 m (3,549 ft) Table Mountain, its deceptively flat-looking top sometimes shrouded by cloud – the tablecloth, as people call it. On either side stand two peaks, Devil's Peak to the east and Lion's Head to the west. It's not easy to get oneself orientated in Cape Town but the maps in this chapter should help as would the panoramic aerial view postcards on sale. The city and the harbour face north. Signal Hill, which forms the rump of Lion's Head, separates the city from the resort suburbs of Sea Point and Clifton. Round to the east, on the far side of Devil's Peak, are the snobbier residential areas of Newlands, Claremont, Kenilworth, Bishopscourt and Wynberg. The dramatic, ever present, Table Mountain, makes Cape Town visually one of the world's most exciting cities, second only perhaps to Rio de Janeiro.

The city was founded in 1652 by Jan van Riebeeck. Today, though jealously preserving some of its fine old buildings, like the Castle van Riebeeck initiated, it is a modern thriving metropolis of just on 1·2 million people (380,000 whites). The foreshore near the harbour has been reclaimed and the freeways are way ahead of most European capitals' road systems, though there is no escape from parking meters in the centre and, increasingly, shopping centres are being established in the suburbs.

The Gardens

The focal shopping and business thoroughfare is Adderley Street, of which more in a moment; at the end of it lie the Gardens, correctly the Botanical Gardens. Grouped round them are the cool, white classical South African Art Gallery and the Parliament Buildings, largely designed by Sir Herbert Baker. Above towers the huge mass of Table Mountain. The Museum nearby holds Bushman paintings among its many exhibits of Africana, while the Gardens were the Cape settlement's original vegetable patch. They now have 8,000 different species of plants, flowers and trees, plus an aviary and a tea house. The tame squirrels and doves are a great attraction to children.

Parliament

The Houses of Parliament can be seen during the recess (July–December) by applying to the Chief Messenger. They contain many relics of British rule, such as the solid gold mace. To listen to debates you have to ask the Gentleman Usher of the Black Rod for tickets. Historically, however, there are several more interesting buildings nearby.

Cultural History Museum

The Cultural History Museum, in Upper Adderley Street, was originally built as a slave lodge for the Dutch East India Company and later became the Supreme Court. Today it houses, *inter alia*, early Cape treasures, weapons, stamps and coins. Another fine old house is Michaelis on Greenmarket Square, where impeccably kept rooms reveal the dignity with which early settlers lived – the

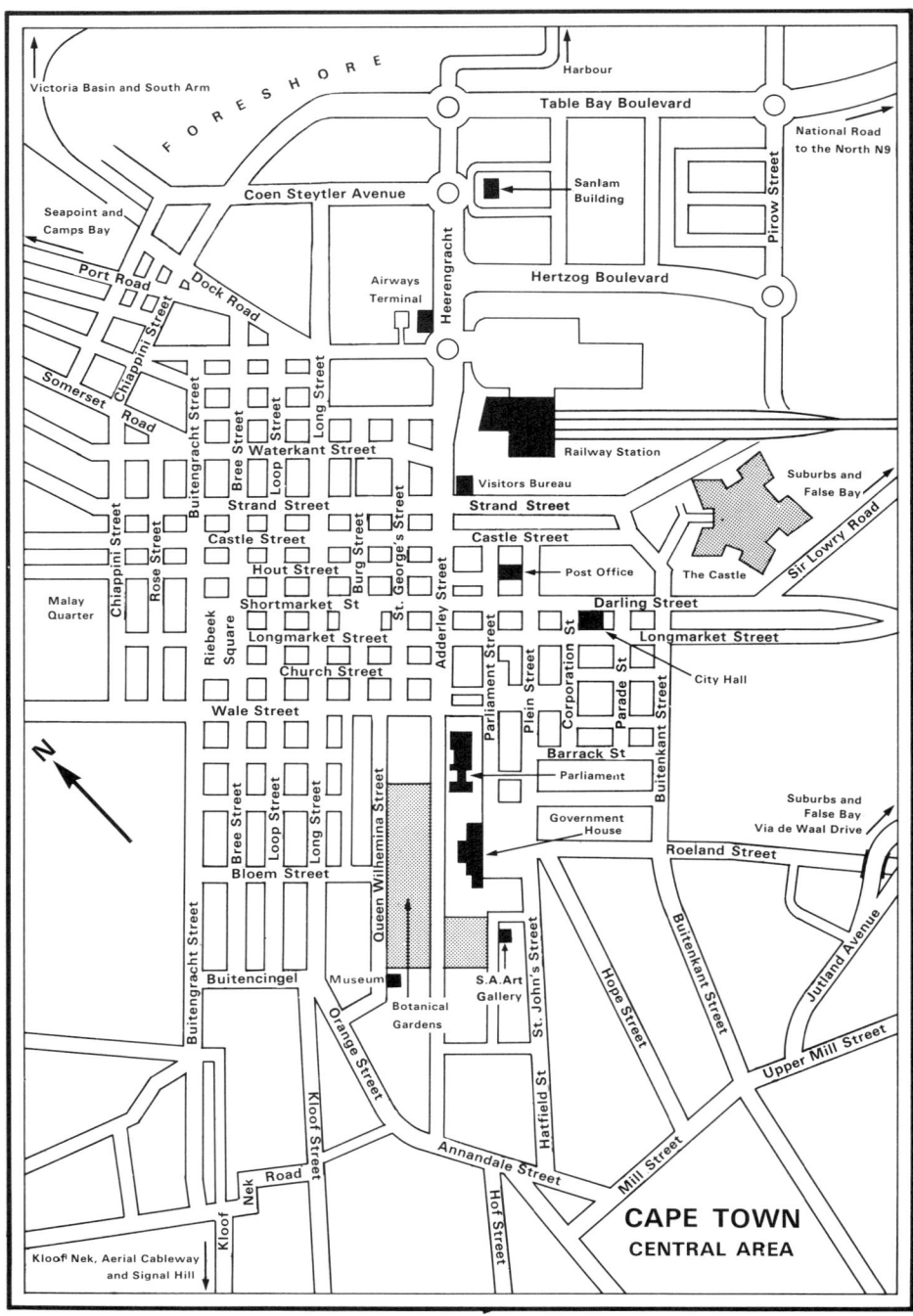

FORESHORE

Victoria Basin and South Arm

Harbour

Table Bay Boulevard

National Road
to the North N9

Coen Steytler Avenue

Sanlam
Building

Seapoint and
Camps Bay

Pirow Street

Port Road

Dock Road

Airways
Terminal

Heerengracht

Hertzog Boulevard

Somerset
Road

Chiappini Street

Buitengracht Street

Bree Street

Loop Street

Long Street

Waterkant Street

Railway Station

Suburbs and
False Bay

Visitors Bureau

Strand Street

Strand Street

Sir Lowry Road

Chiappini Street

Rose Street

Castle Street

St. George's Street

Burg Street

Castle Street

Post Office

The Castle

Malay
Quarter

Riebeek
Square

Hout Street

Shortmarket St

Longmarket Street

Church Street

Adderley Street

Parliament Street

Plein Street

Corporation St

Darling Street

Longmarket Street

Parade St

City Hall

Buitenkant Street

Wale Street

Barrack St

Parliament

Bree Street

Loop Street

Long Street

Queen Wilhemina Street

Bloem Street

Government
House

Roeland Street

Suburbs and
False Bay
Via de Waal Drive

Jutland Avenue

Buitencingel

Buitengracht Street

Museum

Botanical
Gardens

S.A. Art
Gallery

St. John's Street

Hatfield St

Hope Street

Buitenkant Street

Upper Mill Street

Orange Street

Kloof Street

Annandale Street

Hot Street

Mill Street

Kloof Nek Road

Kloof Nek, Aerial Cableway
and Signal Hill

N

CAPE TOWN
CENTRAL AREA

Dutch paintings on show are frankly less intriguing. The whole of Greenmarket
Greenmarket Square is now protected as a national monument, Square
including the hotel called the Inn on the Square.

The Castle is South Africa's oldest building. It was begun in 1666 Castle
and has some graceful eighteenth century additions, notably the
Kat Balcony. Now, after an eventful life, it houses historical
paintings, china, glass and antique furniture. Its shape of a
five-pointed star made it virtually impregnable three hundred
years ago. It is well worth visiting. So is Koopman de Wet's house
at 35 Strand Street, which dates from 1701 and contains one of the
finest collections of Colonial Dutch antiques to be seen anywhere.
Admission is 10c. Both this house and the Castle are closed on
Sundays.

The Malay quarter, on the slopes of Lion's Head, is the home of Malay
descendants of the slaves brought to the Cape from the East in the Quarter
seventeenth century by the Dutch East India Company. Its veiled
women, minarets, narrow streets, and the dilapidated elegance of
its old houses, all give it a special atmosphere which most Cape
Town people cherish. The Malays hold their own Music Festival at
Christmas.

Returning to Adderley Street, there is a small flower market in
Trafalgar Place which gives some idea of the Cape's wealth of
flora. Although this street is still the focal point of the city, there has
been tremendous development at the foreshore end, where the
SAA terminal and the railway station are. A series of underground
malls connect some of the larger department stores and the
CAPTOUR Tourist Information Bureau is in one of these, called the
Strand concourse (telephone 41 2521). CAPTOUR can provide a Information
bucketful of free literature and maps.

Normal business hours in Cape Town are 0900 to 1730 Mondays to
Fridays and 0900 to 1300 on Saturdays. There are so many shops Shops
that to make recommendations would be almost invidious.
However Garlicks and OK Bazaars are two well-known department
stores in Adderley Street. Two good ladies hairdressers are the
Salon in Stuttafords and Lorraine in Markham's Building, Hout
Street.

Major banks include Barclays National Bank Ltd, Standard Bank Banks
Ltd, Volkskas Beperk, First National City Bank, Nedbank Ltd and the
Trust Bank. Banking hours are 0900 to 1530 on Monday, Tuesday,
Thursday and Friday, 0900 to 1300 on Wednesday and 0900 to 1100
on Saturday. The Trust Bank has longer banking hours.

The Central Post Office is in Parliament Street between its Post Office
junctions with Castle and Darling Streets.

Although Cape Town and its suburbs have a mass of hotels you Hotels
need to make reservations well in advance during the November–

March holiday season. SATOUR will give you a hotel guide with prices and gradings. In the city itself the five star Mount Nelson in Orange Street is the best known, with its own seven acre grounds, swimming pool, tennis court and bowling green. It charges from R 26.50 a day. Another good hotel is the five star Heerengracht in St. George's Street which charges from R 47.00 a day. In Mill Street is the four star De Waal, while on the foreshore is the three star Capetonian Hotel.

However most local residents work in the city but live outside. Equally some of the best hotels are in the suburbs, from which there are frequent bus and train services into town (buses are not racially segregated in Cape Town). Round at Sea Point, on the Atlantic side, are the five star President Hotel (R 33 room only) and several good three star hotels, notably the Century, the Ambassador and the Winchester Mansions.

In the other direction from the city, round behind Table Mountain, are three excellent country hotels (see *Excursions* below), namely the Vineyard Hotel (three star) in Newlands; the Alphen (three star), a former Cape Dutch farmhouse in the lovely Constantia Valley, which is more expensive, and in the same valley the two star Hohenort. You need a car if you stay out at Constantia. Cheaper places that give good value for money are the Silver Sands or Surfcrest at Sea Point; and in central Cape Town, the Tudor in Greenmarket Square and the Helmsley in Hoff Street.

Restaurants Quite apart from hotels, restaurants in the city and in Sea Point are plentiful, with lobster, crayfish and seacrab among the seafoods that are a natural Cape Town speciality. For Chinese food we recommend the Dragon Inn Restaurant at Mouille Point, and the Nanking Restaurant at Paarden Island. For indigenous dishes try the Anglo Dutch in Barnett Street, while the Cape Kitchen in Queen Victoria Street and Lacey's out at Sea Point also serve traditional Cape food. Out to the north, at Bloubergstrand, only 25 minutes' drive from the city, is the Blue Peter Restaurant – incidentally, a wonderful place from which to watch the sun set and then the lights of Cape Town come up across Table Bay – as well as Ons Huisie Restaurant. At Sea Point there is the Roundhouse, or, for both grills and seafood, the Algambero. Out at Hout Bay is the Kronendam and at Muizenberg The Cavery. At any of these R 20–R 25 will buy a first class meal with wine for two. Most restaurants in Cape Town are licensed, but it is always wise to check beforehand.

Nightlife For nightclubs try Club 604 at the Top of the Heerengracht, Chatterleys in the Sanlam Building, or out at Sea Point Millionaires in the Century Hotel and Charlie Parker on Main Road. A good disco is Tramps in the Elizabeth Hotel. Like any big port Cape Town has its clip joints with white and coloured hostesses, mostly on the fringe of 'coloured areas', and periodically raided by the police. If you do go to one do not forget that sexual relationships between non-whites and whites are illegal in South Africa, even though restaurants, cinemas and theatres are multi-racial.

56

Professional companies, and sometimes amateur ones, play at the *Theatres*
Hofmeyr Theatre, 39 Adderley Street, the Little Theatre in
Government Avenue or the Three Arts in Plumstead. The Space
offers indigenous theatre, while productions at the Baxter in
Rondebosch compare with the best in South Africa. A new
entertainment complex on the foreshore includes the Nico Malan
opera house and theatre. There is an open air theatre at the
Maynardville Estate, in the suburb of Wynberg. From time to time
there are ballet performances, operas, and symphony recitals in
the City Hall, where there are also organ recitals most Tuesdays at
1315.

If you are in Cape Town over the New Year watch out for the Coon *Coon Carnival*
Carnival, when bands of gaily costumed Cape Coloured people go
singing and dancing at Green Point. The origins of this traditional
festival are obscure, but that hardly worries the revellers. The Cape
Coloured people are a centuries-old mixture of Hottentots and
Asians, with a small addition of African and European blood.

In February the Cape Show is held at the Goodwood showground. *Cape Show*
This is an agricultural and industrial exhibition which includes
galloping mule and horse team competitions, wine tastings, and
sporting events. The wine show part maintains very high
standards which may prove an agreeable surprise to strangers.

A newer event in the Cape Town year, but a major one, is the Arts *Arts Festival*
Festival, held for two weeks in April. Incorporating a circus on the
Grand Parade, open air theatre in the Gardens and other events in
which all communities participate.

Increasingly Cape Town is the centre for visiting the wide
attractions of this part of the Republic. For a start one can go up
Table Mountain for a spectacular view of the city. The summit *Table Mountain*
(1,164 m/3,549 ft) is easily reached by a seven-minute ride in the
cable car, which starts from the station in Kloof Nek Road, plus a
short walk. There is a restaurant at the upper station. The mountain
can be climbed too, but be careful, some of the ways up are
dangerous and need a guide. There is one signposted walk up a
deep cleft in the Platteklip Gorge. Other magnificent views,
particularly of the lights at night, can be had from the road that
winds up Signal Hill. If that is too much of an effort, then go to the
Observation Tower in the Sanlam Building in the Heerengracht,
open weekdays 1015 to 1515.

The South African Railway Travel Bureau, in Adderley Street, *Tours*
arranges coach excursions varying from a tour of Hout Bay and
Groot Constantia at R 14.00 for three hours to five or seven day
tours of the Garden Route. Springbok Atlas operate a variety of
tours. Reputable travel agents are numerous; among them are
branches of the American Express, Cooks and Musgrove and
Watson.

Car Hire	Car hire firms include Budget Rent-a-Car on the foreshore at BP Centre (telephone 21 7610); Hertz on Strand Street (telephone 21 5190); and Avis, 84 Strand Street (telephone 21 6650).
Excursions	Outside Cape Town you should try to see the world-famous Kirstenbosch Botanical Gardens which shelter 6,000 of South Africa's 20,000 species of flora. They are open from sunrise to sunset, with tea and refreshments available; and Groote Schuur (Great Barn), the property which Cecil Rhodes presented to the nation and which is now the home of the Prime Ministers of South Africa. Another splendid example of a Cape farm house is Groot Constantia, former home of the Dutch Governors, in the charming Constantia Valley. It is now a museum maintained by the Government, having been faithfully rebuilt after a fire in 1925. The lovely old wine cellars behind were untouched and you can now buy the produce of Constantia's own vineyards in them, notably
Constantia	Cabernet Sauvignon. Historically Constantia wines have long been renowned and are now being revived, although the vineyards themselves are only a fraction of the size they were when Governor Simon van der Stel began planting this land in 1685.
Bird Sanctuary	For bird lovers there is the Ronde Vlei Bird Sanctuary, only 21 km (13 miles) from the city. One hundred and seventy species of birds have been noted on the Vlei, the pelicans and flamingoes being the most spectacular. Zeekoe ('Hippopotamus') Vlei, bordering on Ronde Vlei, is the largest of the fresh-water lakes on the Cape Flats and yachting and speed-boating are popular there.

The Cape Peninsula

The rest of the Peninsula, which stretches 51 km (32 miles) south of Cape Town, and is approximately 16 km (10 miles) wide, has a series of resorts amid magnificent bays and mountains.

The most spectacular route to Cape Point from the city, taking in 142 km (89 miles), is via the Great Marine Drive. You leave Cape Town via Sea Point, Camps Bay, along the foot of the cliffs called the Twelve Apostles to the beautiful curve of Hout Bay. There is a good restaurant here, the Kronendaal, and you can go by boat out to watch the seal colony on the point. On the way to Hout Bay you pass a pleasant seaside village, Llandudno, and the adjacent Sandy Bay, patronised by nudists though total exposure is illegal.

Kommetjie Beach	Hout Bay marks the start of the Chapman's Peak drive – the mountain itself towering above – past Noordhoek to Kommetjie, where there is a glorious beach, little frequented because of the cold Atlantic water. This beach was used as a location in the filming of *Ryan's Daughter*, because the weather is more reliable than it would have been in Ireland. The fishing along this coast is good too.
Nature Reserve	The Cape of Good Hope Nature Reserve occupies 77 sq km (30 sq miles) of the southern tip of the Peninsula. It is stocked with

58

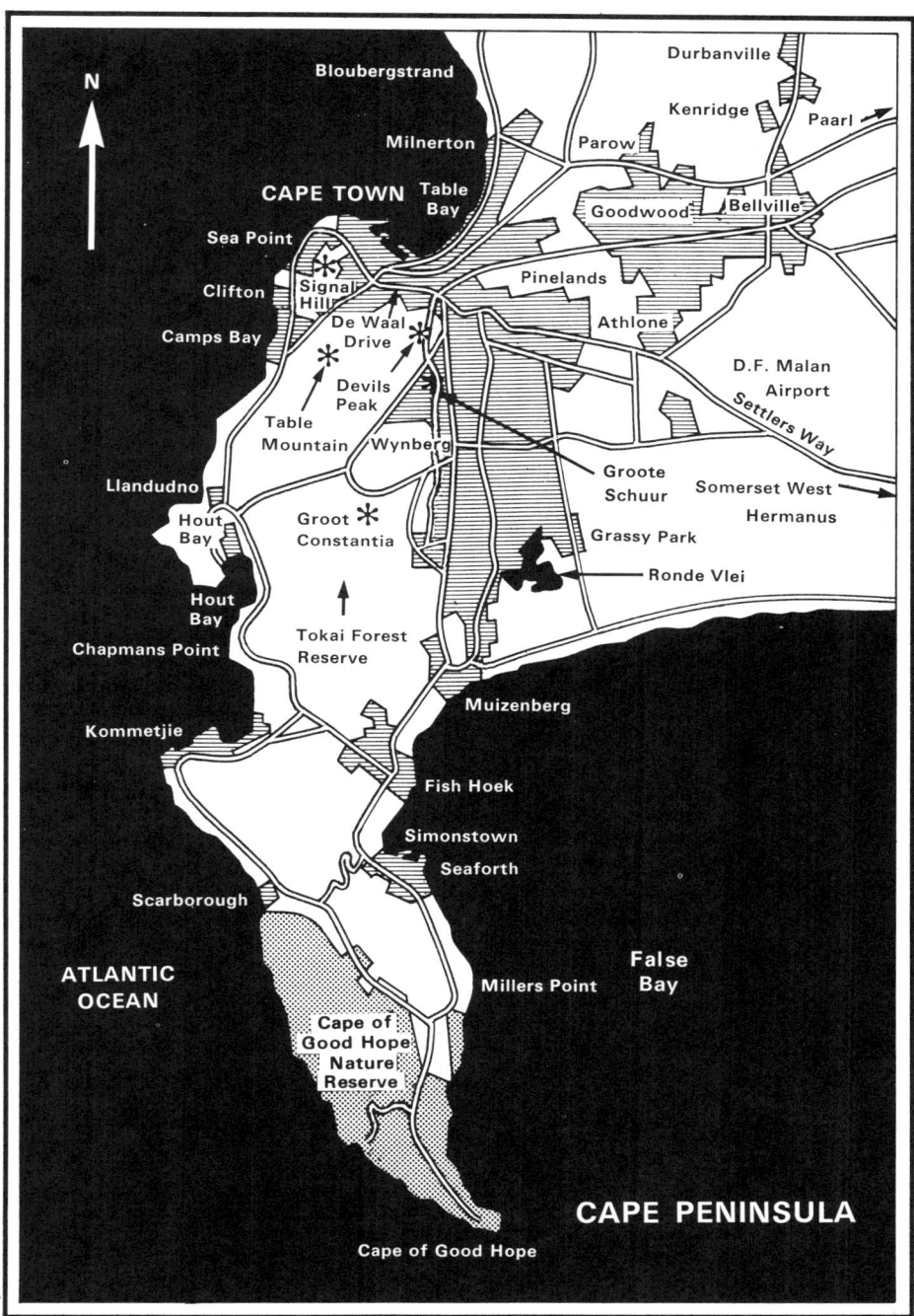

CAPE PENINSULA

antelope, zebra, baboons and other game, shelters 90 species of birds, is known for its flora, especially proteas, and is an excellent place for picnics and fishing. There is a small entrance fee. The road to it eventually ends in a parking area, and you have to walk the rest of the short distance along the old military road to the lighthouse, where you can see Cape Point. It is often thought that Cape Point divides the Atlantic from the Indian Ocean. Certainly the waters to the east of it are several degrees warmer than those to the west. But Cape Agulhas, 200 km (125 miles) to the east, is the real dividing point of the two oceans. You can return via the same route as far as Red Hill, and then take the road to the right. There is a tea room here (closed on Mondays).

Crossing the hump of the peninsula, through scenery that could be in the Mediterranean, the hillsides scented with shrubs and herbs, the M65 road takes you to the recreation area of Millers Point and then you go back north to Simonstown, on the Indian Ocean side of the peninsula.

Simonstown

Fish Hoek

Simonstown is an attractive fishing town with cobbled streets and buildings dating from 1687. It is the headquarters of the South African Navy. From Simonstown follow the curve of False Bay to Fish Hoek. There is a very good surfing beach, a caravan park, and a golf course at Fish Hoek, where incidentally liquor is unobtainable, even in hotels, owing to an old municipal bye-law. Tunny and big-game fishing can easily be organised in the summer months in False Bay and the boating of a 272 kg (600 lb) blue fin is not unusual these days. Yachting and other water sports are popular, while within a few miles of the town are many glorious stretches of safe beach. False Bay's name originates from the first settlers belief that it would provide a deep anchorage, and the reality that it was too shallow (even Simonstown has limitations).

Kalk Bay

Muizenberg

Kalk Bay is the next place; it has an attractive harbour of fishing boats and you can take a launch trip round Seal Island during the summer. Leaving Kalk Bay follow Boyes Drive, which has excellent views of the surrounding bays, past St James, a holiday resort, to Muizenberg. This is a popular town with a long sandy beach and many entertainment facilities. The sea is particularly safe for children. The Information Bureau is in the Municipal Offices, Atlantic Road. The main road from Muizenberg leads to the suburb of Wynberg and on to Cape Town. There is also a good train service down this side of the peninsula.

The Wine Country and the Western Cape

North and east of Cape Town, inland from the peninsula, lies some of the most lovely countryside in South Africa. The valleys among the mountains shelter vineyards and orchards. A few estates produce and sell their own wines, like Bellingham and Nederburg; others like Bergkelder are sold through one or other of the two co-operatives that have become predominant, KWV at Paarl, and the Stellenbosch Farmers Winery. Both welcome visitors. If you have any doubts about the quality of South African brandies, sherries and wines you should go and taste them on the spot. The vineyards were started by Jan van Riebeeck. Thirty years later, in 1688, Huguenot immigrants brought vine seedlings with them from France, and with their expertise developed viticulture in this ideal climate. On the whole the white wines and rosés are better than the red wines, though the last decade has seen a great increase in the sophistication of the business.

Architecturally the whitewashed homesteads are of a disting- *Cape Dutch* uished vintage too. In its simplest form the Cape Dutch house is a *Houses* single storey, thatched structure, dignified by a high decorative gable over the front door, which holds a single upstairs room. We mention various especially graceful houses below. Another of their features is the stoep, a verandah that runs the length of the house. Back in Holland it is a small space by the front door. Transplanted here it is expanded into an open-air living room which is a feature of South African homes.

For simplicity we will describe the Western Cape in a series of directions which cover the more interesting and scenic places, the first two of which are the established 'Wine Routes'. CAPTOUR in Cape Town provides a useful leaflet and map on the area too. An important point about the Wine Routes is that you can follow them as you wish. Many estates participate, usually having two guided tours a day, so you could spend a week going round in your car, or commit yourself only to a Springbok Atlas eight hour coach trip.

One enjoyable drive is to Stellenbosch, 48 km (30 miles) from Cape *Route 1* Town. This attractive university town was founded in 1679 by Governor Simon van der Stel, who originally planted its avenues *Stellenbosch* of oaks. The University has given South Africa many of the rugby players of the famous Springbok teams. Among historic houses are the perfect little Burgher's House by the post office (admission 20c); the old Powder Magazine on the Braak, or village green; La Gratitude in Dorp Street, Libertas and the Rhenish Mission church. The Stellenbosch Farmers Winery is a mile or so west of the town and the Jonkershoek valley to the east has a trout hatchery. At the entrance to the valley, set among vineyards, is Rawdon's three star Lanzerac Hotel (PO Box 4, Stellenbosch), a superbly modernised Cape Dutch homestead, with its own swimming pool, a country house atmosphere, and excellent food, especially the smörgås-bord style Sunday night dinners. It charges from R 16 per day.

Strictly speaking the Stellenbosch Wine Route comprises 12 estates and four co-operatives all within 12 km (7½ miles) of the town. Among them is die Bergkelder in Stellenbosch, which has cellars in the hillside and magnificently carved storage casks. Don't miss the small Wine Museum in the town either, though the best way to learn about the wines is by tasting them. The route we now describe extends beyond the confines of the Stellenbosch Route.

Franschhoek	Leaving Stellenbosch eastwards cross the Helshoogte Pass (Hell's Heights) by the Ida's Valley Dam, and down through the Banhoek valley to Franschhoek, which means 'Corner of France', and has a marble monument to the Huguenot settlers of 1688. The Excelsior Hotel, a two star Swiss type hotel on a farm just outside the town, is good. Franschhoek is at the very bottom of the pass of the same name, which forms part of the wonderful 'Four Pass' drive, the others being Viljoen's Pass, Sir Lowry's Pass, and Helshoogte Pass. A day devoted to moving quietly and coolly through these fascinating parts of the Cape is one well spent. There is a breathtaking view from the winding Viljoen's Pass, after which you turn right on to the National Road to Sir Lowry's Pass towards Cape Town. The Hottentots Holland Mountains, through which you are driving here, are so called because in the early days the Dutch always talked of going home to Holland and the native Hottentots adopted the word for *their* home territory of the hills.

Somerset West   Just off this road is Somerset West, prettily placed in a U-shaped valley of the Hottentots Holland Mountains, the highest point of which is Sneeukop (Snow Peak). The town was the home of the authors H. V. Morton and Stuart Cloete. It is five km (three miles)

Strand   from the Strand, a major holiday and sea-bathing resort. From the mountain drive along the eastern side of False Bay where you have a magnificent view of the Cape Peninsula across the water. This road leads to Cape Hangklip and a series of delightful beaches (see page 64), while the N2 freeway heads you swiftly back to Cape Town.

Route 2   The second Wine Route goes through fruit orchards, to the busy country town of Paarl, 57 km (36 miles) from Cape Town. Set under

Paarl   the craggy Drakenstein Mountains, Paarl is named after the granite outcrops which glisten after rain like huge pearls. The Paarl Publicity Association at 264 Main Street arranges tours of the Cape Dutch homesteads on weekdays. You can also go round KWV's vast winery, and the Huguenot Museum and the Wild Flower Reserve. The Picardie Hotel (one star) in Main Street is a good place to stop for a meal (charges from R 18.50 per day inclusive), though the outstanding place in the area for lunch is the restaurant at Boschendal, an old manor house set in the shadow of the Simonsberg Mountains some 11 km (seven miles) from Paarl towards Franschhoek. The food is excellent and the estate, where wine making began in 1715, is a delight to visit. Boschendal is one of the Paarl Wine Route estates, which include the Franschhoek co-operative, geographically equally near Stellenbosch. More information on the route can be had from the PR Dept, KWV, PO Box 528, Suider Paarl. It also runs north to Wellington, where the climate is ideal for producing sherry and fortified wines.

Wellington   Wellington lies at the foot of the Hawequas and Drakenstein Mountains. It has a fine old church and there are several hotels and restaurants. From here Bain's Kloof Pass takes you through high

Ceres   mountains to Ceres, where in winter there is skiing. The air is crisp, fresh and invigorating. The Belmont Hotel (two star) in Porter

Street (from R 17.50 per day all inclusive) is comfortable and there are several holiday farms in the vicinity. A wild flower show is held in October to which excursions are run from Cape Town. There are radioactive hot springs at Goudini Road.

About 32 km (20 miles) from Ceres is Tulbagh, first settled in 1699. *Tulbagh* It has an interesting collection of antiques in the old church Volksmuseum, built in 1743. One of the vineyards in the valley makes a first rate white wine called Twee Jongezellen.

From Paarl you can take the road through du Toit's Kloof Pass, an exciting but twisting drive over the Great Drakenstein range to Worcester 115 km (72 miles) from Cape Town, in the centre of *Worcester* great wine and fruit districts and dramatically hemmed in by mountains. Its attractions include mountaineering, the Karoo Gardens, the Afrikaner Museum and the Joubert Park Wildlife Sanctuary, which has some black swans given it by Queen Elizabeth the British Queen Mother.

Just under 48 km (30 miles) east of Worcester is Robertson, on the *Robertson* lovely Breede River, which has a mile's length of white beach called the 'Silver Strand'. Holiday accommodation in the form of quaint wooden houses is available, and there is an excellent restaurant. The winter climate, like that of Worcester, is particularly pleasant.

At Montagu, a short drive from Robertson past the oddly coloured *Montagu* rock formations of Kogmanskloof, there are medicinal hot springs. The celebrated Montagu Baths Hotel (one star) is three km (two miles) outside the town.

Driving directly north from Cape Town on the coastal highway past *Route 3* Milnerton you come to the popular Bloubergstrand with its magnificent beaches. Inland are mile upon mile of rolling fertile hills, intensively farmed and still called 'The Granary of South Africa', despite the increasing value of the eastern Orange Free State's wheat. Malmesbury, 56 km (35 miles) from Cape Town, *Malmesbury* was laid out in 1745 round hot sulphur springs. It was then known as Het Zwarte Land (the Black Country) but was renamed by the Earl of Malmesbury in 1829. It is a wine-producing centre and the birthplace of General Smuts, the internationally respected former Prime Minister.

Passing through Moorreesburg and Piketberg, two small grain towns, you reach Citrusdal at the foot of the Cedarberg Mountains. *Citrusdal* It has a hotel. Further along the main road, 240 km (150 miles) from Cape Town, is Clanwilliam, a Namaqualand village noted for its *Clanwilliam* wild flowers in the spring, including literally square miles of big Namaqualand daisies. An attractive diversion on the way back is to turn right at Piketberg towards the little fishing village along St Helena Bay, and Langebaan on Saldanha Bay. Saldanha is *Saldanha* undergoing expansion and is now a major port for the export of iron-ore. There are two two star hotels charging from R 10.40 for

63

bed and breakfast. More interestingly, several animal sanctuaries are being created in the area. And you can treasure hunt: in April 1702 a Dutch East Indiaman, the *Merestyn*, was wrecked on Jutten Island in the bay and ducatoon coins are still washed up on the beaches in stormy weather. You can return to Malmesbury on the secondary road, and so back to Cape Town.

Route 4
Our fourth suggested trip explores towards Mossel Bay and the Garden Route (see below). Taking advantage of the freeway, you can head east towards Sir Lowry's Pass and Hermanus, with a choice of ways as you pass Somerset West. If you are in no hurry then swing along the coast through the attractive fishing village of Gordon's Bay and along past the mouth of the Steenbras river towards the tiny resort of Betty's Bay, passing numerous beaches and the spectacular rock formation at Hangklip, said to be geologically unique. The Harold Porter Botanical Reserve is near Betty's Bay, a noted place to see the flora of the Cape. But there are also flowers and varieties of protea all along the road (remember picking wild flowers is illegal).

This drive takes you round to Bot River. Before going on along the coast to Hermanus, you might stop for lunch at the old coaching inn at Houw Hoek, just off the main Caledon–Cape Town road. Founded in 1834 the inn, though it is only rated one star, has excellent cuisine, riding, tennis and swimming. From here it is 48 km (30 miles) to Hermanus.

Hermanus itself is a favourite seaside resort, with plenty of amenities and several good hotels, notably the Birkenhead (two star) and the Marine. There is excellent fishing, a championship golf course and both the scenery and the wild flowers are beautiful.

Caledon, inland over the hills on the main road, is best known for its wild flower garden just outside the town and for the mission station at Genadendal (Valley of Grace) established 32 km (20 miles) away in 1737.

Cape Agulhas
Cape Agulhas ('Needles') is the most southerly point in Africa. The worst disaster on its saw-edged rocks occurred when the troop-ship *Birkenhead* struck the reef at Danger Point in 1852. Three hundred and fifty-seven soldiers and 57 of the crew lost their lives, but their self sacrifice saved all the women and children. There is a small hotel at Struisbaai; and Bredasdorp, 41 km (26 miles) inland, has adequate accommodation.

Inland to the Karoo

Addo
Elephant Park
The Times, of London, once asked: 'Why should it be that among all herds of wild elephants, only those of the Addo bush have become famous?' The story of the Addo elephant is, indeed, an epic of wildlife preservation. The elephants, now 100 in number,

Opposite top: Protea Repens or Sugarbush, South Africa's national flower
Bottom: Garden at Sabie, Transvaal. Photographs SATOUR

64

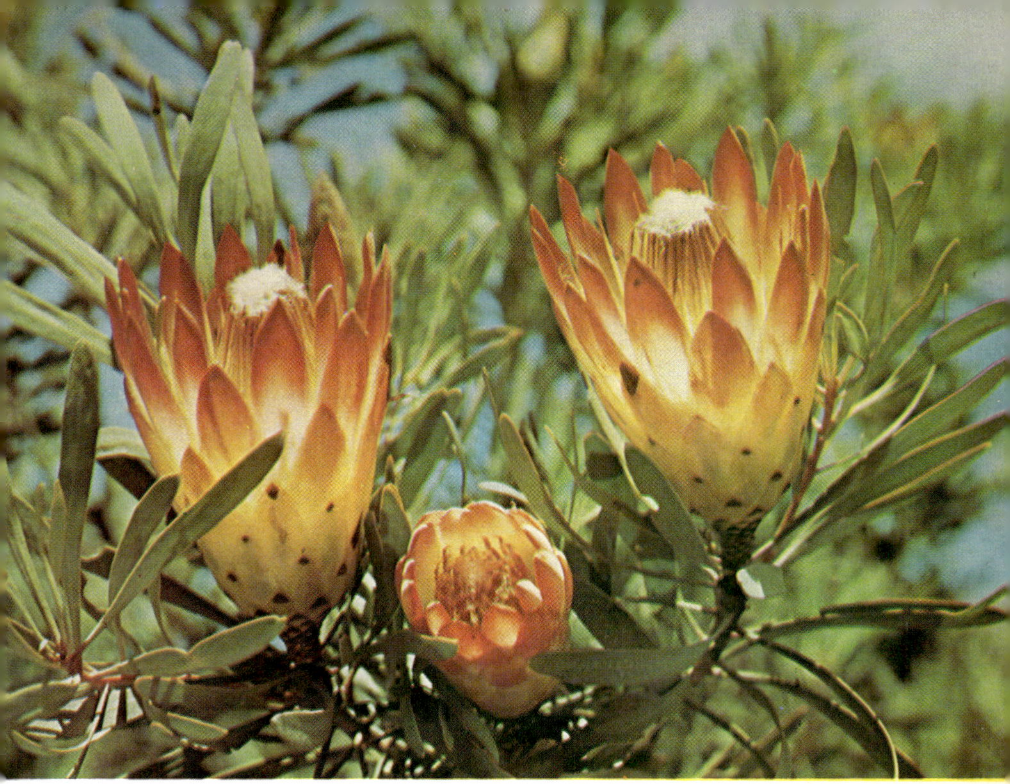

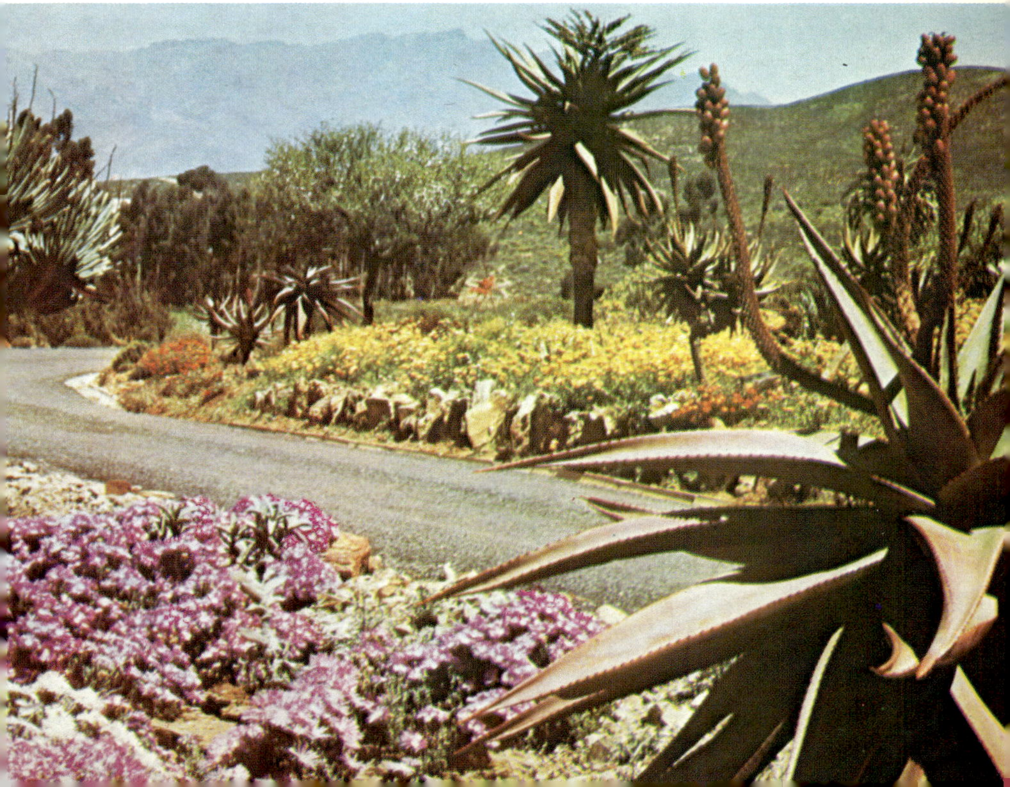

once roamed the citrus-growing Sundays River Valley in big herds and were almost entirely destroyed by irate farmers. The herd has now been fenced in (tram tracks and steel cable were used), and is free to roam in an 8,000-acre reserve. The park is some 69 km (34 miles) from Port Elizabeth, and can be reached by car in one hour.

There is a 19 km (12 mile) road around the elephant camp, and ten viewing ramps. The herd may be viewed at almost point blank range throughout the year. The camp also contains 200 buffalo. Adjacent to these are reserves containing indigenous wildlife, from the tiny steenbok, which stands only about 508 mm (20 ins) high, to lumbering rhinos and hippos.

Beyond Addo, about 256 km (160 miles) north of Port Elizabeth, off the main national road to the Transvaal and in the heart of the Great Karoo, is the unique Zebra Park at Cradock, a sanctuary for one of the last known herds of Cape mountain zebra. The mountain zebra, standing only 1·22 m (4 ft) high, is the smallest of the species. The park also has numerous species of indigenous antelope and 146 species of wild bird. The park has sleeping accommodation for visitors.
Mountain Zebra Park

The Karoo (a Hottentot word meaning arid), rainless in summer and covering hundreds of thousands of square miles, is so dry in places that up to five acres are needed to support one sheep. It is in this area that most of South Africa's rich harvest of merino wool is produced. Physically it is a plateau, criss-crossed by mountain ranges. After rain the whole area changes almost overnight to a rich green, covered with wild flowers. The Little Karoo is a narrow stretch divided from the Great Karoo by mountain ranges, and runs east to west not far inland from Port Elizabeth.
The Karoo

Desolate as much of this bush area is, one must mention an extraordinary piece of restoration at Matjiesfontein, an insignificant railway station on the line between Cape Town and Beaufort West. In 1883 a Scot called Jimmy Logan obtained a refreshment room concession there to serve the travellers bound for the Kimberley diamond fields. It became famous. Cecil Rhodes was a frequent visitor. Logan became rich. But after he died in 1920 the venture declined. Now the building has been restored as the Lord Milner hotel, and the village – conveniently situated on the main Cape Town to Johannesburg road – has revived with it.
Matjiesfontein

The gem of the Karoo is Graaff-Reinet, founded in 1786. It nestles in a large, fertile valley near the Sneeuberg (Snow mountain) range in the north. The town has rare examples of old Cape Dutch architecture, and also a grape vine said to be larger than that at Hampton Court, England, and possibly the biggest in the world. Like Swellendam, the town was once an independent republic. It is well worth an overnight stay in Graaff Reinet at the newly
Graaff-Reinet

Opposite top left: Hertzog Tower, Johannesburg
Top right: Stellenbosch house, Cape Province. Photographs Picturepoint
Bottom: Fort Namutoni, a game lodge at Etosha Pan, Namibia

renovated Drostdy Hotel in Church Street. The rooms are said to be former slave quarters, but today they are furnished with antiques.

Valley of Desolation
About 10 km (six miles) from Graaff-Reinet lies the Valley of Desolation, a grouping of columnular basaltic pillars rising to a height of 455 m (400 ft) above the valley floor, in dramatic confusion. The Valley has made a magnificent film set on occasion.

Thirty-two km (20 miles) from Graaff-Reinet is the farm 'Wellwood' owned by Dr Sidney Rubidge, who has possibly the largest private collection of fossils in the world.

Kimberley, Mafikeng, the Kalahari Gemsbok Park

Diamonds
Kimberley, named after John Wodehouse, first Earl of Kimberley, is the capital of the 259,000 sq km (100,000 sq miles) that stretch from the Karoo (page 65) north to Botswana, and from the Transvaal west to the Atlantic. Most of the northern Cape is arid by nature, but tremendous irrigation schemes are transforming large tracts of it into prosperous farms. The Orange River Scheme alone involves five massive dams and is costing R 600 million.

Kimberley itself is a legend still living, a mining town sprawling around the Big Hole, and the focal point of the world's diamond selling. The gems themselves, formed out of carbon by extreme heat and pressure, are usually found in the throats of old volcanoes. These sections of intensely hard ground are called 'pipes'. The finding of the Star of South Africa diamond in 1868 heralded the rush to the district. Some alluvial diamonds were located in the Vaal River. But the big find was in a small kopje or hill. Gradually this was changed into a vast hole by hundreds of diggers working individual claims, while a mining camp grew up round it. As it reached deeper it became chaotic, and dangerous. The miners amalgamated into combines, of which two major groups emerged – de Beers controlled by Cecil Rhodes, and Kimberley Mine run by a Whitechapel Jew called Barney Barnato. Both men were millionaires before they were thirty.

The Big Hole
However, Rhodes realised that the market had to be controlled or the price would fall, and won overall control, bringing all Kimberley mining under the aegis of de Beers Consolidated Mines Ltd. Subsequently it was from here that the development of Johannesburg and the Rand was planned and modern South Africa sprang. When working in the Big Hole ceased in 1914, it was 457 m (500 yards) wide, 183 m (3,600 ft) deep, and had yielded 14,500,000 carats. Today it is partly full of water. The observation post for visitors to it is at the Mine Museum.

Today Kimberley is the headquarters of the Central Selling Organisation, which handles 80 percent of the world's output of diamonds, including those from Namibia. Illicit diamond buying – IDB – is one of its major worries. If you find a diamond you must hand it over to the police. You will get 50 percent of its value. This can happen. One company prospers on the concession to exploit

all building sites in the town. You can see them at work crushing
and sieving after any house is demolished. Another place to watch
the old style of digging is 32 km (20 miles) away at Barkly West,   *Digging*
where in the winter months prospectors are out looking for alluvial
diamonds in the river.

Modern Kimberley has 100,000 inhabitants. Yet it retains a dusty,
slightly Victorian outback air. The office of de Beers still has a steep
and corrugated iron roof. Outside the club there is still a brass
arrow set in the path to show Rhodes which direction was north.
The streets still wind as they had to originally to avoid the diggings.
However, there are several good hotels, notably the Kimberley on
Dutoitspan Road (four star) and the Savoy in De Beers Road (three
star). Prices range from R 18.50 upwards. The Public Library has a
famous collection of Africana, while the Duggan Cronin Bantu
Gallery is worth a visit. In a sporting sense the city is very well off,
with plenty of facilities.

Although Kimberley was besieged during the Boer War from
October 1899 to mid-February 1900, the town that captured the eye
of the world was Mafikeng, further north. Colonel Baden-Powell,   *Mafikeng*
who later founded the Boy Scouts and instilled in them the value of
the bushcraft he learnt in South Africa, held Mafikeng for 217 days
with 800 men. It was not a particularly important garrison.
However, Baden-Powell's stratagems for its defence, and the
length of the siege, made it seem emotionally the lynch-pin of the
British Empire. Later it was for many years the administrative
capital of Bechuanaland (now Botswana) though not in that
territory. It has a hotel, and is on the route to Gaborone, which
replaced it as the capital. Its English church was designed by Sir
Herbert Baker.

Mafikeng is now the capital of the independent State of   *Bophuthatswana*
Bophuthatswana, a country whose components are scattered
across this part of the Republic and which has no frontier controls.
The main change that came with independence, apart from African
government and the new spelling of Mafeking, was the ending of
racial segregation and the licensing of casinos. The upshot is an
extraordinary pleasure complex called Sun City, run by Southern
Sun Hotels, and including every kind of sport, the Pilanesburg
Game Reserve, gambling, cabarets and lavish restaurants: in other
words a fantasy world for the citizens of Johannesburg to escape
to. Sun City is on the borders of the new State, two and a half hours
drive from Johannesburg, while the Mabatho Sun Hotel, another
luxurious oasis, is 10 km (six miles) from Mafikeng.

Three hundred and twenty km (200 miles) west of Mafikeng,
through Vryburg, is Kuruman, which has a natural fountain of clear   *Kuruman*
water called the Eye of Kuruman, rising in a dolomite cave and
yielding four million gallons a day. Nearby are remarkable
prehistoric rock engravings of animals now extinct, and also the
missionary church built by Robert Moffat, whose daughter
married the famous Dr Livingstone.

Upington	Still further west is Upington, the railway centre on the Cape Town–Windhoek line, also served by scheduled airline flights. It straggles 18 km (10 miles) along the north banks of the Orange River, the islands of which are being developed as a pleasure resort. There is one two star hotel, the Oranje and two one star hotels, the Gordonia and Upington, charging from R 9.00 for bed and breakfast. The town is the starting point for visits to Augrabies and the Kalahari, as well as being a great fruit-growing area.
Augrabies National Park	The Augrabies Falls cascade down a total drop of 89 m (620 ft) into an 11 km (seven mile) gorge and are the fifth largest falls in the world. This wild and savage locale is a National Park, which has stopped prospectors who believe it to be lined with diamonds washed down the river, from investigating the pool beneath the Falls. The small Augrabies Falls Hotel is good (telephone Augrabies 18). For more about the Orange River see under Namibia.
Kalahari Gemsbok Park	The Kalahari Gemsbok Park is 320 km (200 miles) from Upington. The effort involved in getting there is worthwhile as the Park is unique. In its two and a half million acres the noble gemsbok, or oryx, a big animal with long straight V-shaped horns, wanders among the drifting sand dunes. So do lion, herds of springbok, hartebeest, ground birds and many other species. Strange trees, like the kameeldoring (camel thorn) dot the Kalahari landscape. The southern entrance at Twee Rivieren has one rest camp, and the entrance from Namibia at Mata-Mata has another. The third camp is called Nossob. There are no restaurants at any of the camps but meat and supplies of tinned goods as well as petrol and diesel are available. Frozen vegetables are available at Twee Rivieren only. Entrance fee is R 3.30 and accommodation charges range from R 6.00 to R 17.00.

The Garden Route

The name 'Garden Route' is slightly deceptive. The route runs along a beautiful strip of land between mountains and sea that has a temperate climate, forests, green valleys, lagoons and long clean beaches excellent for surfing. But it is a 'garden' only by comparison with the aridity of the Karoo further inland. Basically the route follows the highway from Mossel Bay to Plettenberg Bay, though it's also served by the railway as far as Knysna and by scheduled air services to Oudtshoorn, George, Plettenberg Bay and then Port Elizabeth.

Swellendam	Following the National Road 2 from Cape Town to Mossel Bay you pass Swellendam, a town that was briefly an independent republic in 1795 when its burghers broke away from the Cape Colony's rule. This gives exhibits in the old Drostdy Museum a special interest. The Drostdy was the home of the Dutch East India Company's Administrator. Above the town rear hills which the early farmers used as natural sundials, and are still called Ten O'clock, Eleven O'clock, Twelve O'clock and One O'clock Peaks. Three kilometres

(two miles) away is the Bontebok National Park. The last 34 of these   *Bontebok*
once widespread chocolate brown and black antelope were
surviving at Bredasdorp. In 1961 they were moved to this new Park,
where they quickly multiplied to over 200, while pairs of them are
also put out on the land of preservation-minded farmers.

On towards Mossel Bay you get excellent food at the two star   *Mossel Bay*
Golden Rendezvous and there is good surfing and fishing on the
coast at Still Bay. Mossel Bay itself is a seaport on the slopes of
Cape St Blaize, and centre for big game fishing (for boat hire
consult the Publicity Association). A curiosity is the Post Office
Tree, a venerable milkwood on which a Portuguese navigator
hung a shoe in 1500, leaving inside it an account of the storm that
had wrecked his fleet. Later seafarers collected letters from, and
posted them in, a seaboot nailed to the tree. There are fine beaches
at Santos and Die Bakke, the modern one star Santos Hotel (from
R 14 per day) being by the former. A series of tunnel caves lead
from one bay to the next, but they are dangerous when the tide
rises. Seal Island, the home of thousands of penguins and seals,
can be visited by tug from the port. The ochre factory, curiously,
supplies the Xhosa tribe with their traditional red ochre 'make-up'.

Good beaches en route to George are at Great Brak River and   *George*
Herolds Bay, both little holiday resorts on their own account.
George itself is a quiet inland town, named after King George III,
with a fine white Regency church. Above rises the Cradock Peak
1,698 m (5,562 ft) of the Outeniqua Mountains, which from here on
form a backdrop to the Garden Route. The golf course at George is
first class and there are several hotels. By convention and the
itineraries of coach tours, the Route has come to include
Oudtshoorn, on the other side of these mountains in the dryer and
hotter landscape of the Little Karoo.

Oudtshoorn made its fortune on ostrich farming in 1860–85 and   *Oudtshoorn*
1905–14 when ostrich plumes were ragingly fashionable in
Europe, and 1 lb of feathers fetched R 250. 'Ostrich Palaces' were
built on the proceeds. But the Great War and then motoring killed
the fashion. However, the Safari Ostrich Farm and the Highgate
Ostrich Farm, both on the Mossel Bay road outside the town, still
show visitors the whole business for a fee of R 1.50 – and you can
try riding an ostrich if you want! They are open daily 0730–1700.
The town also boasts a small crocodile farm and a golf course.
Eighteen miles the other side of Oudtshoorn, on the way to the
famous Swartberg Pass, are the Cango Caves, with their extraor-   *Cango Caves*
dinary coloured formations of stalactites (growing downwards)
and stalagmites (growing upwards). A series of 80 caverns extend
for three km (two miles) underground, the first so large that
concerts are held in it. Admission is R 1.75 and there is a
restaurant, and a crèche. Hotels in the area include a Holiday Inn at
Oudtshoorn and the Riempi Motel on the Cango road.

Wilderness, between George and Knysna, is basically a splendid   *Wilderness*
beach (but beware the current) and a series of lakes set among

forested hills. Three good hotels, the two star Wilderness Hotel, the two star Holiday Inn and the one star Fairy Knowe charge from R 12.00 per day upwards. The Wilderness Hotel has a private reserve where you can see the scarlet winged Knysna lourie. The Swartvlei lagoon is noted for leerfish and waterbirds, and the Groenvlei, beyond Sedgefield, for black bass fishing.

Knysna

Knysna offers a lot. It was founded by one of the most intriguing characters ever to set foot in South Africa, George Rex, who arrived at the Cape at the turn of the eighteenth century and established an estate here in 1804. Why the Cape Governor treated him as a VIP was never recorded, but substance has now been added to the belief that he was the illegitimate son of George III and a London Quakeress called Hannah Lightfoot. One book about him is *George Rex of Knysna*. He certainly chose an attractive spot to settle. Knysna lagoon, by which the town stands, runs out to the sea between two sheer red sandstone cliffs called the Heads. The eastern of the two is easily accessible and gives splendid views and good rock fishing. On the way to it is Leisure Island, facing Knysna across the lagoon. Oysters are a local speciality in season. The rambling Leisure Island Hotel (two star) is very comfortable (from R 19.00 per day). In the town are several excellent cabinetmakers' shops. Being among 100,000 acres of hardwood forests, Knysna is the centre for making South Africa's highly

Stinkwood

prized traditional stinkwood furniture. Stinkwood is rare, fetching as much as R 40 per cubic foot in log form. Its hard, fine grain gives it a satiny finish, usually oiled rather than polished. Yellowwood furniture is also attractive, and cheaper.

You can swim either in the lagoon or on the beaches at Buffalo Bay and Noetsie and the Publicity Association provides a useful list of possible excursions. Three interesting ones are to the Homtini Gorge, a natural bird sanctuary; to the abandoned goldmines at Millwood; and to the Garden of Eden Forest Reserve. This latter is a stretch of truly primeval forest 19 km (12 miles) out on the road to Plettenberg Bay.

Plettenberg Bay

Plettenberg Bay itself is, in our opinion, the most attractive small resort in the Republic. The village, on a promontory, was founded in 1778 by the Dutch East India Company. The old timber yard, rectory and chapel still remain down the track marked 'Van Plettenberg Park' off the road to Beacon Island. The new three star Beacon Island Hotel (from R 40.00 per day upwards) is excellent, right on the beach and reached along a short causeway. The Formosa Inn Motel (two stars) is pleasant too. Sea and rock fishing are particularly good off Robberg, eight km (five miles) away. Tackle can be hired from Jock Hunter's shop in the village, and boats from the Plettenberg Bay Angling Club. The peak season here is December–January, and you need to book ahead.

The Eastern Cape and Port Elizabeth

Continuing along the coast from Plettenberg Bay to Port Elizabeth, you pass various places worth stopping at, and much of the way is

70

through scenically magnificent country, like Nature's Valley at the foot of the Grootrivier Pass.

The Tsitsikama Forest and Coastal National Park, around the Storms River, consists of two parts, a 75 km (47 mile) stretch of virgin coast and a section of indigenous forest. Three km (two miles) west of the striking new Storms River bridge you can turn off into the forest and see the Big Tree, a 46 m (150 ft) high, 2,000-year-old yellowwood. There is a restaurant by the bridge. The pleasant Forest Inn (R 14.00 per day) is off the main road, but signposted. You can reach the coastal stretch of the Park by turning off nine km (five and a half miles) west of the bridge. Angling and swimming are allowed and there is a rest camp at Storm-srivermouth. 'Tsitsikama' means 'clear water' and there is a great variety of marine life to be seen.

Cape St Francis, 96 km (60 miles) west of Port Elizabeth, is a growing surfing resort with a good three star hotel. The surfing was recently reckoned the world's best by a Californian team. Oyster Bay, on the eastern fringe of the Tsitsikama Park is another small resort, while Jeffreys Bay is a fishing village, known for its exceptional sea shells and long beach. It has several small hotels.

Gamtoos River Mouth, 61 km (38 miles) from Port Elizabeth, is a fishing resort, reached off the main road via Thornhill. A slow narrow-gauge train optimistically called the Apple Express meanders through the Gamtoos Valley on its way from Port Elizabeth to Uniondale in the Langkloof, a great apple orchard district. It is an amusing way of seeing some picturesque hills and forests.

From Van Staadens Pass, on the main road 40 km (24 miles) from Port Elizabeth, you can get down to the mouth of the Van Staadens River, with its extensive lagoon, miles of beaches and camping resort.

The 'Friendly City' is the commercial capital of the Eastern Cape and the centre of the Republic's motor industry, as well as a resort. It lies on Algoa Bay, the name being a corruption of Bahia Da Lagas (Bay of the Lagoons), given it by Bartholomew Diaz in 1488.

The next event of real significance for Port Elizabeth occurred in 1820, with the arrival of 4,000 British settlers, intended for the Albany District (see Grahamstown). What they found was a huddle of fishermen's hovels, a few rudimentary dwellings, British military storehouses, and a fort. Unknown to them their political function was to form a buffer between the Cape Colony and the African tribes.

Their arrival was the turning point in the history of the Eastern Cape. The settlement was named Port Elizabeth, after Elizabeth Francis, wife of the Acting Governor of the Cape Colony, Sir Rufane Donkin. She had, sadly, died of fever in India in 1818. The Donkin Memorial, a pyramid by the lighthouse, is inscribed 'To the memory of one of the most perfect human beings'.

Since then Port Elizabeth has grown to a thriving metropolis, with over 700 factories, concentrated mainly in the north, among them plants of General Motors, Ford, Firestone, and General Tyre. Because Port Elizabeth was founded at the mouth of a valley, down-town commercial and business development has had to follow a ribbon-like pattern between the foreshore and the hills behind. As a result the down-town area has been concentrated on both sides of the wide Main Street, with the hill behind it.

Information

The principal shopping boulevard is Main Street, where there are big department stores. The Port Elizabeth Publicity Association is in the Library Buildings in Market Street. The town has a variety of hotels, in the city centre, on the hill, and along the beachfront. Among the best beachfront hotels are the five star Elizabeth and the three star Beach and Marine hotels. Prices range upwards from R 19.00 for bed and breakfast. In town, good hotels are the two star Edward in Belmont Terrace and the Griffin (one star) in Griffin Street, north of the City Hall, and just off Main Street. In the suburbs try the Walmer Gardens (two star).

Nightclubs

There are not many nightclubs in Port Elizabeth. The best are Room at the Top and the Champagne Room, the Skyroof in the Marine Hotel, and the Bell in the Beach Hotel. Chinese restaurants include the Hong Kong, Dragon Inn and Lychee. For Italian cooking there is Il Foino and Gino's. There are also many steak houses and we recommend the Fingerlik in Trinder Square, El Cid and Hungry I.

Transport

Taxis are licensed. Minibuses and cars are available for private touring parties from Grosvenor Motors. There are also several car-hire firms, including Hertz. Rates run from R 10.00 per day and 15c per mile. The National Airways Corporation has light aircraft available for charter flights to anywhere in South Africa.

The Museum, Snake Park and Oceanarium form a complex worth at least a full morning or afternoon's visit. The Snake Park is renowned for its fine collection of exotic and indigenous reptiles. Daily demonstrations of snake handling are given, a special feature of which is the milking of venom from puffadders in the summer season. The Tropical House, a unique concept in South Africa, forms part of the snake park. Birds, reptiles and fish can be seen in lush tropical vegetation and visitors may wander through the dense vegetation. Nocturnal animals and birds may be seen under simulated moonlight conditions in the Nocturnal House. The famous performing dolphins and seals in the Oceanarium perform daily at 1100 and 1500. After each performance the seals and fish are fed.

Beaches

Only a ten-minute bus ride from the city centre is the beginning of a glorious three km (two mile) stretch of golden beach, running from King's Beach to Summerstrand, with one or two rocky outcrops. King's Beach is so named because it was here, in 1947, the Royal Family's special train was parked during a visit to the Eastern Cape.

A garden valley runs inland from the promenaded Humewood Beach, midway along the seafront. This is Happy Valley, which is illuminated by coloured lights at night, and is criss-crossed by lovers' walks.

There are two turf clubs operating which hold meetings on alternate Saturdays. These are the Port Elizabeth Turf Club at Fairview on the Cape Road, and the St Andrew's Racing Club at Arlington. The city has five golf courses which are open to the public. The Humewood Links is rated as being one of the finest tests of golfing skill by top international golfers. Others are the Wedgewood Park Club, the Port Elizabeth Golf Club, and a miniature course at the Walmer Golf Club. The nine-hole course at Command Headquarters is by invitation only. *Sport*

Impressive catches of big-game fish have been made in the sea off Port Elizabeth. These include yellow-fin tunny, big-eye tunny, marlin, barracuda, and broadbill swordfish. Boats can be hired in the harbour. *Fishing*

Three monuments deserve special mention, as they are landmarks in Port Elizabeth. The first is the 52 m (170 ft) high Campanile at the harbour entrance, which was erected in memory of the 1820 Settlers. The more energetic should climb the 204 steps to the observation floor for a magnificent panoramic view of the city. Then there is the pyramid next to the lighthouse on the Donkin Reserve which we have already mentioned. But the most famous of all is the Horse Memorial in Cape Road, which commemorates horses killed in the South African War. It has a particularly moving inscription.

The Marine Drive is a winding, 24 km (15 mile) coastal road, through the picturesque village of the Driftsands Forest Reserve, leading to Schoenmakerskop (Shoemaker's Head). Still visible on the rocks is part of the rusted hull of the *Western Knight*, wrecked in the 1920s. Halfway to Schoenmakerskop is the bungalow resort of The Willows. When driving on the Marine Drive, keep an eye open for troops of monkeys. These lovable freebooters often cause traffic holdups as they beg titbits from passing cars. *Marine Drive*

Settlers Park is a striking wild flower reserve in the Baakens Valley, between Port Elizabeth and the neighbouring municipality of Walmer, where a representative collection of indigenous buck and waterfowl has been introduced in natural surroundings.

For yachting and river fishing enthusiasts, a visit to the Swartkops River, 13 km (seven miles) from Port Elizabeth, is a must. This wide, slow flowing tidal river has the villages of Swartkops and Amsterdam Hoek on opposite banks near the mouth, and is a photographer's paradise in early morning, and towards evening, when the harsh African sunlight is mellowed. Further upriver is the village of Redhouse. Both Redhouse and Swartkops have their own yacht clubs. *Amsterdam Hoek and Swartkops*

Merely looking at the map, it is hard to appreciate the extent of the Eastern Cape, stretching as it does up into the Karoo and along the coast to East London. What follows now are brief descriptions of the more interesting places in it, followed by a chapter on the Transkei, now a self-governing African State.

Towards East London

Grahamstown

The blood-curdling war cries of Xhosa warriors and the African sun glistening on spears were daily threats to Grahamstown less than a century ago, though it seems unbelievable now. However, if you look at a town plan you see that the streets radiate from the centre like the spokes of a wheel. This was Colonel John Graham's basic defensive plan when he started a settlement here and it worked when the Xhosas were successfully repulsed in 1832. Colonel Graham, originally of the 93rd Highlanders, wanted to populate this area with Scottish crofters after the Napoleonic Wars, though only a few were sent among the 1820 settlers. Today Grahamstown is a charming old-world cathedral city, full of natural beauty, and the academic and judicial capital of the Eastern Cape. Quite often, though, you see groups of red-blanketed, pipe-smoking Xhosa women, their faces painted and carrying babies on their backs, mingling with shoppers on the streets. Another one-time frontier town is Bathurst, established in 1820 as the original centre of British Settlement, now a charming period piece of a place.

The country here is full of reminders of colonial wars, like Kaffir Drift, once a vital pass, and Cuylversville Church, near Shaw Park. During the war of 1846, 14 families used the church as a refuge against attacks by marauding Xhosa tribesmen. Again, in 1851, some 300 people sheltered there. It is now a national monument. If you are interested in the history of the 1820 Settlers you should read *Story of the British Settlers, 1820* by Hockly.

On the way to East London you also pass the ruins of Fort Dacres near the bridge over the Great Fish River, traditional meeting place of White and Black migratory moves in the nineteenth century. The fort was built in the Kaffir War of 1846 to protect the river crossing, by men of the Royal Navy. At the mouth of the Great Fish River is a small resort and beach on Chapman Bay, named after the ship which brought British settlers to the Eastern Cape in 1820. In the bay Diaz made his last anchorage before turning back to Portugal. The river was the frontier of the Cape Colony during the many Kaffir Wars of the nineteenth century, and, for three km (two miles) upstream, is a bird sanctuary and fishing resort.

Port Alfred

At the mouth of the Kowie River, and a 45 minute drive from Grahamstown, is Port Alfred, a residential and holiday resort. Founded in 1821, it has bathing beaches, a tidal lagoon, miles of river boating in beautiful scenery, fishing, and an 18 hole golf course, and the usual resort amenities. Indeed the whole coast on either side of Port Alfred is well sprinkled with resorts and attractions of historic interest. George river mouth, commonly called the Riet River (Reed River), has a fine beach and a lagoon. Nearby are the Three Sister Rocks, originally named Fountain Rocks by Bartholomew Diaz in 1488, because of the spectacular way waves smashed against them. Further along is Cawood's Bay, where the lagoon and beach are now a holiday resort.

King William's Town 59 km (37 miles) from East London, was the capital of British Kaffraria during the Kaffir Wars of 100 years ago, but today it is a quiet, sedate town with good hotels, among undulating hills and cattle country. We recommend the Central Hotel.

King William's Town

A few kilometres on the East London side of King William's Town is the African township of Zwelitsha ('New Era'), a self-contained westernised community. Some of the privately owned houses cost more than R 13,000 to build in the late sixties. Most African houses, however, are rather austere. A university exclusively for Africans is about 61 km (38 miles) from King William's Town at Fort Hare in a town called Alice. Many East and Central African leaders took their degrees at Fort Hare University.

East London

Coming past a series of villages named Berlin, Potsdam and so on by German settlers, you come to East London, fourth biggest seaport on the South African coast. It is a modern city of 124,000 people (57,000 white) on the Buffalo river mouth. The climate is temperate and the rainfall average is 33 ins a year. It came into being 120 years ago when the British Government of the Cape Colony had to police the border between British Kaffraria and Kaffirland (now Transkei) and was seeking a quicker, safer way of bringing in troops, supplies and ammunition than the arduous, hazardous overland route.

Lieutenant John Bailie, an 1820 settler, formerly of the Royal Navy, who was on board George Rex's brig, *Knysna*, surveying the river mouth, climbed what is now Signal Hill in November 1836 and hoisted the Union Jack. He claimed the port as British territory.

Today East London is a thriving industrial city that also makes a special point of catering for tourists. Its surfing and swimming in the warm Indian Ocean are excellent. There are white sandy beaches right on the city's beachfront, separated from modern, luxurious hotels only by the broad Esplanade. Of the beachfront hotels, Kings (three star) and Kennaway (three star) are the most modern and charge between R 25 and R 30.00 for bed and breakfast. King's Hotel has a private swimming pool, heated in winter, and Ceroy's nightclub which we can vouch for. There is dining and dancing at the Collette in Hotel Kennaway. In the city centre Queens on Currie Street is good and also has its own night spot. All have cocktail bars, and floor shows are put on from time to time. You could have a night out on R 15 a head.

Surfing	If you want to enjoy the seaside in luxury without staying in the city, there is the attractive two star Dolphin Hotel at Nahoon Beach eight km (five miles) from the City Hall. Two minutes' walk down a pathway brings you out on to the Nahoon Beach, where the surfing is really live. There are free changing rooms and also a shark patrol of young men, rather like Australian life-savers. Sharks, you may like to know, usually come in close to the shore only in cloudy weather, when the sea is murky and the temperature over 21°C (70°F). Boats can be hired for boating and fishing on the river that runs out here.
Shopping	East London's main shopping streets are Oxford Street and Terminus Street.
Car Hire	Hertz, Avis, and Budget Rent-a-Car all have offices in the city and at the airport. Rates run from R 10.00 a day and 10c a km for a two door Golf.
Riding	For riding contact the Glenlyn Riding School at Beaconhurst.
Information	The SAR Travel Bureau is at Southern House, Terminus Street and there are various other travel agents. The East London Publicity Association is in the City Hall and is most helpful to visitors.
	Deep-sea fishing trips, with equipment and bait provided, cost R 10.00 per person per day. The boat will buy all you catch unless you want to take the fish away with you. Pollock's Sports Shop will arrange bookings, so will Hughes and Co in Oxford Street.
Coelacanth	But the fish that is really famous in East London, the coelacanth, is in the Museum. The coelacanth is a species of fish (this one is about 1·22 m/4 ft long) thought to have been extinct for fifty million years. A stir was caused in the scientific world at Christmas, 1938, when this one turned up in the nets of a trawler which had been fishing near East London. Miss Marjorie Courtenay-Latimer, who is still Director of the Museum, helped to identify it. 'Old Four Legs', as it is sometimes called, has leg-like fins and is associated with the theory that land animals evolved from fish. Indeed the marine and seashell collection here is quite superb. So are exhibits of native Xhosa life, which include a section on witchdoctors and fertility dolls, and of early German and English settlers' costumes.
Wild Coast	From East London the main N2 road continues straight through the independent State of the Transkei – remember you may need a passport – and you can branch off before the border to the first of the Wild Coast resorts. Haga Haga, Morgan's Bay and Kei Mouth all have hotels and there is more about this justifiably well known stretch of coast in the next chapter.

76

The Bunga, or Parliament, Umtata

Transskei

The National Route from East London to Natal passes plumb through the independent African state of the Transkei and its capital, Umtata. It is tarmac all the way as is the Queenstown to Umtata road. Entering the Transkei you require a valid passport, smallpox vaccination certificate and yellow fever certificate (if you have been in a yellow fever area of Africa). A visa can be purchased at the border for R 2. South African currency is used.

Entry Requirements

The Transkei borders on Lesotho to the north and includes two small separate zones, one to the east in the Witteberg hills and the other to the north east, beyond the Natal town of Kokstad.

On the main road leaving East London you enter the Transkei after crossing the Great Kei River near Butterworth, which has two hotels. The nearby Butterworth River Cascades are attractive, but the real interest lies in the countryside itself, the homeland of the Xhosa people, whose rhythmic 'click' songs have become internationally known through singers such as Miriam Makeba. 'Xhosa' itself is pronounced 'Kosa', with a click on the Xh. They were a strong tribe until in 1857 a prophet declared that if they

Xhosa

77

killed all their cattle and destroyed their crops the white man would be driven out of Africa, and that furthermore God would given them food in plenty. So they slaughtered their cattle. But on the appointed day nothing happened. Subsequently, despite European help, some 60,000 died of starvation, and the tribe's power was broken.

Today the beautiful rolling hills of the Transkei, dotted with groups of huts and villages, reveal a completely different way of life to European South Africans. It has both a dignity and a happiness all its own. On the other hand the erosion that accompanies African methods of farming, largely due to overgrazing, is pitiful to see in a countryside so potentially fruitful.

From a tourist point of view the Transkei is best known for the Wild Coast already mentioned, which has a number of small holiday resorts reached by turnings off the main road. Its rocky, dramatic length runs 241 km (150 miles) from East London in the Cape Province to Port St John's, is divided by 20 rivers and is known for rock fishing, unfrequented beaches and its unspoilt nature.

Wild Coast

'Unspoilt' however means what it says and you must not expect more than simple facilities. Following the coast the resorts include Qora Mouth, with the thatched roof Kob Inn; Coffee Bay with the Ocean View Hotel: and Port St John's, which is the largest town on the coast, situated at the mouth of the Umzimvubu river. Nearby are two high headlands, sheer and forested, called *The Gates*. The whole area is a wildlife sanctuary. The Cape Hermes Hotel is among the best in the Transkei and there is a casino. Further north east is Port Grosvenor, only a village despite its name, where a treasure ship called the *Grosvenor* was wrecked in 1782.

Nature Reserves

Among the best beaches along the Wild Coast are those at Umngazi Mouth, near Port St John's and at the Hluleka Nature Reserve. This reserve, one of four along the coast, has attractive log cabins which can be rented through the Department of Agriculture and Forestry, Private Bag X5002, Umtata. They accommodate six people each and are self-catering. There are also log cabins at the Dwesa Nature Reserve, much further south by the mouth of the Bashee river, and there are many camping sites. The same department issues camping permits, which must be obtained. A fee is payable.

Umtata

Returning to the main road, the very long drive through the country offers an obvious stopping place in the capital. Being 698 m (2,290 ft) above sea level, Umtata has a pleasant climate, but limited facilities. The Parliament, called the Bunga and illustrated at the head of this chapter, can be visited and five km (three miles) off the Kokstad road are the Hillmond Weavers, who produce fine, hand-woven, mohair tapestries and carpets. These are well made and cost anything from R 15 to R 1,500. The best hotel is the Holiday Inn, one km south of the town. The Savoy Hotel is in the centre and there are several other lesser places. Transkei Airways and SAA run flights from Johannesburg to Umtata daily except Sundays.

The Umtata river divides Tembuland from Pondoland and Emboland. Whereas you will notice that Xhosas often wear red blankets, the Pondo people to the north of the river favour blue ones. More prosaically, the Umtata river has had the first of its two falls, formerly worth seeing, converted to hydro-electric production. However the Tsitsa Falls, near Qumbu on the national road to Natal are dramatic enough to be worth a stop as are the easily accessible Magwa Falls near Port St John's and Lusikisiki, which tumble 125 m (466 ft) into a gorge. The name Lusikisiki, incidentally, is an onomatopoeic word, deriving from the sound of wind blowing through the reeds.

Close to the road from Umtata to Port St John's is a high rock called Mlengana, or Execution Rock, from which local chiefs used to have their enemies thrown.

Past Qumbu the National Route passes through Mount Frere, where there are two hotels and good fishing. You cross the Natal border shortly before Kokstad, which the road skirts. The town sits 1,283 m (4,210 ft) up on the slopes of Mt Currie and is named after Adam Kok III, the last of the Griqua chiefs. It has two hotels and offers tennis, bowls, polo, golf, swimming and fishing. There is a useful cafe at the turn off from the main road. From Kokstad you can either drive down to the coast at Port Edward or Port Shepstone, both in Natal, or continue through another part of the Transkei to Ixopo, also in Natal. Between Ixopo and the sea lie large sugar estates.

The Amphitheatre in the Drakensberg

Natal

Though the smallest of South Africa's four provinces, Natal is remarkably varied within the compass of its more than 33,500 sq miles. For a start, there are 46 Game Reserves and National Parks, all the way from the valleys among spectacular peaks and vast natural amphitheatres of the Drakensberg to the sanctuaries of the rare white rhino in the sub-tropical bush of Zululand. The range of flora and fauna preserved here is unparalleled in Southern Africa. By contrast you can visit Zulu kraals, or if you prefer blondes to all other forms of life, take yourself down to the nightclubs of Durban and the miles of unspoilt beaches along the coast, with its many informal holiday resorts.

Climate   The sun shines virtually all the year round with most of the rain in summer. The winter months are cool and dry. Generally speaking the autumn and the spring are the best times for touring.

History   Natal owes its discovery and its name to Vasco da Gama, the Portuguese explorer who pioneered the sea routes to India. Sailing up the Natal coast on Christmas Day, 1498, da Gama christened the land 'Terra Natalis'. But it was not until 1824 that 26 adventurers under F. G. Farewell and H. F. Flynn sailed from Cape Town and landed in Port Natal to establish a trading station. This settlement's early history and development were punctuated by regular skirmishes against the Zulus, a powerful African nation which had come from territories north of the Limpopo River at the end of the 16th century and been welded into a powerful force by their leader, Chaka.

In October 1837, a band of Voortrekkers who had travelled in ox-wagons from the Cape, arrived in Durban. They were warmly welcomed by the existing British settlers, but their leader, Piet Retief, was treacherously murdered when parleying with Dingaan, Chaka's successor, for a grant of land. The Zulus were finally defeated at the Battle of Blood River on 16th December 1838. Shortly afterwards, the Voortrekkers declared Natal to be a Boer Republic with its capital at Pietermaritzburg. This in turn led to conflict between Boer and Briton and in 1844 Natal was annexed to the British Cape settlement and was subsequently created a separate British colony in 1856. It was again fought over during the Boer War, the battles of which are commemorated at various places, including Ladysmith, made famous by its unsuccessful siege by the Boers.

Apart from war memorials and evocative place names like Colenso and Spioen Kop, there is little to remind one of Natal's stormy past. Black and White (both Afrikaans and English) now live peacefully together. Nonetheless it remains the most British of the four provinces in both atmosphere and language though, like the rest of the Republic, the development of its agriculture, industry and communications has been phenomenally energetic and rapid.

Durban is 500 km (312 miles) by air from Johannesburg and there are a number of flights a day by South African Airways. Other flights go to East London, Port Elizabeth and Cape Town. SwaziAir operate twice weekly to Manzini in Swaziland. The train services are also excellent. Johannesburg is a 15 hour overnight journey, while the Orange Express makes the 2,000 km (1,277 miles) to Cape Town in 40 hours via Ladysmith, Kroonstad, Bloemfontein and Kimberley on Mondays and Fridays. The main roads are mostly tarred, except the last stretch to Swaziland and the Umfolozi and Hluhluwe game reserves. If in doubt, consult the Automobile Association offices or SATOUR's Tourist Map of the Republic. *Communications*

National Parks, Game Reserves and Nature Reserves

Not to visit one or more of Natal's reserves, would be an omission you would regret, as they are unique in their scope and excellently maintained. One of the major aims of the Natal Parks Board is to preserve and, if necessary, recreate the conditions in which the area's indigenous flora and fauna lived before human settlement began to affect the balance of nature.

The Board's headquarters are at the Queen Elizabeth Park Nature Reserve, eight km (five miles) outside Pietermaritzburg. Free literature on the parks may be obtained from the Reservations Officer, PO Box 662, Pietermaritzburg, who deals with bookings for all hutted camps, though not for hotels, which handle their own. Similarly, bookings may be made through travel agents. Usually you have to bring your own food to the hutted camps, at which accommodation is from R 5.50 a day.

Entrance charges to Reserves are R 3 per vehicle, 50c per adult and 25c per child. The services of a game guard can be invaluable in showing you exactly where to find different species.

Wilderness Trails If you have time, we strongly recommend the wilderness trails. These are treks on foot round otherwise inaccessible parts of the reserves. Three days cost R 50 a person, but you need to be fit (see text on Game Reserves). It is always worth looking out for tropical flowers and birds as well as game. Firearms and domestic pets are prohibited, by the way.

Fishing The Drakensberg mountain streams are excellent both for brown and rainbow trout. Largemouth and smallmouth black bass and bluehill sun fish thrive in warmer waters. Bream are numerous in coastal waters and in Zululand. The best fishing seasons are September, October and March to May. You want to avoid the summer rains when rivers are in spate (November to February). For inland fishing, you need a licence, obtainable from any Receiver of Revenue and certain sporting goods dealers. No licence is needed for sea fishing, except in Durban Bay.

Of Natal's 46 reserves, those most worth visiting are broadly divisible into the mountain reserves around the Drakensberg and the KwaZulu reserves, where you find rhino, hippo and buffalo, as well as buck and antelope. The larger Drakensberg reserves, both open all the year, are:

THE ROYAL NATAL NATIONAL PARK

It is 40 km (26 miles) south-west of Bergville. Total area 42 sq miles. Spectacular mountain scenery, riding, fishing, mountain-climbing. Wildebeeste, buck, lynx, birds, magnificent wild flowers. Hotel, hutted camp, camping. See page 92. It incorporates the Rugged Glen Nature Reserve.

GIANT'S CASTLE GAME RESERVE

Area: 100 sq miles, 70 km (43 miles) south-west of Estcourt. On plateau below the Drakensberg escarpment. Eland, wildebeeste, various buck. Flowers, birds, fishing. Hutted camp. Horse riding trails can be arranged. See page 94.

The KwaZulu reserves, all sub-tropical bush north of the Tugela River, include:

THE HLUHLUWE GAME RESERVE

This is pronounced Shlush-shloowy. Via Mtubatuba, it is 290 km (182 miles) north of Durban and is open all the year round. Black and white rhino, buffalo, zebra and other species are found there and many tropical birds. 89 sq miles. Hutted camp. See also page 97.

UMFOLOZI GAME RESERVE

305 km (195 miles) north of Durban with lions, rhino, buffalo, crocodiles, warthogs etc. Hutted camp. Wilderness trails, 187 sq miles. See page 97.

ST LUCIA GAME RESERVE AND PARK

This extends 70 km (45 miles) from the St Lucia Estuary, 28 km (18 miles) east of Mtubatuba and totals 189 sq miles. It includes the St Lucia Lakes, Charters Creek and Fanies Island. Hippo, crocodile, buck, prolific bird life. Two hutted camps. Boats, fishing, wilderness trails. Open all the year round. See page 97.

Durban

World travellers have described Durban as one of the most beautiful maritime resorts in the world. In fact it has a second side to its character. It rivals Cape Town as the second biggest city in South Africa, boasts the largest harbour on the continent, has a population of approximately three-quarters of a million and is thoroughly modern and attractively laid out. During World War II its hospitality became a byword among British and American servicemen. Today it is a major port of call for cruise ships.

Climate

The climate is warm and balmy most months of the year, with the hottest temperatures in January, February and March, when the humidity can be uncomfortably high.

Beaches

The city's greatest attraction is undoubtedly its kilometres of golden sandy beaches and the warm waters of the Indian Ocean. The three main beaches are South Beach, North Beach and Country Club, all protected by shark nets. The latter two are excellent for surfing.

Durban is also a great golfing centre and was the home town of Gary Player, the international golf champion.

Shopping

The main shopping zone is along West Street which virtually slices the city in two and ends up at the beach front. At the beach end, there is a multitude of shops stocked with holiday clothing, curios and souvenirs. Don't forget to get certificates of origin for any skins you buy, as customs officers may want them when you leave the Republic.

Nearer the centre of the city, and still in West Street, you will find department stores like Stuttafords, John Orrs, Payne Bros, the OK Bazaars and Woolworths. There are good ladies' hairdressing salons at most of the hotels (like Hotel Edward and EdenRoc), and at the major department stores.

Information Bureau

Before mapping out a plan of action in Durban, it is as well to call at the Visitors Information Bureau (PO Box 1044, telephone 25358) on the corner of Church and West Streets. The staff are helpful and will provide free maps and local pamphlets. The National Tourist Bureau is at 320 West Street (telephone 26410).

You should not miss the Indian and African markets, next to one another in Victoria Street, off Grey Street, in the Indian business section of the city, among mosques and temples. The Indian market specialises in fine wrought jewellery, curios, leather work, subtle blends of curry powders, baskets of all shapes, brass, ivory and filigree silverware. You can buy anything from a hollow lucky bean with a tiny elephant carved inside to carved Chinese camphor kists and massive elephants in ebony. But never pay the first price asked – a little good-natured wrangling may well bring the price down 50 percent. More than 500,000 Indians live in Natal, playing a large part in its trade. You will notice their influence in many places. They are largely descended from labourers brought to Natal's sugar estates because Zulus refused to cut sugar cane.

Markets

The African market has a completely different character. Here you can buy assegais, carved masks, miniature shields made of toughened cowhide, the ingredients for witchcraft potions, elaborate walking sticks and other African curios. Prices are not high, though they tend to rise if the stallholder realises you are a tourist. Again, do not be afraid to argue the toss. A more sophisticated place to get African carvings is the African Art Centre in Syfret House, Gardiner Street. It is run under the auspices of the South African Institute of Race Relations.

Hotels

Because of its year-round equable climate, Durban attracts visitors in spring, summer and autumn as well as during the fashionable winter season (mid-May to mid-August), though the high seasons are short. For this reason, the hotels are of a higher standard and considerably cheaper than those at resorts depending on a seasonal trade. Durban's two five star hotels are the Maharani on the Marine Parade, and the Royal on Smith Street. For bed only they charge from R 25 to R 65. A well known hotel is the four star Edward on the Marine Parade where the daily rate for bed and breakfast is R 21.75. Among other hotels we recommend are the Elangeni (four star), Blue Waters (three star), Malibu (three star), Lonsdale (two star) and the Park View (two star). All these are near the sea and charge from R 13.50–R 22 a day for bed and breakfast.

Lesser hotels charge as little as R 5 a day for a room only. For instance the President, MiraMar, Los Angeles or Crown. All are one star hotels.

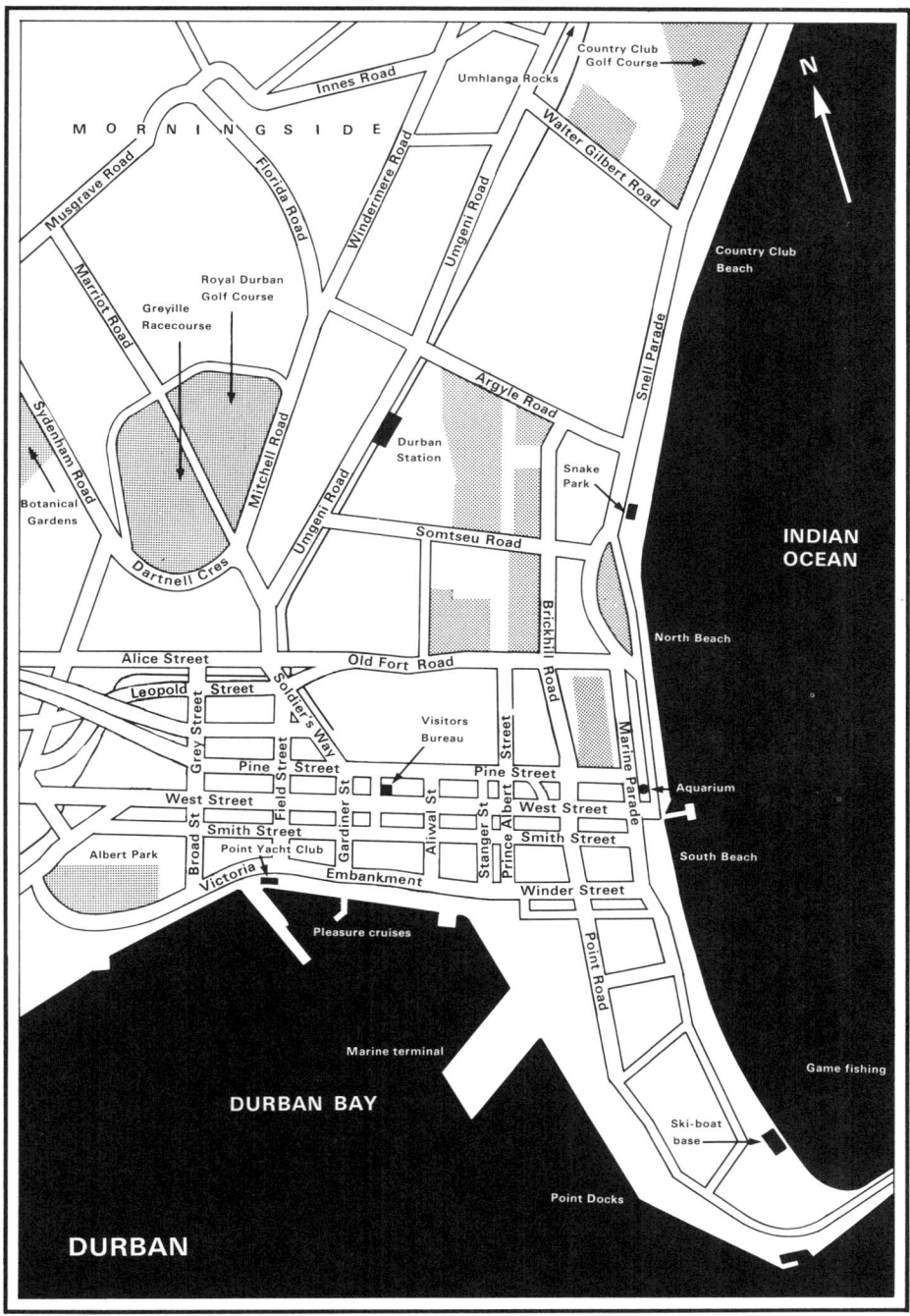

Two hotels outside Durban which deserve special mention are the Oyster Box (three star) and the Beverly Hills (five star), both at Umhlanga Rocks (pronounced Umshlanga), an attractive spot 16 km (10 miles) north of the city on a fast road. The Beverly Hills is of international standard with iced water on tap, three restaurants and a nightclub, swimming pool, hairdressing salon and so on. The tariff is upwards of R 37.50 bed and breakfast per person per day or R 46.50 full board. By comparison the Oyster Box, which charges R 19.80 a day is homelier, though more renowned for its food. There is a protected beach at Umhlanga Rocks.

Restaurants Good restaurants are the Red Rooster in Point Road, the Smorgasbord at the Edward, the Napoleon, the Roma, and the 67 in Albany Grove. For Indian food there is the Goodwill Lounge in Victoria Street. The Edward has, too, a first class Chinese restaurant. Surprisingly the Golden Egg on the Marine Parade serves excellent seafood.

Nightclubs At night Durban becomes a fairyland of lights, with fun fairs and amusement arcades in full swing along the beach front. The night clubs vary. Happily we did not come across any clip joints, although one or two are pretty far down the market. For an evening out, most South Africans go to a good restaurant with a resident band such as the New Causerie at the Edward Hotel, the plush Copacobana at the Beverly Hills, the Cascades at the Blue Waters, the Bali Hai at the Elangeni or the Café de Paris at Claridges. You should eat and drink well and dance for around R 15 to R 20 a head.

Cinemas There are half a dozen air-conditioned cinemas, but little regular live theatre.

The Oceanarium At the sea front end of West Street is one of South Africa's finest Oceanariums, for which admission is 50c. If you are there at eleven in the morning or three in the afternoon, you can see a thousand fish being fed underwater by hand. The light is good, so take a camera. The sharks, in their own special tank, are fed every second day by an astonishingly fearless diver.

The Orchid House Durban's famous Orchid House, in the Botanical Gardens above Curries Fountain, now an Indian sports centre and five minutes' drive from the city centre, houses the finest collection under one roof in the whole of Africa, with more than 3,000 plants and hundreds of exotic varieties in a breathtakingly beautiful setting.

The Snake Park The Snake Park on the beach front is open all day, and whenever the number of visitors warrants it an employee at the park climbs right in among the snakes and picks them up to display their fangs. You can see the cobra, the deadly ringhals and fat, bloated puff adders by the score. If you are not squeamish, ask an attendant to drape a three m (nine ft) python around your neck for a picture.

The Harbour Harbours are always fascinating and as the Port of Durban is the biggest and busiest in Africa, it is worth a visit at any time of the day. The departure of big ships from Durban is a festive occasion. Operating from Dick King jetty, on the Esplanade, near Dick King's statue, are fast, fully equipped and very comfortable boats which can take you on sight-seeing cruises around the Bay and docks. (Dick King is commemorated for his 960 km ride to Grahamstown in 1842 to seek re-inforcements for the besieged Durban garrison. He and a Zulu companion achieved the ride in 10 days.) If you prefer it, you can go deep-sea fishing – rod, line and bait are supplied. A day's run after salmon, barracuda or '74' will cost about R 10 a head and R 5 for spectators. Alternatively people have caught a wide variety of fish – even sharks – off the South Pier.

Not the least of Durban's attractions are the 16 flower-filled parks that spread over 76 ha (189 acres). Chief among them is the Japanese water garden, at Durban North, Jameson Park, famed for its roses, Albert Park, Mitchell Park and the Botanical Gardens. Depending on the time of year, you will find bougainvillea in profusion, azaleas, even daffodils in the spring. Other worthwhile visits would be to the amphitheatre on the beach front, the Museum with its fine collection of native crafts, butterflies and birds eggs, and the art gallery. At the Blue Lagoon, you can learn to waterski, play mini golf, cruise up the river or drive a go-kart and nearby is the Durban Country Club, where facilities include one of the finest golf courses, eight tennis courts, croquet, numerous squash courts, a swimming pool and the best food in town.

Parks and Gardens

On Sunday afternoons, teams of 35 or more Zulu dancers in tribal dress give demonstrations of Ngoma dancing at the African dance ground in Somtseu Road. The Visitors Bureau can give you more details of motor coach trips to see this exciting spectacle.

Zulu Dancers

In March and April the Indian community holds fire-walking ceremonies and rituals near the Hindu temples and the Indian Quarter is always full of strange sights and sounds, the smells of exotic cooking and incense, the sight of the women in beautiful Benares silk saris.

Indian Ceremonies

One of the chief attractions during the winter season is horse racing. The Durban Turf Club, at Greyville, encircles the Royal Durban Golf Course, not five minutes from the business centre of the city. It is here that the R 50,000 Durban July Handicap takes place each year on the first Saturday in July. Like Ascot in England, it is South Africa's most fashionable race meeting of the year and tens of thousands of people come from all over the country for the event. The Gold Cup meeting, four weeks later, is another elegant occasion.

Racing

A full list of tour operators can best be obtained from the Durban Publicity Association. Hertz, Budget and Avis, all central, offer cars for hire and arrange special tours to various parts of South Africa with a uniformed driver and courier.

Tour Operators and Car Hire

The South African Railways operate first class coach tours to the game reserves and down the coast as far as Cape Town as do Springbok Safaris at 69 Guildhall Arcade, Gardiner Street.

Taxis are plentiful in Durban, but they do not drive around the streets in search of a fare. You will find them at special ranks.

Air Charter
There are two airports. Scheduled services operate out of Louis Botha, while Virginia is the smaller civil airport. There are two major air charter companies – Commercial Air Services (at Virginia Airport) and Rennies Air Natal (at Louis Botha Airport). Single-engined aircraft can be chartered for about R 80 per hour, including pilot.

Medical Care
The city has a number of good doctors and dentists, a large provincial hospital, Addington Hospital, and many private nursing homes.

Durban's Neighbourhood and Coastal Resorts

Durban has three nature reserves in its immediate vicinity, as well as stretches of coast both north and south that make an easy day trip for a picnic. Coach tours run to most of them – consult the Visitors Bureau about them.

One of the most interesting reserves is the Stainbank Reserve at Yellow Wood Park, a suburb of Durban, 10 minutes by car from the city centre, which not only has impressive indigenous bush and flowers, but birds and several species of game, including zebra. Going inland towards Pietermaritzburg (described under Inland Natal), don't let yourself be confused by the succession of townships along the National road. You pass the 28 ha (70 acre)

Paradise Valley Paradise Valley Nature Reserve 17 km (11 miles) from the city centre and further on, five km (three miles) from Kloof, is the larger

Krantzkloof Nature Reserve Krantzkloof Nature Reserve. This comprises more than 40 ha (100 acres) of a spectacular forested gorge on the Emolweni River. Bushpig, bushbuck, reedbuck and duiker are among the wild life and there is an attractive picnic site immediately above the Kloof Falls. Further on again, if you take the old Pietermaritzburg road beyond Hillcrest, you drive up into the rolling landscape of the

Valley of a Thousand Hills Valley of a Thousand Hills and the Inanda Zulu Reserve. There is a good hotel named after the valley. The area has, deservedly, become a major tourist attraction.

Shembe Festival
Once a year, on the Sunday nearest 25th July, the Shembe Festival is held at Ekuphakameni village in the Inanda district. This is the festival of a Zulu religious sect started by Isaiah Shembe, a convert to Christianity and later led by his son, Johannes. Zulu tribal rites have been adapted into the sect's Christian ceremonies.

North of Durban
There is still a distinct contrast between the resorts north of Durban and those to the south, despite the expansion of the last decade.

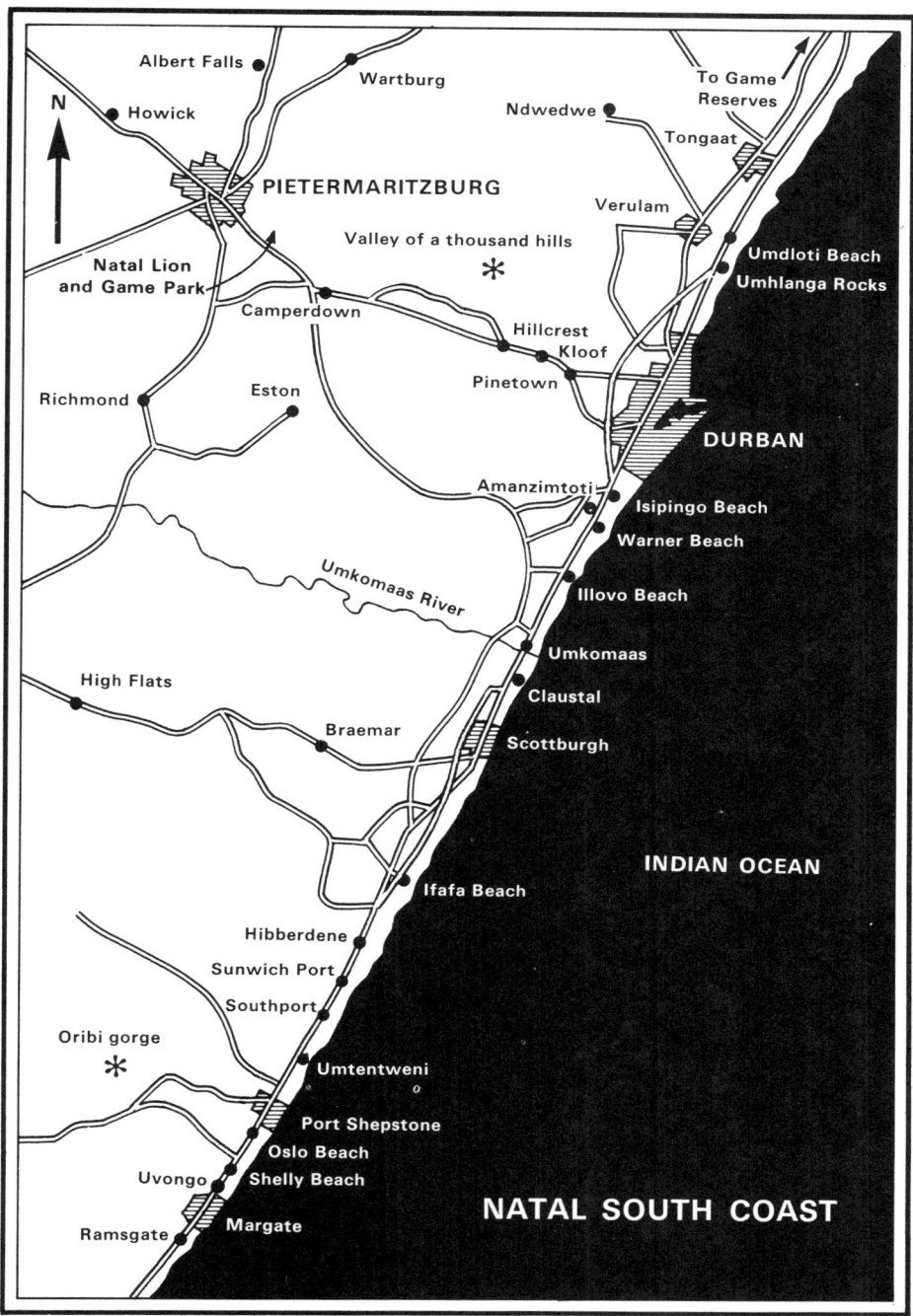

NATAL SOUTH COAST

True Umhlanga Rocks, already mentioned, is highly developed with shopping centres, holiday flats and villas. Its attractions include golf, botanical gardens and the Scarlet Tanager Aviary, a remarkable collection of talking birds of the parrot and parakeet variety. However there is less development further north, where seaside villages like Compensation Beach, Ballito Bay, Willard Beach, Thompson's Beach, Chaka's Rock, Salt Rock and Sheffield Beach offer excellent surf and rock fishing. At Stanger there is a monument to the famous Zulu King Chaka, who was murdered by his half brother Dingaan, at the great kraal Dukuza – see later in this chapter. Much further up the coast Richards Bay has a three star hotel and there is a Nature Reserve, though the town is industrial.

South of Durban South of Durban, the road passes through the port and industrial area. Once clear of this, you come to slightly more sophisticated resorts similar to those on the Hibiscus Coast described further on.

Amanzimtoti Of these resorts, Amanzimtoti, 27 km (17 miles) from Durban is the most progressive. It has its own zoo, golf course and several fine hotels, among the best being the Lagoon, and the Beach. At the Inyoni Bird Sanctuary there are hundreds of wildfowl, peacocks and aquatic birds, with interesting indigenous trees like oleander, wild banana, kaffirboom and umdoni.

Umkomaas At Umkomaas there are several hotels, including the Lido Hotel which has a good table, a championship golf course and swimming pool heated in winter.

Further on, Scottburgh has a particularly good beach, with four hotels, excellent camping sites and golf. Indeed most of the resorts on the south coast have golf courses. A normal green fee for the day is from R 2.

Inland from the coast, both north and south of Durban, are extensive sugar plantations, among the rolling hills. The Mount Edgecombe Estate, close to Durban is well worth a visit.

The Hibiscus Coast

The Hibiscus Coast is one of the most popular holiday playgrounds in Southern Africa. It stretches from south of Durban to Port Edward. The coastline is ruggedly attractive and all resorts have their own nets to protect bathers from sharks. Because of the warm Agulhas Current which flows down the coast, the sea is warm throughout the year and is ideal for bathing.

Fishing Fishing is excellent, especially in late June or early July, when millions and millions of sardines make their annual migration up the coast, hotly pursued by game fish of all kinds. At many of the towns along the Hibiscus Coast, the sardines are forced ashore in their thousands by their pursuers and can be collected in baskets or any other receptacle that is handy. Grilled over hot coals, or fried in butter, they are delicious!

Margate

The main resort in this region of Natal is Margate, an attractive little town that has pleasant hotels, holiday flats, camping sites and well laid out caravan parks. The town caters especially for teenagers and families and has all the amenities and attractions expected of a popular and modern beach resort. In May every year a Hibiscus Festival is held where a beauty queen is chosen.

Not far from Margate is the Oribi Gorge, an awesome chasm cut out of solid rock by a river over thousands of years. Twenty km long (12 miles) and five km (three miles) wide, and with a sheer drop of 364 m (1,200 ft) at some places, the gorge is an unforgettable sight. It can be reached by car or bus.

Many other lovely resorts dot the coastline – Ramsgate, Port Edward, Southbroom, Uvongo, Banana Beach, Shelly Beach, St Michael's-on-Sea to mention just a few. Hotels cater for all types of visitor and children are usually very welcome. A tourism committee is active in the area and is based in Margate. All inquiries are welcome (PO Box 25, Margate). Hotel prices range between R 14 to R 19, a day, inclusive.

The Drakensberg and Inland Natal

Drakensberg Mountains

It is a debatable question whether more people go to the Drakensberg from Johannesburg or from Durban. If you arrive in the country by air, via Johannesburg, you would take the N 16 route through the north-east corner of the Free State and Harrismith (see page 46). The Voortrekkers who came into Natal this way from the high veld, thought the vast escarpment above the lush green hills of Natal resembled the saw-toothed spines of a dragon. So they named it the Drakensberg. It is the most spectacular range of mountains in Southern Africa, with peaks towering to 3,248 m (10,763 ft) at Mont aux Sources, where the Orange and Tugela Rivers have their source.

The entire range provides a constant challenge to mountaineers and is a magnet to hikers and nature lovers. There are crystal-clear mountain streams, tumbling waterfalls, wild flowers in profusion, ferns and forests with ancient yellow woods. There are baboons, dassies (quaint rock-rabbits) and several species of buck to watch. Fishing is superb as both rainbow and brown trout were introduced into the rivers at the turn of the century and the streams are constantly being restocked.

Today the Drakensberg is one of South Africa's favourite playgrounds, with a chain of nature reserves and first-rate hotels running along the escarpment from Royal Natal National Park in the north to the Loteni Nature Reserve in the south. Being high in the mountains, there are no direct routes between them, except on horseback, and they are reached by road through various towns in the valleys below.

Virtually all the hotels offer horse-riding, fishing, swimming, tennis, bowls and other amusements, both indoor and outdoor. There are also a number of guest farms. For a complete list of them, write to the Publicity Association, Pietermaritzburg, Natal. Remember that you need warm clothing at night and stout shoes for hiking in the mountains.

Royal Natal National Park

The Royal Natal National Park, which includes Rugged Glen Nature Reserve, covers some 31 sq miles of absolutely magnificent mountain scenery between 1,500 m (4,700 ft) and 3,300 m (11,050 ft) above sea level. It is being restored botanically to its primeval state; its wildlife includes black wildebeest, various species of buck and baboon. There are many waterfalls, including the delightful cascades, deep ravines and great mountain bluffs that are snow-covered in winter. Two of these mountains, the Sentinel and the Eastern Buttress, flank a huge natural amphitheatre, over the edge of which the Tugela river falls 853 m in three dramatic stages.

The only way to travel in the park is on foot or horseback. We strongly recommend the guided patrols run by the Rangers here. The authorities also publish an excellent guide to the park.

The film *Zulu*, starring Stanley Baker, was shot with the great amphitheatre in the background. At Tendele there is a hutted camp, which may be reached by road (three km/two miles from the hotel) and there is a beautiful camping park. For details contact the Senior Warden, Royal Natal National Park, PO Mont aux Sources (telephone Mont-aux-Sources 3) or the Reservations Officer, Natal Parks Board, PO Box 662, Pietermaritzburg.

Hotels

If you have an opportunity to chat to one of the Wardens, take it. They are very knowledgeable about nature conservation. The Warden's Office adjoins the Royal Natal National Park Hotel (two stars). It has the same address. The telephone is Mont-aux-Sources 1, and rates run from R 20 a day. The British Royal Family stayed here in 1947 during their extensive tour of South Africa, after which the hotel became 'Royal'. Virtually all the rooms have wall-to-wall carpeting and private bathrooms and accommodation is in such demand all the year round that it is essential to book ahead. Just outside the park, adjoining Rugged Glen, is another hotel, Mont aux Sources Hotel (one star) (telephone Mont-aux-Sources 7), with rates from about R 18 a day. It has horse-riding, bowls, tennis and swimming facilities. Both hotels are served by SAR luxury touring buses from Durban and Johannesburg and by daily buses to Ladysmith railway station.

The access road to the Park, slippery in wet weather, can be reached either from Harrismith through the Oliviershoek Pass or through Bergville and Ladysmith. The Pass road is not tarmacked and can be bad after heavy rain. The longer route, through Ladysmith, is tarmacked as far as Bergville, a small village with the Walter Hotel, a petrol station and a couple of stores. This is the direct route to Durban (290 km/181 miles). There are three Andrews Motels near Ladysmith which we recommend – one at Estcourt, one at Fort Mistake and a particularly attractive one on the road from Harrismith near Van Reenen's Pass. Rates are R 9.80 a night, meals cost extra and all are two star establishments.

Ladysmith is certainly worth a visit. Originally a transport riders' camp and now growing industrially, its fame derives from its 118 day siege during the Boer War, when the British held out despite lack of water and the attentions of a siege gun called Long Tom, mounted on the hill above by the Boers. The British actually employed an Indian to stand on an adjacent part of the hill and wave a flag every time Long Tom was fired so that residents could take cover – there were no high velocity shells in those days. *Ladysmith*

The town centre retains many of the pleasant old Victorian houses of the last century. All Saints Church has memorials to the British who fell, as do the surrounding hills, like Caesar's Camp. The Town Hall has an interesting historical collection. The hotels include the Royal and the Crown, which charge in the region of R 11 a day.

If you are interested in history, you could spend some time here. Not only were hills like Spioen Kop everyday words around the world in 1900, but earlier the Zulu Wars gave bloody renown to Rorke's Drift and Blood River, to the east near Dundee. At the battle of Isandhlwana, the Zulus massacred nearly 4,000 British soldiers under Lord Chelmsford who despised the Boers 'laager' method of defence. Soon after, the Zulus attacked the hospital at Rorke's Drift on the Buffalo River. Eighty men turned it into a laager by forming a traditional square and held it, earning the greatest number of Victoria Crosses ever awarded for one action – nine. *Rorke's Drift*

Further north, near Volksrust, is the extraordinary conical mountain, Majuba, where the British General, Sir George Colley, fell. And at the foot of the mountain is another national monument, O'Neill's Cottage, where the agreement to end the first Boer War was signed in 1883, a piece of history that is often forgotten.

Returning to Ladysmith, which is to be by-passed by a freeway section of the N 3, you could go south to Colenso, another battlefield with a Museum, and go on to the Armoured Train memorial near Chieveley, the place where Winston Churchill, then a war reporter, was taken prisoner in a Boer ambush.

More peaceful pleasures lie up at Cathedral Peak, reached via Winterton, and part of a series of mountain resorts south of the Royal National Park. The two star Cathedral Peak Hotel (PO Winterton, telephone Cathedral Peak 1), charges from R 17 a day. It *Cathedral Peak* is set in superb scenery and has good facilities. Also reached from Winterton, but by a different road, are Cathkin Park, a forest reserve, Champagne Castle, El Mirador and The Nest.

Giant's Castle
Game Reserve

Loskop is on the main road between the resorts and Estcourt, from which a branch road leads to the Giant's Castle Game Reserve, 70 km (43 miles) from Estcourt. The road is potentially tricky in wet weather. The reserve's 96 sq miles lie under the Giant's Castle Peak 3,280 m (10,000 ft) of the Drakensberg, its grassy plateau intersected by many streams and valleys. There are numerous Bushman paintings. Guides are available. The bird life is fascinating and includes eagles, lammergeyer and giant kingfishers, while game includes eland, mountain reedbuck, duiker and an occasional leopard. The fishing is excellent. There is a hutted camp in beautiful surroundings run by the Natal Parks Board and costing from R 4.50 a night. Bookings must be made through the Parks Board, PO Box 662, Pietermaritzburg or the Camp Superintendent, PB, Estcourt.

Kamberg
Nature Reserve

A smaller reserve, the Kamberg Nature Reserve of eight sq miles is situated among the foothills, by Mooi River, with 13 km (eight miles) of trout fishing. The reserve is now the home of the Zulu Royal cattle and of reedbuck, eland, duiker and oribi. There is a small rest camp where bedding, etc, is provided but you bring your own food. Bookings to the Camp Superintendent at PO Rosetta.

Loteni

The next in the line of reserves is the Loteni Nature Reserve, 80 km (49 miles) from Nottingham Road, off the route from there to Himeville. You can also reach Loteni through Pietermaritzburg, via Impendhle. The wildlife is similar to that of Giant's Castle and the scenery in the valley of the Loteni River and of the Umkomaas, into which it runs, is magnificent. There is a hutted camp, run by the Parks Board.

Another small sanctuary is the Himeville Nature Reserve, where the lakes attract a lot of wildfowl. It is two km from Himeville, a village with a hotel which will arrange landrover trips up the spectacular Sani Pass and into Lesotho (Basutoland), weather permitting.

Sani Pass

The Sani Pass itself ascends 610 m (2,000 ft) in three km (two miles) by a series of tortuous bends, finishing 2,700 m (9,000 ft) above sea level. People go to the top by jeep not only to enjoy the fabulous scenery and exhilarating air, but to ski down the upper slopes of the Drakensberg, which are covered in snow for many months of the year. A ski lift is in operation and a small chalet has been built for mountaineers who wish to spend the night at the top of the mountain. Remember to take your passport with you if you decide to go to the top of the pass – it will be needed when you cross the border between Natal and Lesotho.

However the main resort is the Sani Pass Hotel, a luxurious hotel below the pass, with a fine range of facilities, including squash, tennis, swimming, horse-riding, golf and air flips over the pass. Visitors can be met off the SAR bus at Himeville, or off the train at Underberg, as can visitors to the Drakensberg Gardens Hotel, another popular holiday centre in the area. Both have air strips.

From Underberg you can drive via Bulwer down to Pietermaritz-burg on the main road through country where many of the Africans cut fine figures riding their horses across the countryside and through the glorious deep valley of the Umkomaas River. Near Elandskop, at Majunza location, there is an annual Festival of First Fruits, at the time of the new moon, towards the end of March. This is a harvest festival with ceremonial African dancing at sunset. Do not forget that you need a permit to enter African tribal areas.

Festival of First Fruits

The capital of Natal, Pietermaritzburg, was founded in 1838 by a party of Voortrekkers, looking for a new home after the Battle of Blood River. It is a pleasant city, full of parks and gardens and small compared with Durban which is 80 km (50 miles) away on a fast road. Although at an altitude of 610 m (2,000 ft), Pietermaritzburg can get hot and sticky in summer, but at other times has a wonderful climate. There are a number of hotels of which the Camden, Capital Towers, and Hilton are all three star charging up to R 35 for bed and breakfast. Two star hotels such as the Imperial and the Ansonia charge from R 9 to R 11 for bed and breakfast. The information office (telephone 22196) is in Church Street, just behind the City Hall.

Pietermaritz-burg

There is a fair variety of shops. Among the things to see in the city are the Church of the Vow, built by the Voortrekkers to commemorate the victory at Blood River, and now a Museum and the Botanic Gardens, known for their flowering trees and shrubs, especially azaleas. There is an Azalea Festival every year, early in September, when a queen is chosen.

Pietermaritzburg is also the headquarters of the Natal Parks Board, whose offices are at Queen Elizabeth Park Nature Reserve, eight km (five miles) north-west of the city. This is particularly notable for its flora and has quite a few tame buck and a couple of rhino in an enclosure. The Parks Board publishes some very good wildlife drawings that are well worth buying to have framed.

Queen Elizabeth Park

Further up the main freeway is Howick with, according to the National Geographic Magazine, the second healthiest climate in the world (the most healthy is in Australia). The Howick Falls dropping 110 m (365 ft) are famous, as are two other spectacular water falls – the Albert Falls 22 km (14 miles) from Pietermaritz-burg on the Greytown road and the Karkloof Falls, 40 km (25 miles) from the city. The Midmar Dam, on the Umgeni River 19 km (12 miles) west of the city is a newly developed centre for yachting and fishing. En route the luxurious Hilton Hotel at Hilton Road, between Pietermaritzburg and Midmar, is a popular stopping place.

Howick Falls

Northern Natal and Zululand (KwaZulu)

The coastal region of the north is a country of green, rolling hills, studded with beehive-shaped native huts. It stretches to the borders of Swaziland and Mozambique and is the home of that once powerful warrior race, the Zulus, whose impis fought the white man so tenaciously a century ago (see also Inland Natal). Gradually the whole of Zululand's 10,425 sq miles are being consolidated into the self-governing African state of KwaZulu.

If you have any of the traditional preconceived ideas about Africa, then Zululand is the place where you will find them justified. It is all feature-film material – long beaches, sub-tropical vegetation, an abundance of wildlife in seven reserves and the legendary Zulus themselves, tall handsome men, quite often decked out in their magnificently beaded tribal dress. One other thing to remember there is that dirt roads can also be the making of travellers' tales – as they are often impassable after heavy rains. An energetic programme of tarring them is now being carried out.

If in any doubt about these roads, consult the AA before you set out. There are various coach tours to the game reserves, in particular the South African Railways five day tour is good value.

Zulu King

The N 2 road brings you north from Durban and you enter KwaZulu as you cross the long modern bridge over the Tugela River. A few miles before the bridge you pass Stanger, once a centre of ivory hunters and now surrounded by green sugar estates. Here there is a memorial to Chaka, the Zulu king, on the site of his great kraal, Duzuka – which means Labyrinth, where he lived with his regiments and his concubines and where he was finally assassinated by Dingaan. His career began about 1818 and under his cruel dictatorship the Zulus were welded into a great military nation. His impis wore leopard skins and ostrich feather crests and could not marry until they had killed. Every kraal was effectively an army camp, until the British finally broke the Zulu power at Ulundi in 1879. It seems a far cry from the women you now see working happily in the mealie fields, while their men tend cattle in the hills.

KwaZulu

Much of the Tugela basin is being developed as part of the plan under which KwaZulu is becoming a self-governing African state, like the Transkei. To reach Eshowe, 150 km (93 miles) from Durban, you turn off the N 2 and climb into the hills. The town is 500 m (1,700 ft) above sea level and it derives its name from the gentle sighing of the wind in the forests that surround it. There are two hotels and a few shops. Dingaan's Kraal is nearby and the whole area is steeped in Zulu history. However the capital of KwaZulu is at Ulindi, 160 km (100 miles) from Durban and the seat of the KwaZulu Parliament. It lies some distance inland.

Opposite top: Bushmen hunters in the Kalahari
Bottom: Zebra in Mountain Zebra National Park. Photographs SATOUR

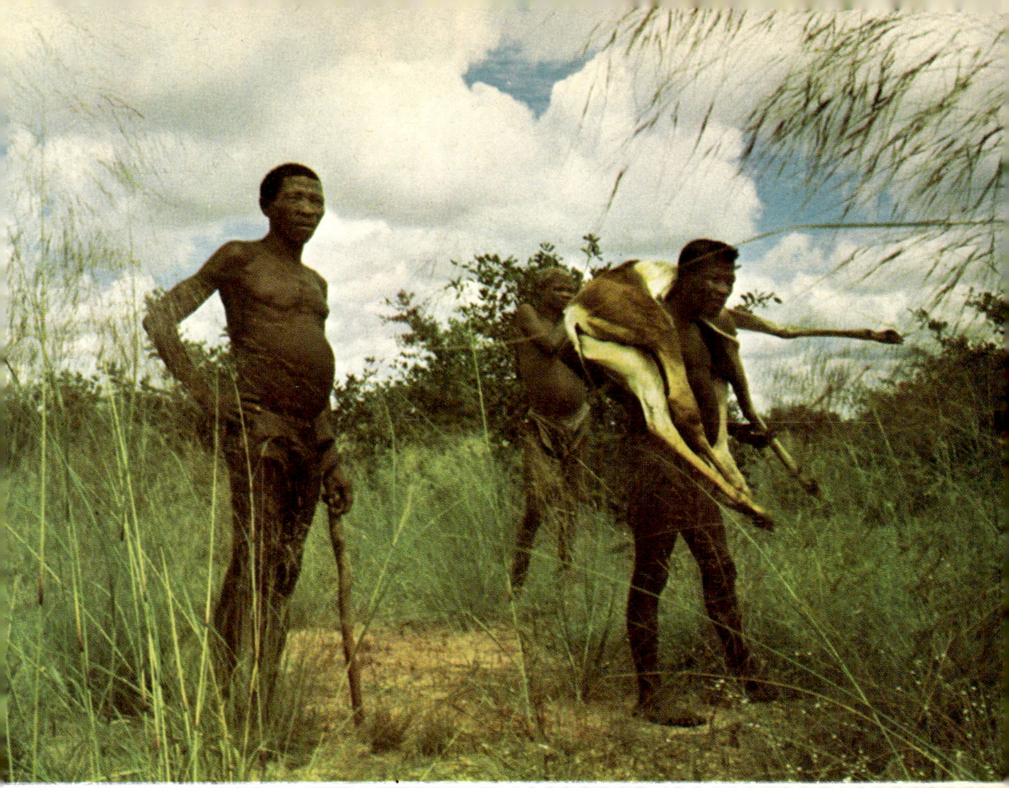
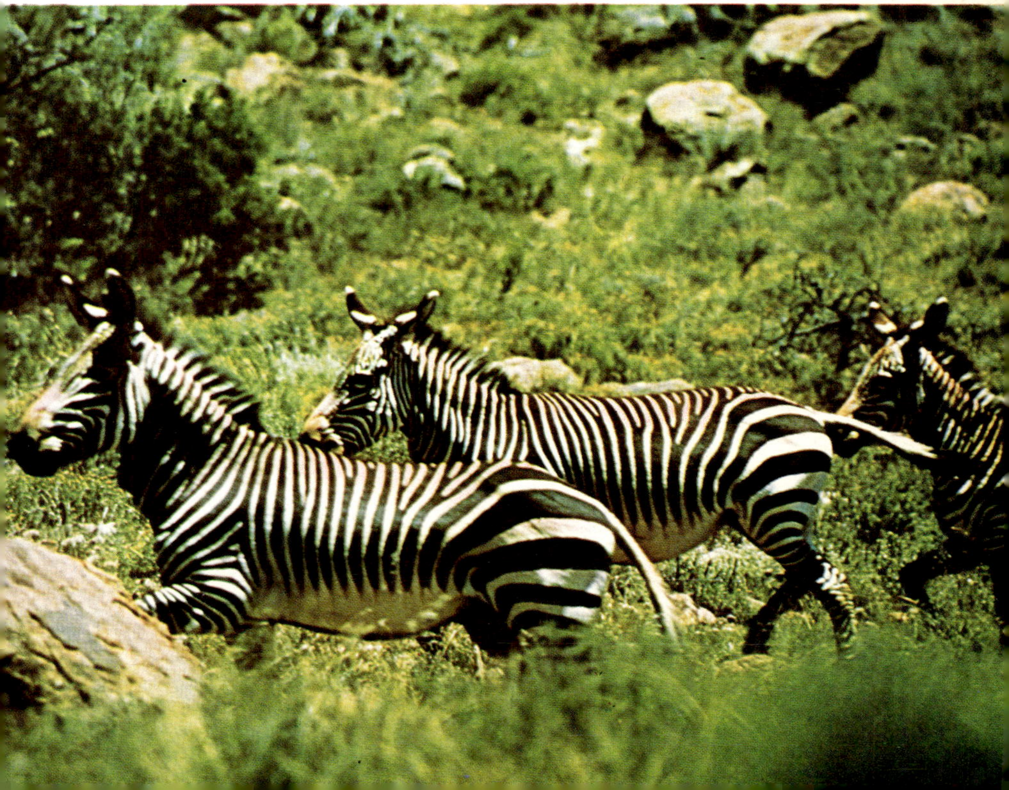

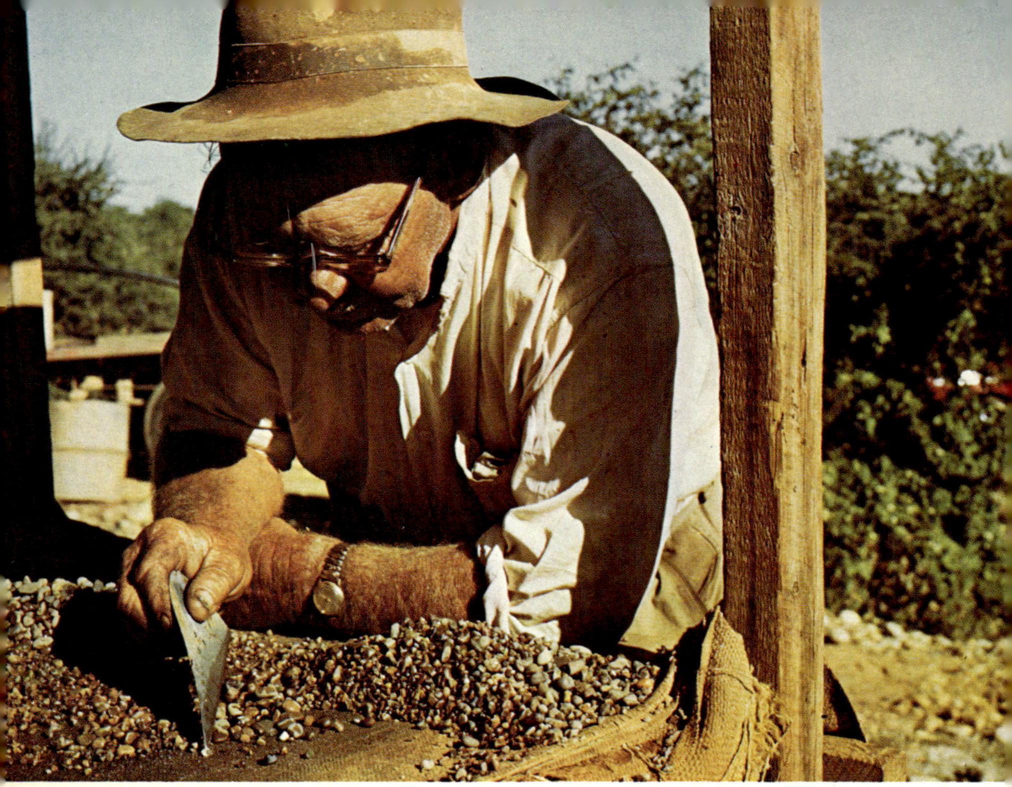

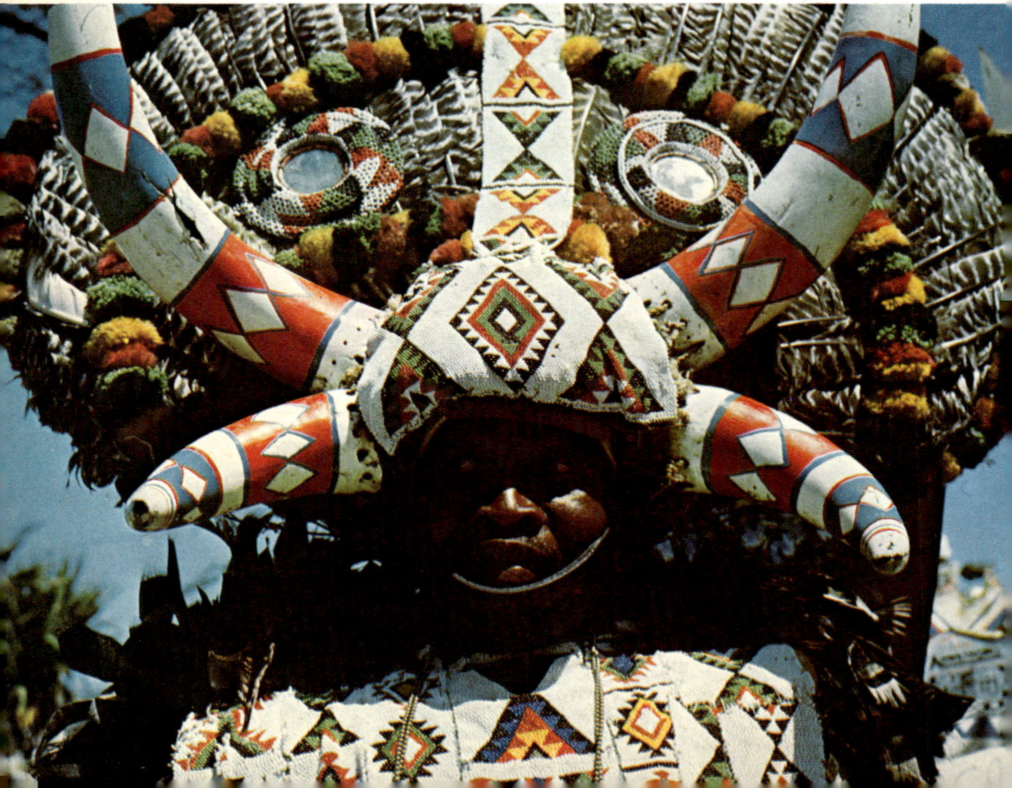

Following the N 2 up the coast takes you through Empangeni, Zululand's largest town in a sugar growing area and near Richards Bay, with its new port and industrial centre.

Beyond you come into the region of game reserves and untarmacked roads. The vast and beautiful St Lucia Bay is a fishing paradise, dotted with tiny islands, coves and inlets. The St Lucia lake is the largest inland lake in South Africa and is the focal point of the 1,903 sq miles St Lucia Game Reserve and Park, which extends some 72 km (45 miles) north from the estuary at the end of the lake. Hippo abound and the bird life includes pelicans, goliath herons, white-bellied korhaan, saddlebill and spoonbill.

St Lucia Reserve

There are two hutted camps and two camping sites in the Reserve (R 4.50 a night) and two hotels outside at St Lucia Bay. These are the Lake View (two star) and the Estuary (one star). Both charge from R 11 to R 18 a day. For reservations at the camps, contact the Ranger, St Lucia Estuary. From Charters Creek, where one of the camps is, wilderness trails set out under a Park Ranger. You spend one of the three days moving around by boat and will see a lot of wildlife. Boats can be hired.

East of the lake are two magnificent game reserves, Umfolozi and Hluhluwe, linked by a 'corridor' for the game. They are open all year round and are famous for their rhino.

Hluhluwe, which is pronounced 'Shlushshloowy', is 290 km (182 miles) from Durban via Mtubatuba. It has more black than white rhino and as there are no carnivores you are allowed out of your car, though it is still unwise to argue with a rhino. Other game includes buffalo, zebra, brindled gnu, kudu, impala, bushbuck, waterbuck, steenbuck, reedbuck, duiker, giraffe, warthog, bush-pig, leopard and baboon. Among the numerous birds are maribou stork, vultures, bateleur, crested guineafowl, quail, sunbirds, fish eagles and ground hornbill. The reserve's 89 sq miles are undulating bush, rising to 610 m (2,000 ft) above sea level. Accommodation consists of picturesque furnished cottages and rondavels, with cooks and servants available. You bring your own food, easily obtainable en route. Charges are from R 3 a person. Bookings through the Reservations Officer, Natal Parks Board, PO Box 662, Pietermaritzburg. You can make a one day tour to the Reserve from Durban.

Hluhluwe Reserve

Near Hluhluwe is a private 39 sq mile game reserve centred on the Zululand Safari Lodge (bookings through Southern Sun Hotels). Walking safaris are organised for game viewing.

The larger Umfolozi Reserve has similar accommodation to Hluhluwe, booked through the Parks Board. It is primarily a

Umfolozi Reserve

*Opposite top: Kimberley prospector sorting diamonds. Photograph SATOUR
Bottom: Traditional headress of Zulu rickshaw boy, now less often seen, Durban.
Photograph Picturepoint*

sanctuary for the largest herd of white rhino in Africa, 800-strong, and well worth seeing. Recently white rhino from the 'corridor', which may become a reserve, have been moved to the Kruger Park. Others have gone to the Addo Park in the Cape, to Zimbabwe and to zoos in London, New York and Germany. It would cost you R 6,000 to buy a white rhino – as well as giving convincing assurances about its future welfare. A feature of the Umfolozi Reserve is the three day walking tours led by game rangers into areas where cars are not allowed. These wilderness trails operate throughout the year. Each trail party consists of six people at a cost of R 50 each, providing their own food, though sleeping bags, tents, pots and cutlery are supplied.

Mkuzi Reserve Finally the N 2 road takes you past the Mkuzi Game Reserve (96 sq miles) with black rhino, leopard and a wealth of other game. It has a hutted camp (bookings through the Parks Board), but it is not as developed as Hluhluwe or Umfolozi. Up here on the Mozambique border, you are in wild country for which you need to go prepared, but there is a lot to reward the adventurous.

Ndumu Reserve Sordwana Bay and Kosi Bay are both places where you can camp, fish and bird watch. At the 39 sq miles Ndumu Game Reserve, there are hippos and crocodile as well as bird life. The hutted camp has a kitchen and washing facilities. Bookings are as for the others.

German Castle in Windhoek

Namibia

(South West Africa)

If you look at a map of South West, as Namibia was known, you see some strange names – 'Bushman's Paradise', 'Kokerboom Forest', 'Fish River Canyon', 'Skeleton Coast'. This great chunk of territory, bounded to the west by the Atlantic and the Namib Desert, and to the east by the Kalahari, is no ordinary country. Much of its 322,000 sq miles are the primeval Africa, thick with game and only imperfectly explored, that still makes travellers' tales even in the twentieth century. You can watch elephant at sunset, stumble on primitive Bushman paintings in caves, find jaspers and agates lying on the beach. Although the German style living in the towns is good, there is nothing soft about South West. But if it remains politically stable it will continue to be one of the most rewarding countries in Africa to visit.

The most ancient inhabitants are Khoisan peoples, including Bushmen and the Nama Hottentots. The Damaras introduced iron and copper smelting. During the sixteenth to eighteenth centuries the Bantu speaking Ovambo and Okavango moved into the north, while Herero came to the west and south of the Etosha Pan. However the drought of 1829/30 forced the Herero south to the Okahandja and Windhoek areas.

Diego Cam, a Portuguese, was the first recorded explorer to land here, in 1484. But it was another 200 years before traders,

History

99

prospectors and missionaries began to discover the upland veld which the shifting sand dunes of the desert shore protected from intrusion. During the nineteenth century there were continual wars between the Herero tribe moving south and Hottentots from the Cape Colony moving north. In 1872 Maherero, the Chief of the Hereros, appealed to the Cape for protection – the outcome was the Port and Settlement of Walvis Bay, which is to this day part of the Republic of South Africa, an enclave on the coast of 1,124 sq km (434 sq miles).

In 1885 treaties made by a merchant from Bremen named Luderitz resulted in the territory becoming a German Protectorate, except for Walvis Bay. Settlers flowed in from the Fatherland. But in 1915 South African forces under General Botha defeated the local German colonial army. After the Great War the League of Nations handed South West over to South Africa as a Mandate. It is still administered by the Republic, although the United Nations is pressing for its independence.

Immigration Health and immigration requirements are the same as for South Africa and, at the time of writing, there were no controls between the two countries. The currency is the same (Rand), so are public holidays and most laws. However, South West has its own stamps, allows bars to open on Sundays and is completely multi-racial. More significantly, the character of the place is quite different.

German Influence The strong German influence has added another dimension to life here. German is an officially recognised language, while Afrikaans and English are official, and people switch among the three in conversation. Windhoek, Swakopmund and Walvis Bay are three of the few places in the world where the British and German dead of the two world wars are commemorated on the same memorial.

The People The total population is just under a million, including 100,000 whites. The largest native tribe is the Ovambo who occupy a vast part in the north, south of the Angola border; the Herero are the most advanced; and the Bushmen, only 15,000 strong, some still hunting with bow and arrow, the most interesting. There is also a community of Coloureds, known locally as Basters, who run their own region centred on Rehoboth (see page 112).

Climate The climate inland up on the plateau is magnificent, with daytime temperatures up to 35°C (95°F) and cool nights. Indeed the farmers would like far more rain than the pittance they get. Down at the coast the air is kept fresh by the Atlantic. In the Namib, the 110 km (70 mile) wide stretch of desert that separates the plateau from the coast, it is hot, with temperatures up to 40°C (104°F). Temperatures can also be as low as 2°C (35·6°F) at night in winter.

Communica-tions In spite of the rugged terrain millions of Rand have been spent on road and rail improvements. However, flying remains the most convenient way to travel. South African Airways has daily flights

from Windhoek to Johannesburg and Cape Town and a weekly *Air*
service to Frankfurt. Windhoek's international airport is 42 km (26 miles) east of the capital. The local airport is Eros, close to the town. Internal air services and charters are operated by Namib Air.

There are passenger trains twice a week to and from South Africa *Rail*
via Upington, with sleeping berths and a restaurant car. The journey takes two days. Internal rail services link Windhoek with Gobabis, Grootfontein, Keetmanshoop, Outjo, Swakopmund and Walvis Bay. A branch line runs from Keetmanshoop to Luderitz.

To Windhoek by road from Cape Town is 1,556 km (973 miles) via *Road*
Springbok and from Johannesburg is 1,846 km (1,154 miles) via Upington. Main roads are tarmacked. Cars can be rented in Keetmanshoop, Swakopmund, Walvis Bay and Windhoek – see under those towns. Taxis are available in Swakopmund, Walvis Bay and Windhoek. You drive on the left. Seat belts are compulsory. Overseas visitors need an international driving licence.

Hotels are graded from one to five star, on a similar basis to South *Hotels*
Africa. The SWA/Namibia Information Service (PO Box 2160, Windhoek) can provide a complete list of hotels, motels, guest farms and caravan parks. National Park accommodation is usually self catering (see below).

Angling is popular at the coast. Other sports available include *Sport*
cricket, flying, squash, swimming and tennis.

National Parks

The teeming wildlife in the north of the country deserves to be better known internationally. All the classic big game are there, as well as several 'specialities'. These are the gemsbok, or giant oryx, a strikingly handsome desert animal that weighs up to 193 kg (450 lb); the southern greater kudu, one of the largest antelopes; also the magnificent eland which are 'Royal Game' and the mountain zebra, seldom found elsewhere. The advisory board that runs the Game Parks follows the principles of the International Union for the Conservation of Nature, and facilities have been greatly improved lately. On the spot organisation is by white game wardens and rangers, aided by African trackers, usually Bushmen.

No hunting is allowed in the Parks, but photography is unrestricted. There are speed limits of 56 kph (35 mph) everywhere and 16 kph (10 mph) in camp. Charges are made for admission. Generally speaking it's best to look for game in the early morning and late afternoon. The principal parks are:

THE ETOSHA NATIONAL PARK
22,270 sq km (14,771 sq miles) around the Etosha salt pan in the north. 1,524m (5,000 ft) above sea level. Lion, elephant, rhino,

giraffe and enormous herds of other game. Three rest camps. Open 16th March–31st October. See also page 106.

NAMIB DESERT PARK

Part of the oldest desert in the world, in which the prehistoric *Welwitschia Mirabilis* grows. Its 7,497 sq km (4,657 sq miles) run inland from near Walvis Bay to the escarpment, where you see gemsbok, ostrich, zebra, springbok, etc. Open all year round. Camping facilities and hotels in Walvis Bay and Swakopmund. See also page 110.

DAAN VILJOEN GAME PARK

Seventeen sq miles in the hills 24 km (15 miles) west of Windhoek. Eland, kudu, impala, gemsbok, etc. Bungalows. Open all year round. It is in pleasant, hilly country, and easily accessible. See page 105.

HARDAP NATURE RESERVE

Fifty-four sq miles around a dam on the Great Fish River 22 km (14 miles) west of Mariental. Wonderful birds. Some animals. Excellent freshwater angling, boating. Rest camp. Open all year round.

SKELETON COAST PARK

Averaging only 25 km (15 miles) in width, this runs between Ugab river in the south and the Kunene river in the north. There are December/January holiday camps at Torra Bay and Terrace Bay, but the north is a private concession.

In addition to the above the Waterberg Plateau Park is being developed east of Otjiwarongo to protect threatened species of game; the Cape Cross Seal Reserve, north of Henties Bay has restricted access (see page 109) and the Ai-Ais Nature Reserve is really a health resort, with hot springs and bungalows close to the Fish River Canyon (page 112).

Rest Camps

Accommodation in all Parks can be booked through the Reservations Office, Department of Nature Conservation, Private Bag 13267, Windhoek 9000 (telephone 29251, telex 3180). Prices are very reasonable, but you should book in advance and you normally need your own cooking utensils and crockery. Shops at the rest camps sell foodstuffs, including fresh meat, butter, bread and eggs. Only cash or South African travel cheques are accepted, not foreign currencies.

Hiking

The only official hiking trails are at Naukluft in the Namib Park area and at the Fish River Canyon.

Hunting is allowed all the year round for overseas visitors, though only on private land. The best season is April to November. Licence fees are no longer payable in advance – only after you have secured trophies. You are allowed two of each species and gamebirds are free. But elephant, rhino, giraffe and buffalo are protected throughout the country. Basie Maartens Safaris (PO Box 11212, Windhoek), is the best known safari company. For advice on hunting generally write to the Association of SWA Professional Hunters and Hunting Guides, PO Box 11292, Windhoek. *Hunting*

Afro Ventures (Pty) Ltd, PO Box 10848, Johannesburg 2000, who run 15 day desert safaris from Johannesburg, and SWA Safaris, PO Box 20373, Windhoek, are well known local firms. *Photographic Safaris*

Windhoek

This small capital city of only 80,000 people is situated 1,650 m (5,400 ft) above sea level in the country's central highlands. Both the climate and the place itself are enviably pleasant. It has new hotels and shops, yet the modern buildings have blended well with the attractive old German colonial houses. The city has two traditional German festivals, each of which lasts for several days. These are the Carnival in early May, with processions and a masked ball, and the beer-drinking Oktoberfest, when the streets are hung with decorations. In further contrast you will see the tall and stately Herero women in colourful Victorian style dresses which they copied from missionaries over a century ago and still consider fashionable. *Carnival*

Windhoek was founded in 1890 by Major Kurt von Francois, who hoisted the German flag and built the Alte Fest (the Old Fort) in Leutwein Street, now part of the Museum. But the city owes its name to the Hottentot leader Jonker Afrikaner, who called it Winterhoek after the farm in the Cape where he worked as a boy. Eventually it contracted to Windhoek. Formerly it had been known as Ai-gams, a native word for hot springs, while Sir James Alexander, the famous explorer, tried to name it Queen Adelaide's Baths. The springs, in the suburb of Klein Windhoek, long supplied the town with water.

Kaiser Street is the main thoroughfare and business and shopping centre. Business starts early at 0800 and ends at 1730. South West's most famous products are diamonds, semi-precious stones, and Karakul, or Persian Lamb, pelts. Overseas visitors do not have to pay the local sales tax. *Shopping*

Diamonds are barely cheaper than elsewhere, but you will get purer quality for your money. Semi-precious stones like agate, jasper, rose quartz, chalcedony, amethyst, amazonite and tiger's eye are gratifyingly cheap – after all, the territory is stiff with them. The tourmalines here are the world's finest, the most valuable being those with emerald or ruby lights in them. You can get semi-precious stones roughly polished by 'tumbling' very cheaply. A well made gold ring, set with a properly cut stone, will cost substantially less than in Europe. Among curiosities one of the most interesting is the many faceted 'Desert Rose'.

Persian Lamb   Karakui sheep originated in Afghanistan and Bokhara, Southern Russia, but today Namibia exports more than two million of the world's annual production of ten million pelts. Naturally, tailoring them is a speciality here. A full-length Persian lamb coat uses 20–28 pelts, while broadtail coats are relatively more expensive.

There are plenty of good photographic and chemists' shops. For fishing and sporting tackle we recommend Metje and Ziegler, while A. Rosenthal is a gunsmith. Both are in Kaiser Street. Local curios include Ovambo baskets, and Bushman quivers for arrows, made of the bark of the curious Kokerboom tree that grows in the semi-desert.

Information   The SWA/Namibia Information Service (PO Box 2160, Windhoek) is in the centre of town and has various publications available, including colour brochures on National Parks and towns.

Hotels   The only three star hotel is the Kalahari Sands (PO Box 2254), but the older two star Thüringer Hof (PO Box 112) in Kaiser Street is very pleasant, with an outdoor restaurant in a shady courtyard. In all Windhoek has eight hotels, normally clean, comfortable and with good cuisine. In a two star hotel you will pay R 12 to R 20 bed and breakfast.

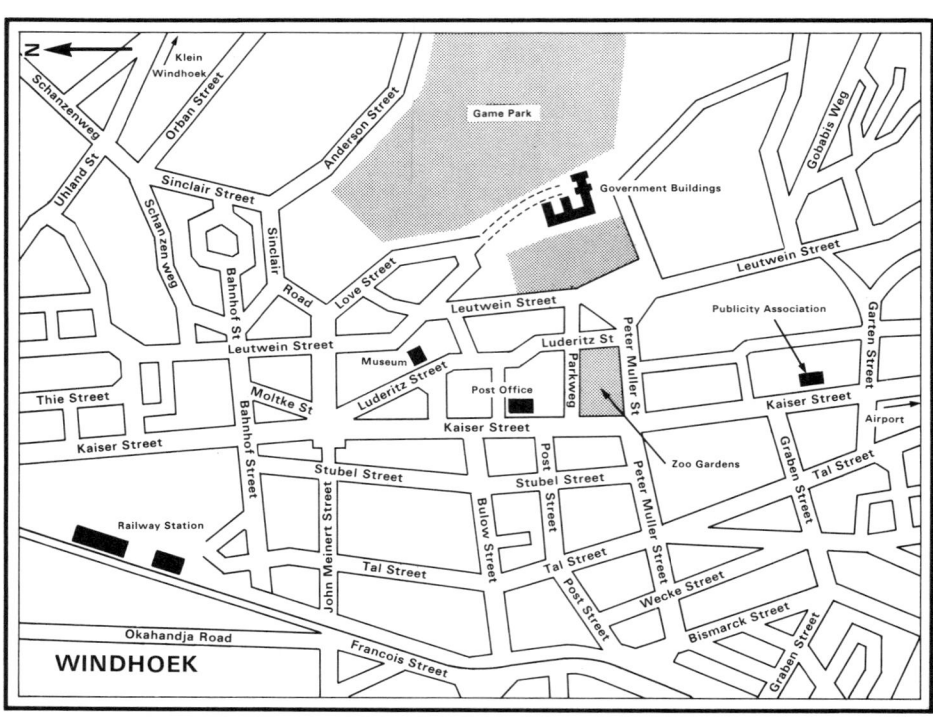

There are several restaurants in the town. Bars are open on Sundays, though only from 1200–1400 and 1800–2100. We recommend the local lager type beers, Hansa and Windhoek. The courtyard of the Thüringer Hof and the terrace of the Continental Hotel are favourite meeting places for a drink. There are no nightclubs in Windhoek.

Taxis are few. You must telephone for one in good time, as you can rarely hail one on the street. *Transport*

Tours to the Game Reserves and elsewhere are run by South African Railways Travel Bureau (PO Box 415), SWA Safaris (PO Box 20373), Springbok Atlas Safaris (PO Box 2058) and others, while tours in the immediate neighbourhood are run by City Tours (PO Box 21203).

There are several car hire firms, and you can rent a car at the international airport. Avis (PO Box 2057), Hertz (PO Box 1387) and Budget Rent-a-Car (PO Box 1754) are international firms. Trip Car Hire (PO Box 100) is a local one. *Car Hire*

SAA and Namib Air have offices in the town. One tip worth knowing is that you can sometimes buy a spare seat on someone else's air charter. Be sure to distinguish between the two airports. Local flights and charters run from Eros, close to the town. The JG Strijdom international airport is 42 km (26 miles) away. *Air Charter*

The Windhoek area has a number of attractions. The Railway Station, unexpectedly, has great character. It was built in 1912. There is an art gallery close to the Windhoek theatre. Near the town are three small Rhineland style castles, each on a hill, called Schwerinsburg, Heinitzburg and Sanderburg. They are privately owned. Heinitzburg is the home of Mrs Olga Levinson, the authoress who wrote *The Ageless Land* about this country. The Roman Catholic church's vineyard in the suburb of Klein Windhoek deserves a visit. The pleasant Garden in the centre of the town has a fine collection of meteorites, and the remains of a prehistoric elephant. The Zoo itself is now behind the Administration Buildings and harbours antelope, giraffe, zebra and ostrich in natural surroundings. The Museum, on Luderitz Street near the centre of town, has fine examples of Herero and Ovambo native crafts. The old German fort, the Alte Feste, is interesting in itself. *Native Crafts*

The Daan Viljoen Game Park, in the Khomas Hochland west of Windhoek, is only a short drive away, 24 km (14 miles) and one of its features is that you can hike over the rolling hills viewing the game, because there are no dangerous predators. It has a delightful camping/bungalow site by a lake.

The North and the Etosha Pan

In the north are the native tribes and the wildlife, particularly round the famous Etosha salt pan. The road, now tarred most of the way to Tsumeb, initially is also the principal route to the coast. It runs to Okahandja 72 km (45 miles) from Windhoek, where you can stop for a beer at one of the hotels. This is a farming town and also the site of the graves of both Jonker Afrikaner and of the great Herero chief, Maherero. At the time of the full moon in August the tribe gathers here in tribute to its dead chief. Near Okahandja are hot springs at Gross Barmen, which have been developed as a spa. There are bungalows to rent and a restaurant. There is also a resort based on the Von Bach dam in the hills near Okahandja, with fishing for black bass, carp and bream.

Okahandja

From Okahandja you can either turn west to Karibib and then north to the Brandberg or go straight on north to Otjiwarongo, 'the place where the fat cattle graze'. The Hamburger Hof hotel here is good.

Tsumeb

Tsumeb has the largest base mineral mine south of the Zambezi, and a pleasant hotel to stop at, the Minen Hotel (PO Box 244, Tsumeb). The largest known meteorite ever found, 82 percent iron and 16 percent nickel and weighing 70 tons, is not far off on a farm called Hoba West near Grootfontien. As you get nearer Etosha the country becomes more tropical, mostly mopane bush and veld grass.

Etosha National Park

From Tsumeb to the Namutoni rest camp in the Etosha National Park is only 119 km (74 miles). The Etosha Pan itself is a truly fantastic 1,690 sq mile salt pan, near which there are other smaller ones, all of which attract game like flies to a jampot. Thousands of years ago the Pan was fed by the Kunene River, but the river changed its course, the lake shrank and dried up. Indeed the name Etosha means 'the place of dry water' on account of the heat mirages and the pan is now only under water after rain. When it is wet, waterbirds also flock to it. After the rainy season (January–March) the veld around Etosha is green. May onwards is the best time to go there, although the Park is open to the public from March 16 to October 31 every year.

At a recent count the numbers of game here were estimated at: elephant 1,200, lion 500, giraffe 1,000, springbok 25,000, wildebeeste 30,000, Burchell's zebra 35,000, kudu 7,000, gemsbok 6,000, hartebeest 3,000. These figures speak louder than superlatives, and there are leopard, rhino, the tiny 18 inch damara dikdik (an antelope species), cheetahs, ostriches, secretary birds, and many other birds. After the first rains a large percentage of the zebra, wildebeeste, gemsbok and springbok leave the southern border of the Pan and trek west, right into Ovamboland. The apparent reason is that the grass is literally greener on the other side, being of an annual and not a perennial kind, and when it comes up they move across to it.

Namutoni

There are three rest camps, at Namutoni, Okaukuejo and Halali. Namutoni is a spectacular Beau Geste style fort, built in 1903, where seven German soldiers once successfully held out against

500 Ovambo tribesmen. Renovated, it now has a Museum, shop, restaurant, and 40 furnished rooms, bathrooms and hot and cold running water. There is an adjacent camping site. Okaukuejo has bungalows and luxury rondavels, student dormitories and camping sites. Tents can be hired. Halali, situated geographically between the other two camps, has luxury bungalows, dormitories and camp sites. The name 'halali' means a single bugle call after the hunt is over. All three places have airstrips, first aid posts, swimming pools and shops, and sell booklets about Etosha. Bookings for them can be made through travel agents or to the Director of Nature Conservation, Private Bag 13267, Windhoek. They must be reached before sunset. Bedding has to be hired at a modest charge and you buy food from the shop and cook it yourself – there are barbecues provided – unless of course you are on a tour. The South African Railways five-day tour from Windhoek is especially good value. You can book at any SAR Travel Bureau.

Okaukuejo is the administrative centre with an Ecological Institute. *Okaukuejo*
To the west is the Haunted Forest, a dense stand of a curious tree unique to Namibia called *Moringa Ovalifolia*: it looks like a thinner baobab. This area also protects several thousand pelicans at breeding time. Incredibly they bring fish for their young from Lake Oponomo, 100 km (62 miles) away, each parent taking it in turn and riding thermals to make the long journey.

The whole of the country beyond the Etosha Pan has long been a closed area, because it was tribal territory. It includes the spectacular Ruacana Falls, on the Kunene River, which forms the frontier with Angola. At the time of writing this was also a military area but it may one day be opened.

Returning from Okaukuejo to Windhoek you drive through Outjo, a tiny cattle town, and Otjiwarongo. The Fransfontein Nature Reserve is 138 km (86 miles) west of Outjo, while the Waterberg *Waterberg*
Plateau Park lies east of Otjiwarongo. At Waterberg rare species *Plateau Park*
such as sable antelope, black faced impala and white rhino have been brought in for their preservation. A camp site is being established near the red sandstone cliffs in the south of the Park. The area also has historical significance, if of a grim kind. It was here that the German army finally defeated the 1903 African rebellion, a subjugation in which 75 percent of the Herero and 50 percent of the Nama perished and which permanently altered the population structure of the country.

The Coast

The coast, as the map shows you, is enormously long and one of the strangest in the world. It has only three towns, the delightful and unexpected resort of Swakopmund, the port of Walvis Bay, and Luderitz. From Swakopmund north to Cape Cross is comparatively tame. But from there to the Angolan border is known as the

Skeleton Coast, with good reason. The bones of both ships and men lie entombed in the dunes there, from sailing ships to passenger liners and freighters. It has been designated a National Park. Inland from it lies the Kaokoveld, largely territory reserved for Africans. It supports some game, and is partly diamondiferous. You can only go there with police permission.

Namib Desert

South from Sandwich Bay, near Walvis Bay, right down to the Orange River, is a diamond mining area, protected from intrusion both by the law and by the 145 km (90 mile) wide Namib Desert. The Namib's shifting dunes, some as much as 304 m (1,000 ft) high, are the result of the cold Benguela current in the Atlantic preventing rain from falling on the interior. There is often coastal mist, but very seldom rain. The only place open to visitors on this part of the coast is Luderitz. The town of Oranjemond right down in the south is the private property of the diamond mining company. Adolf Luderitz, after whom the town is named, bought the whole coastal area from the Orange River to 26°south, up to a distance of 20 miles inland, in 1883. For it he paid £500 and 60 rifles, acquiring one of the richest diamond areas in the world.

Swakopmund

Swakopmund, founded in 1892 as a port by the Germans because the British held Walvis Bay, is a highly individual, intriguing and friendly small resort. During its October–March season it is socially very much alive, especially when the Administrator moves down from Windhoek in December and January. Swakopmunders are at all times proud of their town, which architecturally is a complete turn-of-the-century period piece. Many of the houses have towers from which their merchant owners used to watch for arriving ships, just like their counterparts in Baltic seaports and many buildings are now protected as national monuments. Among notable ones are the Administrator's summer residence, the jail – designed to look like a country house – and the imposing railway station.

Getting to Swakopmund is easy. Daily trains run overnight from Windhoek and there are regular flights by Namib Air, but be sure you order a taxi to meet you at the airstrip. The taxi telephone number is 2205.

The main road is 363 km (226 miles) via Okahandja and Karibib. An alternative route is across the scenically splendid Khomas Highlands and down along the side of the Namib Desert Park, but there is only one garage en route and it is best to go in company with another vehicle.

Hotels

The best hotel unquestionably is the three star Hansa (PO Box 44). Its German cooking is excellent. The hotel was the home of Susannah York, Stanley Baker and other stars when *Sands of the Kalahari* was being shot out in the desert near the Khan mine. Another good hotel is the Strand (two star) or you can stay more cheaply in one of several *pensions*. North of the town is a modern caravan park, a reflection of Swakopmund becoming the centre for the National West Coast Tourist Recreation Area, a 200 km (125 mile) long strip of the coast terminating in the north at the Uchab river.

Recreation Area

The town has plenty of shops, hairdressers and garages. Car hire firms include Budget Rent-a-Car (PO Box 1510) and Car Hire Swakopmund (PO Box 695). Local tours are arranged by Charly's Atlantic Tours (PO Box 882). The Walvis Bay Bus Line also has an office.

Car Hire

Local attractions include the beach, which has the unusual habit of shifting all the time. 'It's a good beach this year,' someone remarked to us. In the course of its wanderings it has silted up the harbour. The Museum covers the coast's natural history and is well worth a visit. Close by it is the Namib Garden, where most plants known in the desert are grown.

Any botanist will want to see the extraordinary desert plant, the *Welwitschia mirabilis*. One place to do so is about 80 km (50 miles) out near the Khan mine. This relation of the conifer lives for hundreds of years and has leaves over three m (12 ft) long. The Khan mine, now disused, is nine km (six miles) off the Swakop-mund–Usakos road.

We will return in a moment to the Namib and the *Welwitschia*, first looking north of Swakopmund. Driving along the coast you come to Henties Bay, a small holiday resort with one hotel. From here you could venture inland up to the Brandberg mountains via Uis. The most famous Bushman painting of all, the White Lady of the Brandberg, is to be found by going along the road to the Uis mine. This is actually a group of paintings, Mediterranean in style. They are in a cave that is a four km (three mile) walk from the road, signposted, though with no facilities. Other Bushman paintings are at Bushman's Paradise, near Usakos, but the trip involves rock climbing.

Brandberg

Alternatively continue along the coast until 131 km (82 miles) from Swakopmund you reach the Cape Cross Seal Reserve. An estimated 18,000 seals live and breed on the rocks here, but you must ask about visiting times, since it may be closed in the second half of the year. Travel agents organise special tours to it.

Cape Cross Seal Reserve

Further on you reach the Skeleton Coast Park, already mentioned. The north is a private concession. You can obtain details from Skeleton Coast Safaris, PO Box 2195, Windhoek. In the nearer, southern, part there are holiday camps at Torra Bay and Terrace Bay, the latter offering all inclusive facilities. The Nature Conservation Department runs them. Terrace Bay is known for its surf fishing. Indeed the whole coast offers good angling for kabeljou, steenbras and galjoen. If you are going up to the Skeleton Coast and intend to explore you need a four wheel drive vehicle.

Skeleton Coast Park

Namib Desert Park

Two rather easier trips from Swakopmund are to the Goanikontes oasis, a good camping spot 40 km (25 miles) away, and to the Namib Desert Park. The game in the Park – gemsbok, ostrich, zebra and buck – tend to concentrate near the escarpment. There are roads and bungalow camps administered by the Nature Conservation Department. The Namib is not only one of the oldest deserts in the world, it is one of the most fascinating. Extraordinary weathered rock formations, and vegetation along the Swakop and Kuiseb rivers, contrast with mile upon mile of sand dunes in which you would think life impossible. The secret is the fog which sweeps in off the Atlantic and which condenses on plants, keeping both them and insects alive, while springs enable animals to drink.

Sandvis Lagoon

At the coast, the Sandvis area has a reed lined lagoon with little salinity which attracts many species of freshwater birds. Its secret is that it is largely fed by water from the Kuiseb River, percolating through the sand dunes, far from the river's actual course.

Naukluft

Sossusvlei

Incorporated in the Namib Park are two further areas: the Naukluft Mountain Zebra Park to the south east and Sossusvlei, where the Tsauchab River disappears into some of the highest sand dunes in the world. Naukluft is on the escarpment at the desert's edge. Hiking trails and camping sites are being established. Sossusvlei, however, is only open to day trips as it lies in the diamond concession area. It is a photographer's paradise because of the dramatic, windblown ridges of the dunes.

Walvis Bay

You can also enter the Namib Park at Walvis Bay, which is 33 km (21 miles) from Swakopmund, down a fast road that, although it looks like tarmac, is actually made of compacted salt. On the way, driving through the high dunes, you pass Rand Rifles, a deserted 1914 war army camp, and enter the South African territory of the Walvis Bay enclave. There is no frontier post but you come under South African law.

Walvis Bay – which means Whalefish Bay – lies below sea level. It is a port and commercial centre, the terminal of the railway, and the home of a vast fishing industry. So rich is the ocean here that trawling fleets come down from Europe. There were an estimated 400 Russian trawlers offshore during our visit. The town has several hotels, notably the Mermaid and the Flamingo (from R 12 bed and breakfast), shops and other facilities, including an active travel firm, the Walvis Bay Busline (PO Box 429, telephone 2929). This company arranges car hire, operates tours to the game reserves, and safaris.

Sandwich Bay

Flamingoes gather in hundreds on the lagoon. There is a most unusual desert golf course where the fairways are marked by pegs, and the surf fishing along the coast is excellent. One of the best places is at Sandwich Bay. Although in the diamond concession area, you can easily get a permit to go there from the Walvis Bay magistrate.

This brings us to the subject of diamonds. All the way from here to *Diamonds* the Orange River there are diamonds lying on the bedrock beneath the sand, and on a marine terrace underwater formed during the Second Ice Age. They are thought to have been brought down the Orange River aeons ago, and gradually washed up the coast by the Benguela current. Certainly the largest stones are nearest the river mouth. Originally they could be picked up on the sand, and sometimes still can. This has led both to intricate security precautions by the concessionaires, the Consolidated Diamond Mines of SWA Ltd, and an unending series of smuggling attempts – plus a vast output of journalistic nonsense. The facts are as hard as the stones themselves; firstly, when uncleaned these diamonds are extremely hard for an amateur to identify; secondly, the fine for going more than 20 yards from the road without a permit in a concession area is R 1,000. If you find stones in Namibia you must hand them in to the police. Nonetheless smuggling attempts continue. One bold pilot was jailed after landing on a deserted beach to pick up a 'parcel' of diamonds hidden there by a CDM employee. Unhappily his aircraft's nosewheel stuck in the sand – and security men caught him. People joke that the only successful smugglers are the security men themselves. The whole huge district is known as the Sperregebiet – the Forbidden Area.

Stories about this R 160 million business are legion and if you want to walk into the atmosphere of a Hammond Innes novel the place to go is Luderitz. This town, perched on the rocks, often plagued by *Luderitz* a howling wind, is quite unique. Even fresh water is priced per cubic metre. Luderitz used to live off mining, and you can get a permit from the CDM office to visit the fascinating ghost diamond mining town at Kolmanskop, abandoned almost overnight in 1938. *Kolmanskop* Founded in 1908, it had a casino, a skittle alley and a school. Some buildings are being restored, though others will remain filled with drifting sand, as memorials of how a boom can end.

Luderitz itself has many examples of German colonial architecture, notably the Lutheran church and the Magistrate's house, a Museum and a golf club. Jackass penguins congregate on nearby Halifax island and the fishing is excellent: the town's prosperity depends today on the rock lobster catch.

A natural curiosity 160 km (100 miles) to the south is the rock arch by the sea at Bogenfels.

Kapps Hotel at Luderitz (from R 8.50 bed and breakfast) is well run, and usually full of mining men on their way to the camps down the coast. Namib Air have regular flights from Windhoek, Walvis Bay and Cape Town, or you can drive from Keetmanshoop. By train from Windhoek takes up to a week.

The South

Fish River Canyon

The real attractions of the south are round the Fish River. The gigantic 64 km (40 mile) long Fish River Canyon, reached from the main Keetmanshoop–Karasburg road, is a spectacle that rivals the Grand Canyon in the United States. It is 609 m (2,000 ft) deep, savage, and so sheer and unexpected in the landscape that you could walk into it by accident. Part of the country round it is a National Park, with leopard, zebra, rockrabbits and antelope. There

Ai-Ais

are radioactive hot springs near the Canyon, at Klein Ai-Ais, 91 m (300 ft) above sea level, which is a modern health resort open from mid-March to October 31. There are flats, a restaurant, bungalows, tents, camping facilities, a shop, bottle store, etc. Vehicles are free but there is a 50c entrance charge for each occupant. Flats cost R 4 a night. You must bring your own crockery but not bedding. An 86 km (54 miles) hiking trail has been created between Ai-Ais and the main vantage point on the canyon. It takes four days.

Keetmanshoop

Keetmanshoop is a small town, a centre of communications and of a karakul farming district. It has hotels. To the east you can drive through to the Kalahari Gemsbok National Park (see page 68). The savannah country here is a vast, never-ending plain. To the

Kokerbooms

north-east of Keetmanshoop grows the weird Kokerboom forest, spiky, euphorbia-like trees from the bark of which Bushmen traditionally make their quivers. Further north, near Asab, is a spectacular balancing rock formation called the Finger of God.

Hardap

Mariental is another small town on the Keetmanshoop–Windhoek road and railway, near which the Hardap Dam has created fishing and watersport facilities. A more curious construction, over near the Naukluft mountains, some 80 km (50 miles) west of Maltahöhe,

Schloss Duwisib

is the German Rhineland style castle called the Schloss Duwisib. It was built by the Baron Hansheinrich von Wolf, who when serving with the German army allowed himself to be defeated near here by a force of Hottentots. He was sent home in disgrace, but returned in 1909 after marrying a wealthy American lady and began farming. He acquired 130,000 acres for about R 1,400 and erected the Schloss, which he furnished with antiques. He was killed in the Great War, but the castle is still maintained by a company and can be visited.

Rehoboth

His story, and that of the Rehoboth Republic, are told by Lawrence Green in his book *Lords of the Last Frontier*, published by Howard Timmins in Cape Town. The Rehoboth 'Basters' are a coloured people, a mixture of Europeans and Hottentots, who still largely rule themselves in the wide karakul farming lands between Mariental and Windhoek.

Opposite: Oryx at the Etosha Pan, Namibia. Photograph SATOUR

Useful Facts—SOUTH AFRICA and NAMIBIA

Banks

Banking hours in cities are 0900 to 1530 daily except Wednesdays and Saturdays when banks close at 1100. In the country, banks open from 0900 to 1245 and 1400 to 1530 with the same early closing on Wednesdays and Saturdays as in the cities.

Banks having branches throughout South Africa are: Barclays National Bank Ltd; The Standard Bank of South Africa Ltd; Volkskas Beperk, The Netherlands Bank of South America Ltd; The Trust Bank of Africa Ltd. The Trust National City Bank of New York Ltd and the Chase Manhattan Bank Ltd also have branches.

Climate

Coastal regions: From Cape Town to Port Elizabeth, dry summer, rain in winter. September to May are the best months. Average temperatures, summer 21°C–22°C (70°–72°F), winter 11°C–12°C (52°–54°F).

Inland: Natal and Transkei and Eastern Transvaal, rain in summer with high temperatures. Winters dry. Average temperatures 22°C (72°F) summer, 11°C (52°F) winter. Natal coast is sub-tropical and midwinter (June, July and August) are the best months. Average temperatures 24°C (76°F) summer, 16°C (61°F) winter.

Currency

The currency unit in South Africa is the Rand (R 1), divided into 100c. There are banknotes for R 20, R 10, and R 2. Coins are a nickel R 1 piece and 50c, 20c, 10c, and 5c pieces with copper 2c and 1c pieces.

R 1 equals approximately 55p Sterling, $ US 1.28, DM 3.75, Fr 6, It. Lire 686, Dutch guilders 3.80, Portuguese escudos 32$00, Sw. Fr. 4.45.

Currency Regulations

There is no limit on bringing in travellers' cheques, letters of credit, bank drafts, etc., but banknotes of some foreign countries may be hard to exchange. Sterling and dollars are acceptable. You may only take out of South Africa R 20 or cash amounting to the amount you brought in. It is advisable to change your spare currency before leaving.

Opposite: Cheetah. Photograph SATOUR

Customs

All articles of clothing, jewellery, cameras, binoculars, guns and tackle for sporting purposes and camping equipment are free of duty whether new or used provided they are your personal property. You can also bring in one bottle of wine and one litre of spirits, 300 ml of perfume, 400 cigarettes, 50 cigars and 250 gms of tobacco.

Firearms must be accompanied by a permit, obtainable at point of entry, which is valid for six months. The firearm must have a number stamped into the metal. When leaving the country you must have a certificate of origin for taking out skins or any article made of skins. Note that *no skins or articles made of skin* are allowed into Australia or New Zealand.

Diplomatic Representation

There are South African diplomatic missions in: Port Louis (Mauritius), Ottawa, New York, New Orleans and San Francisco, Buenos Aires, Rio de Janeiro, Hong Kong, Tokyo, Beirut, Canberra, Wellington, Vienna, Brussels, London, Copenhagen, Dublin, Paris, Cologne, Athens, Rome and Milan, The Hague, Oslo, Lisbon, Madrid, Stockholm, Berne, Las Palmas.

The majority of countries, except independent African states, are represented in Pretoria.

Driving

You drive on the left. Traffic lights are called 'robots'. International Drivers' Licence essential.

Health Requirements

A valid International Certificate of Vaccination must be produced, also ones for cholera and yellow fever if you have been in or passed through a country where these are endemic, unless you did not leave the airport whilst in transit.

Language

English and Afrikaans are the official languages. In Namibia, German is a third officially recognised language.

Passports and Visas

Category A. Citizens of the UK and Colonies, Canada, Australia, and the Republic of Ireland of pure European descent require a passport but no visa. This goes also for nationals of Portugal resident in Mozambique, nationals of Switzerland and Liechtenstein. Cypriots and Maltese of European descent or extraction

114

must obtain permission from nearest representative of South Africa to enter.

Category B. Passports with visas are required by everyone else. If not obtainable in your own country write to: Secretary for the Interior, Private Bag 114, Pretoria, South Africa. Leave plenty of time to obtain a visa.

All visitors entering in Category A must have a return ticket and enough money for their stay or someone to stand surety for them. If you stay longer than six months, you must be registered as an alien.

Visitors in Category B must also obtain an Aliens Temporary Permit at the point of entry which states the length of stay permitted, usually 90 days.

Postal Services

Post Offices open from 0830 to 1530 and stamps are sold to 1700. On Saturdays they close at noon and stamp counters at 1300.

Postal rates for South Africa and neighbouring States are 5c for a letter, 2c postcards. Airmail 5c a letter.

Overseas letters per ½ oz: Britain 20c, Europe 20c, Americas 25c, Australia and New Zealand 25c.

Telegrams 75c for 15 words inland.

Cables 9c per word to Europe – R 1.98 for 22 words at non-urgent rates (ie: they are transmitted during off-peak hours).

Public Holidays

New Year's Day (January 1), Founders Day (April 6), Good Friday, Family Day, Ascension Day, Republic Day (May 31), Kruger Day (October 10), Day of the Vow (December 16), Christmas Day (December 25), Day of Goodwill (December 26, or 27 when it falls on a Sunday).

Family Day is Easter Monday.

Shopping Hours

0830 to 1700 on weekdays, and to 1300 on Saturdays, except Public Holidays. In Namibia 0800 to 1300 and 1430 to 1730 in winter. In summer the afternoon hours are 1500 to 1800.

Time

South African Standard Time is two hours ahead of GMT.

Bushmen in the Kalahari

Botswana

Botswana's wildlife areas are becoming more and more popular the world over. It is one of the few places left where game sanctuaries have remained completely unspoilt by so-called civilisation and where you can get the feeling of being truly in the wilds.

Botswana has designated 80,000 sq km (30,000 sq miles) as permanent game sanctuaries – 16 percent of the whole country – and some of the best known safari companies have opened here and have built lodges designed to blend with the natural surroundings. There are endless perfect camping sites for those who want 'do it yourself' safaris, which offer little in the way of luxury, but everything imaginable for the true nature lover.

Physically, Botswana covers 231,804 sq miles of tableland, a huge chunk of Southern Africa about the size of France, and is entirely landlocked and bordered by South Africa, Zambia, Zimbabwe and Namibia. It lies on the Tropic of Capricorn and has a mean altitude of 1,000 m (3,300 ft) above sea level. However there are wide variations of climate and vegetation.

In the north west is the Okavango delta, 320 km (200 miles) wide at its greatest and covering more than 18,000 sq km (7,000 sq miles).

The great Okavango river, flowing into the area from the Angolan highlands, then empties into the semi-desert, creating a complex system of waterways and a superb environment for game of all kinds. The river rises in December and reaches its full flow in February/March, both filling the delta and going further to create the ephemeral Lake Ngami and reach the Makigadikgadi salt pans and Lake Xau.

In the extreme north the Chobe river, also attracting great herds of game, runs out of the delta and into the Zambezi.

By contrast the seemingly never ending Kalahari desert stretches right across the south west of the country. A desert in name only, the Kalahari consists of vast stretches of arid thorn veld. It is the home of the Bushman, whom the authorities nowadays prefer to call Remote Area Dwellers. Much of it lies in the Ghanzi and Kgalagadi districts.

The best agricultural land lies along the country's eastern borders.

Climate

The climate is generally sub-tropical, but varies considerably with latitude and altitude. The northern part of the country is in the tropics. The southern and western areas vary between hot steppes with summer rains, to desert or semi-desert climates.

The winter days are warm and the nights cool to cold, with occasional frosts in the north and heavy frosts in the semi-desert areas. The summer is hot, but tempered by a prevailing north-easterly breeze.

The rains generally begin in late October, ending in April. May to September are usually dry months. Average rainfall is 450 mm but less than 225 mm in the Kalahari.

Population

Some 80 percent of the 726,000 population live in the east: average density is one person per sq km. The vast majority of people are Batswana, consisting of eight main tribes: the Bamangwato, Batawana, Bakgotia, Bakwena, Bangwaketsi, Batlokwa, Baralong and Bamalete. In the past tribal rule was carried out by the chief in association with and aided by the Central Government through District Commissioners appointed to each tribal area. Today the country is divided into nine districts, which follow tribal bound-aries closely, and township areas are defined around Gaborone, *Towns* Lobatse and Francistown. Other main towns are Orapa in the north-west, where the second largest diamond pipe in the world was discovered in 1967; Selebi/Pikwe in the north-east where copper/nickel is being mined, Serowe, Kanye, Mochudi and Molepolole. Mining has transformed Botswana's economy. Orapa is a closed town, not open to casual visitors.

Language

The language of the people is Setswana. However, English is widely spoken and is the country's official language.

History	In the north-east geologists, investigating primitive gold workings, have found fragments of third century oriental glassware. Explorers from the Orient who penetrated East Africa apparently reached as far as here. The coming of Africans is more recent. Folklore has it that they arrived from the north and historians believe that the Tswana are a branch of the Sotho people (see Lesotho) who moved down into southern Africa during the great Bantu migrations of the sixteenth to eighteenth centuries.

The first contact with Europe was through the missionary Robert Moffat in the early nineteenth century, and later through the famous David Livingstone. In 1885, as a result of conflict with the Boers across the border in the Transvaal, the Batswana chiefs appealed to Britain for protection, and the Bechuanaland Protectorate was proclaimed. In 1895 Britain incorporated the southern part of the territory, including the capital, Mafeking, into the Cape Colony. However, Mafeking continued to be the administrative centre until, as independence neared, a new capital was built at Gaborone. The country became independent, with the name Botswana, on 30th September 1966. It is a Republic in the Commonwealth with an Executive President, Sir Seretse Khama, who is also an hereditary chief, and who was for a time exiled by the British in the 1950s.

Communications

The country's huge size means that the town you make the starting point of your visit depends on where you are coming from. The train from Cape Town runs up through Mafikeng (formerly Mafeking) twice a week to Lobatsi, Gaborone and Francistown, going on to Bulawayo and the Victoria Falls.

Air

Botswana Airways link the main towns with several flights weekly. Zambia Airways fly in from Lusaka and SAA from Johannesburg.

Roads

There are some 10,200 km (6,337 miles) of roads. Those in Gaborone, Lobatse and Francistown are tarred, as are the Gaborone to Lobatse road, Francistown to Nata and the new 640 km (400 miles) Nata to Kazungulu road, which links Botswana with Zambia by a ferry across the Zambezi river. The main road west, linking Ghanzi to the eastern centre runs from Lobatse to Kanye and across the Kalahari Desert and is suitable only for four wheel drive vehicles or trucks. Although some of the main roads are sandy in places and become slippery when wet they present no problems under normal conditions. However, away from the main roads system, particularly in the west and north, the roads are liable to be very heavy sand and tracks are suitable for trucks and four wheel drive vehicles only.

For the more adventurous the routes of the early hunters and missionaries such as van Zyl, Selous, Andersson, Livingstone and Price still remain to be followed.

Car Hire

Vehicles can be hired from: Cliff Engineering, PO Box 282, Gaborone; Botswana Game Industries, Post Bag 30, Francistown;

118

Botswana Safari and Tours, PO Box 118, Francistown; Botswana Development Corporation, PO Box 438, Gaborone. Various safari companies offer transport but it must be booked well in advance.

A useful hotel list is published by the Division of Tourism, *Hotels* Department of Wildlife, National Parks and Tourism, PO Box 131, Gaborone. Hotels are not graded. The list does not cover campsites.

National Parks and Game Reserves

Botswana's game areas are among the finest in Africa and are certainly less spoiled by tourism than most. The National Parks include:

CHOBE NATIONAL PARK

11,007 sq km (4,250 sq miles) around the Chobe river, including the Savuti Channel. Closed November to April. See page 124.

CENTRAL KALAHARI NATIONAL PARK

A vast area in the centre of Botswana, home both to large herds of game and to the Bushman.

MOREMI NATIONAL PARK

1,813 sq km (700 sq miles) north of Maun in the Okavango delta. Elephant, buffalo, antelope, lion. See page 122.

Smaller Parks are the Kalahari Gemsbok National Park, half of which is in South Africa; the Khutse National Park, in the southern central part of the country; the Nxai Pan National Park east of the Okavango delta; and the Makigadikgadi Game Reserve (also known as the Makarikari) on the Botletle river between the delta and Lake Xau. The Parks are administered by the Department of Wildlife, National Parks and Tourism, PO Box 131, Gaborone. Information is not easy to obtain outside Botswana, except through safari firms. However the hotel list mentioned above does tell you how to get to the lodges, which are privately owned and *Lodges* run. The best known are mentioned in this text.

Hunting and Photographic Safaris

Most Botswana people are hunters. From the Bushman, to whom it is a way of life, to the cattle owning Bamangwato, they understandably feel the hunting should be reserved for themselves. However visiting sporting hunters are allowed in, provided they are accompanied by a licensed professional hunter. The season is from March 15 to September 30 and bookings must be made before January 15 of the year in which you want to hunt. All hunting is controlled by the Chief Game Warden, PO Box 131, Gaborone. The basic game licence can be added to so that it covers all the Big Five except rhino.

Firearms   To bring firearms into the country you require two permits, the first from your own country to export them and the second from the Chief Game Warden to import and possess them. Safari firms will help with this and make you familiar with the laws on fauna conservation.

The two principal safari centres are Maun and Kasane and the main companies operating are: Safari South, PO Box 40, Maun, who incorporate the Kenya firm of Ker, Downey and Selby; Hunters Africa, PO Box 11, Kasane; Micheletti-Bates, PO Box 119, Maun.

Photographic   Photographic safaris are organised both by the hunting firms and by Gametrackers Botswana (PO Box 100, Maun) who also operate tented safaris in from Johannesburg (279 Ferndale Ave, Randburg, Johannesburg). Seven days in luxury tented camps would cost R 615. Less expensive tented safaris are run by Afro-Ventures (PO Box 10848, Johannesburg 2000). A local firm is Crocodile Camp Safaris (PO Box 46, Maun).

Gaborone, Lobatse and Francistown

Gaborone   Gaborone is the capital of Botswana and the seat of government. It has a population of about 25,000 and is situated on the line of rail in the south-east of the country close to the South African border. It was established in 1963, after independence, and has grown fast since, with a traffic-free pedestrian shopping precinct in the centre and three hotels, the Gaborone, the President and the Holiday Inn. Prices are up to P 30 per night. Holiday Safaris (Pty) Ltd operate to the Kalahari from the Holiday Inn, which also has a casino, golf and tennis. Banks include Barclays Bank International and the Standard Bank.

Amenities within Gaborone include a wide range of shops, a cinema, museum, library, sports and recreational facilities including golf, tennis, bowls and squash. Gaborone Dam, five km (three miles) from the town centre, offers a site for water sports such as yachting and water-skiing. There is a modern hospital and an airport.

Lobatse   Lobatse is a small but attractive town situated amidst a range of low hills, almost midway on the railway line between Mafikeng and Gaborone. It is the site of the Botswana Meat Commission, one of the largest meat processing plants in Africa. It also has several small industries but a shortage of water had prevented the town growing as fast as Gaborone. However, with the completion of the pipeline from Gaborone Dam to Lobatse the water problem has been solved and the population rose to 12,920 by 1976 and is larger now. The town has two hotels, the Cumberland and the Lobatse. Tariff – from about P 25 bed and breakfast.

Francistown lies close to the Zimbabwe border on the railway *Francistown* and is only 192 km (120 miles) from Bulawayo. The traditional industrial centre, it now has a population of 25,000 and with good air connections to neighbouring countries has become a staging post for the game parks in the north as well as for businessmen. There are two hotels, the Grand and the Tati. The Grand charges around P 25 per day full board.

Other towns along the railway line with hotels are Palapye and Mahalapye. Serowe has a small hotel too.

There is one outstanding game lodge in the eastern part of *Tuli* Botswana. Tuli Lodge is set among 29 sq miles of unspoilt bush in the Tuli hunting block on the Limpopo river. It is luxurious, with swimming pools and a large staff. Birds and game abound. It is near the border post at Pont Drift and visitors driving the 512 km (320 miles) from Johannesburg are met there. Bookings can be made through Gametrackers, 279 Ferndale Ave, Randburg, Johannesburg.

Maun, the Okavango and Moremi

Maun, the administrative centre of the area, is a small town, with a *Maun* population of about 13,000. It has a hospital, airfield, shops, and is 499 km (312 miles) from Francistown along a good gravel road. Riley's Hotel is not a luxury establishment, but offers reasonable food and accommodation for P 20 a day. You meet a variety of amiably crazy characters in the bar – not a few visitors have had to extend their holiday in order to recuperate from the hospitality there!

One hunter remarked of Maun that it's 'more a bunch of frenetic dreamers than a boom town'. Nonetheless the safari business is doing well and there are several lodges a short distance away along the Thamalakane river, notably the Crocodile Camp (PO Box 46, Maun), the Island Safari Lodge (PO Box 116, Maun) and the Okavango River Lodge (PO Box 32, Maun). You need four wheel drive. All have thatched huts or bungalows and arrange game viewing, photographic expeditions and fishing. Lodges further *Lodges* into the Okavango delta are mentioned below.

Local tribespeople include tall, dignified Damara nomads, whose wives wear magnificent full length robes and turban headdresses, derived from early German missionaries' styles. You also see Bushmen here, lean and small people with almost apricot-coloured skins. The best souvenirs to buy are reed and gameskin mats, fur karosses, lion and leopard skins, and Bushmen's *majumboro* shirts, fringed with bright beadwork. You can hire a car from Riley's garage.

121

Okavango Delta	Maun lies at the south eastern edge of the delta. This vast basin, watered by the great Okavango River, flows from the Angolan highlands and spreads out to form the Okavango Swamps. The virtually unexplored Okavango is not a true swamp but an inland river delta some 6,500 sq miles in extent. It is surrounded by desert that drains the crystal-clear waters of the elevated regions of Angola, creating a widespread network of waterways opening into lagoons, islands, forests, and vast grass flats. A few intrepid hunters, the Bayei, Bag/Ereku and Vambukushu, have settled on the islands and live by hunting and a little agriculture. The Okavango and adjacent forests are teeming with wildlife. You can move about by dug-out canoe, called a *mokoro*, and see the fantastic bird life, hippopotamus, marsh antelope and the shy and elusive sitatunga.

It is also possible to take a boat from Maun through the narrow waterways for 640 km (400 miles) and come out at the north-west corner of Shakawe, taking four days, unless you camp on any of the islands at night. A most exciting and rewarding trip with a safari fishing camp at the end on the banks of the Okavango River with 200 miles of river and lagoons for fishing, bird watching and shooting. The Shakawe Fishing Camp is run by Okavango Fishing Safaris (PO Box 446, Francistown) and is the nearest accommodation to the Tshodilo hills. You must, however, be accompanied by a guide.

Tshodilo Hills	A ridge of micaceous quartzite schist, rise 378 m (1,260 ft) above the surrounding desert 56 km (35 miles) west of the Okavango Delta. There are on their towering cliffs over 2,000 Bushman rock paintings of wildlife in many styles.

The Delta really has two seasons, as a result of the seasonal changes in the levels of the water. Choose May to August when the river floods the channels and enjoy fishing and exploring but if you are interested in big game specifically, go any time from September onwards. Swap the canoe or dug-out used in July for a four wheel drive vehicle in October.

Lake Ngami	Situated 72 km (45 miles) south-west of Maun, Ngami is one of the finest bird areas in Africa. It is sometimes covered with flocks of flamingoes numbering more than 20,000 and there is an abundance of pelican and countless waterfowl. This lake, however, is drying up and is quite dry on occasions. There is no accommodation at Lake Ngami but camping is permitted.
Moremi	The Moremi Wildlife Reserve lies some 144 km (90 miles) from Maun. Completely wild and unspoilt, this 695 sq mile reserve set in the north-east corner of the Okavango Delta is perhaps the most beautiful and probably the most spectacular of all reserves – the first in Southern Africa to be created and administered by an African tribe on their own land, namely the Batawana.

122

The Moremi contains an incredible spectrum of wildlife and, unlike the majority of parks and reserves, visitors are free to approach the animals on foot, offering a unique opportunity for close-up photography. Visitors must be accompanied in the Reserve by a game scout. Bird-watchers will find the Moremi an ornithologist's dream with virtually every species of Central African bird life represented. The heronry in the Reserve is the only known major nesting site of the Marabou stork.

There are two justifiably well known lodges in the area. San-Ta-Wani Safari Lodge (PO Box 100, Maun) near the Reserve's south gate, and the more famous Kwai River Lodge, near the northern gate and also bookable through Gametrackers in Johannesburg or at PO Box 66, Maun. Both have first class facilities.

The Moremi Reserve extends towards the Chobe National Park, described below. First we should mention two wildlife areas east of Maun, both watered by the Okavango river's seasonal flood.

Makgadikgadi Salt Pans

Makgadikgadi Salt Pans (Makarikari), once a large lake, are now vast white expanses rarely covered by a few inches of water, when large flocks of flamingoes line the shore. Massive herds of springbok, gemsbok, zebra and wildebeest are to be found in the plains to the north of the pans, which are now a Game Reserve. The salt pans lie just south of the Maun–Francistown road.

Nxai Pan National Park

One of the most interesting of the fossil lake beds is Nxai Pan (or Paradise Pan) which lies 32 km (20 miles) north of the main road from Francistown to Maun, covering about 155 sq km (60 sq miles). Large quantities of game visit the pan in the rainy season: gemsbok, springbok, zebra and wildebeest, sometimes herds of up to 5,000.

Driving from Victoria Falls

This area is much more accessible, especially if you have been visiting the Victoria Falls. There are two routes by road. One is to drive 80 km (50 miles) from Livingstone in Zambia to Kazungula at the confluence of the Chobe and the Zambezi Rivers, where four countries meet – Zimbabwe, Zambia, Botswana and the Caprivi Strip of Namibia. You then take the ferry across the river, landing in Botswana's borders close to the great Mazungula Tree (Sausage Tree) where David Livingstone first sighted the Zambezi, and 13 km (eight miles) further on is Kasane. Alternatively, the one and a half hour drive from the Victoria Falls, following the south bank of the Zambezi, avoids the ferry. Thirdly you can drive up the new road from Francistown and Nata.

Kasane, little more than a village, lies close to the Zambian border at the entrance to the Park. At the Kasane store you can buy frozen and tinned foods, films, curios and camping supplies, as well as hire camp equipment, boats and fishing tackle. There is a shady camping and caravan site near the river. Barclays Bank International Ltd operates an agency. There is no hotel, but there are two lodges near (see below).

Chobe
National Park

The 4,250 sq mile Chobe National Park, blessed with abundant grazing and well watered, offers perhaps the biggest variety of game anywhere in Africa. It takes its name from the Chobe River, one of the main tributaries of the Zambezi River. It is possible to see lion, leopard, cheetah, zebra, buffalo, 18 types of antelope including lechwe, roan and sable. One of the Park's main features is its elephant which may be seen at any time. Hippos snort in the water and hundreds of elephant come down to drink and bathe. Inland can be seen giraffe, gemsbok and wildebeest.

The Chobe is a bird-watcher's paradise and contains most types of Central African bird life, particularly aquatic birds, and an almost soundless drifting in a boat through the papyrus and reeds in the many canals will reveal the abundance of rare and exotic birds at close quarters.

The river swarms with tiger fish, often called the freshwater barracuda, bream and barbel – a delight to any fisherman. You may fish anywhere from the boat but fishing from the banks is designated to certain areas as elephant and other big game may get caught on the end of your line! No licence is required for fishing and there is no closed season.

The best time to visit the Park is during winter from May to October.

The Chobe Safari Lodge (PO Box 10, Kasane), is only 200 yards from the National Park entrance. Overlooking the river this hotel offers single or double rooms, thatched rondavels or family cottages and there are attractive camping sites in the grounds. Seven km (four miles) inside the Park is the more luxurious Chobe Game Lodge.

Linyanti

Savuti
Channel

The western end of the Chobe Park has several safari camps – and for good reason. A spillway called Selinda takes water from the Okavango delta to the small Linyanti swamp which feeds the Savuti channel. Linyanti is also fed by tributaries of the Chobe river. For a hundred years Savuti was dry, but since 1959 it has become seasonally wet again. Both it and Linyanti attract enormous concentrations of game, as does the Mababe Depression, where the channel dies.

The Linyanti Tented Camp is run by Gametrackers (PO Box 66, Maun), while Allan's Camp and Savuti South Camp, on the channel, are also used by them. You need to go on an organised safari in this area, unless you are highly experienced. Safari South (PO Box 40, Maun) are experts here too.

The Kalahari Desert

Many books have been written about the Kalahari. Its Bushmen are among Africa's few indigenous peoples and according to legend

124

there is a city buried somewhere beneath its arid wastes. It is not, however, a true desert. It is sandy and dry, but its vast undulating spaces are covered by thorn bushes, grassland and strange trees. When the Spring comes many trees burst into bloom and the rains bring the whole desert to flowering life.

About 4,000 Bushmen, living in small bands, wander in the heart of the Kalahari, hunting with bows and arrows, spears and snares, and searching for edible roots.

Among the herds of game are gemsbok, eland, greater kudu, wildebeest, Cape hartebeest, springbok and ostrich, while predators include lion and leopard.

Ghanzi

The only hotel in the area is at Ghanzi, a village in the desert with a hospital, an airstrip, one or two shops and a weekly agency of Barclays Bank International. Ghanzi is where the roads from Namibia, Maun and Lobatse meet. The 640 km (400 miles) drive from Lobatse needs four wheel drive. There is a scheduled air service. The Kalahari Arms hotel (PO Box 29, Ghanzi) is very small but offers good hospitality.

Kalahari Gems-bok National Park

The Kalahari Gemsbok National Park, half of which is in South Africa, lies in the south west corner of Botswana and the entrance is in the Republic. The South African Parks Board provided facilities and visitors must abide by their regulations (see page 68). However the Central Kalahari Game Reserve is entirely within Botswana. Adjoining it is the Khutse Game Reserve.

Khutse Reserve

This small game reserve is situated in the heart of the Kalahari and offers visitors a unique opportunity of seeing this interesting region of Botswana where all Kalahari game have been recorded. Access to the Reserve is through Molepolole, the main village of the Kweneng Distirct. There is a good gravel road from Gaborone to Molepolole. From Molepolole to the Reserve is a graded sand road suitable only for four wheel drive vehicles and trucks. It takes approximately six hours to reach the Reserve from Gaborone.

Petrol is available at Gaborone and Molepolole as well as food supplies and visitors must come fully equipped as there are no facilities in the Reserve. There are a number of boreholes on the route but it is best to set off with a water supply.

Useful Facts—BOTSWANA

Banks

Barclays Bank International Ltd and the Standard Bank Ltd have branches. Banking hours are 0830 to 1300 Monday to Friday and 0830 to 1100 on Saturdays.

Currency

The basic unit is the Pula, divided into 100c. At the time of writing one Pula was worth approximately US $ 1.20, being tied to the US dollar.

Health

1. Do not drink water without first boiling it and do not bathe in either pools or dams; there is bilharzia in Botswana.
2. There are places in Botswana where it is possible to contract malaria. You are advised to take a prophylactic drug such as Paludrin or Darachlor.
3. If you enter a tsetse fly area and are bitten and later become ill you should advise your doctor immediately that you have been bitten by a tsetse fly and that you may be suffering from Sleeping Sickness.

Immigration

No visas are required by citizens of the Commonwealth or of Austria, Belgium, Denmark, Federal Republic of Germany, Finland, France, Greece, Iceland, Ireland, Israel, Italy, Liechtenstein, Luxembourg, Netherlands, Norway, The Republic of South Africa, San Marino, Switzerland, the United States of America and Uruguay.

Smallpox vaccination certificates are required.

Public Holidays

New Year's Day (January 1), Good Friday, Easter Monday, Ascension Day (May 31), Whit Monday, President's Day (July 13), Botswana Day (September 30), United Nations Day (October 24), Christmas Day (December 25), Boxing Day (December 26).

Representation abroad

Botswana has diplomatic missions in London, Bonn, Lusaka, Moscow, New York, Peking, Seoul and Stockholm. Visas are obtainable from them.

Time

Two hours ahead of GMT.

Tourist Enquiries

Enquiries can be made to the Controller of Tourism, Private Bag 47, Gaborone.

126

Mountain village

Lesotho

Lesotho, formerly called Basutoland, is a tiny mountain kingdom, an enclave within the Republic of South Africa, as San Marino is in Italy. Its 11,716 sq miles lie between, or rather sit above, the borders of Natal, the Free State and the Cape Province. But, although travel brochures often describe it as 'The Switzerland of South Africa', its rugged peaks, 3,352 m (11,000 ft) and more high, seem more Tibetan than Swiss. In fact its breathtaking landscapes might not be in Africa at all. Its great attraction is its total individuality, characterised by the handsome Basuto horsemen, splendid in conical straw hats and multi-coloured blanket cloaks. It is a connoisseur's country in fact, with the added lure of some of the best freshwater fishing in the world, riding through the mountains and climbing.

Basutoland first realised its identity as a country of refuge. In 1818 *History* the remnants of several small tribes escaping from the powerful Zulu and Matabele were rallied here by a Chief called Moshoeshoe. For fifty years they fought to keep the mountainous hinterland to themselves, the biggest threat coming from Boer farmers moving north on the Great Trek, in the 1830s.

In 1868, after numerous appeals from Moshoeshoe, the British Government agreed to take Basutoland under British protection. On 4th October 1966 it became independent, under the name

Lesotho, with Moshoeshoe's direct descendant, His Majesty the King Moshoeshoe II, as its constitutional monarch.

Broadly, the government of the new state of Lesotho is formed on the traditional British pattern. It has a National Assembly of elected members and a Senate or House of Chiefs, in the same mould as the British House of Lords. The capital of the country is Maseru.

The People The present population of Lesotho is about 1,200,000, of whom less than two thousand are non-Basutos. Despite their scattered origin, the Basutos have become very much a nation of their own, and are an extremely colourful people, particularly on horseback. There is no racial segregation.

In many areas, the Basuto pony is the sole means of transport. Owning one of these is a man's prerogative, but most womenfolk can ride and the children learn to sit a saddle almost as soon as they can walk. Indeed, in a recent survey, a German equestrian expert ranked them among the best mountain riders in the world. Surprisingly, in view of the poor communications, Basutos have the highest standard of literacy in the African continent – more than 60 percent at the last census.

Climate In the lowlands, which constitute a quarter of Lesotho, temperatures vary from 32°C (90°F) in summer (October to February) to 13°C (20°F) in winter. It is healthy and there are no tropical diseases.

The mountain climate, however, is far more extreme. Snow may fall in the highlands at any time and in winter some areas may be snowbound for several weeks. Travellers should watch their lines of retreat. If camping make sure you have ample food and fuel as well as warm clothing and bedding. Away from the main towns, there are few points of supply.

The annual rainfall is approximately 71 cm (28 ins), mostly falling between October and April, though every month has its showers. You will need a raincoat.

National Park Lesotho's first National Park, Sehlabathebe, was established in 1970 in the Qacha's Nek district on the country's eastern borders. It covers about 23 sq miles, protecting rare birds, mountain reedbuck and flowers. The scenery is magnificent. The Mountain Lodge and the simpler Park Hostel can both be booked through Sehlabathebe Lodge Reservations, PO Box, Maseru (telephone (0501) 23600). You must bring your own bedding and food.

Travel There are several points of entry by road from the Republic of South Africa. The best is through the capital Maseru via Ladybrand in the Orange Free State. The recommended route from Johannesburg is via Kroonstad – Winburg – Marquard – Clocolan – Ladybrand – Maseru; and from Durban, via Paul Roux – Rosendal –

Opposite: Basuto horseman. Photograph SATOUR

Ficksburg – Clocolan – Ladybrand – Maseru. A bus service links Maseru with the railway at Marseilles, on the Bloemfontein-Natal main road. Butha-Buthe in the north is accessible from Fouriesburg; Leribe from Ficksburg; Mafeteng from Wepener and Quthing from Zastron and Herschel.

There is a precipitous track for four wheel drive vehicles up to Mokhotlong through the Sani Pass, which connects with Maseru via Butha-Buthe and which is currently being upgraded. This road forms part of the route of the annual 900 km (559 miles) Roof of Africa car rally, which starts at Maseru and lasts two days.

Roof of Africa Car Rally

Even if you are not rallying, a four wheel drive vehicle is strongly recommended. The normal maximum speed limit is 90 kph (55 mph) and the wearing of seatbelts is compulsory. Overseas visitors – ie without Southern African licences – need an International Driving Licence. An excellent booklet, *Motoring in Lesotho*, is published by the AA of South Africa, PO Box 596, Johannesburg 2000.

Driving

Maseru is served by a branch line off the Bloemfontein to Durban line, changing at Marseilles. There are two trains a day and one on Sundays.

Rail

Over 30 flights a week by Lesotho Airways and SAA connect Maseru to Johannesburg. There are also flights to Durban and Maputo. There are airstrips throughout the country to which Lesotho Airways (PO Box 10, Maseru) will fly private charters. Rates on application, but not much different from those prevailing in Johannesburg.

Air

As Lesotho is in the same Customs area as South Africa there are few formalities at the frontier, though you do need a passport. Details of requirements are given under the Useful Facts at the end of this chapter. Travellers' cheques are accepted at hotels and shops, though rural people are unfamiliar with them.

Entry

As far as clothing goes the General Information on page 8 holds good. Remember that warm clothing is essential at night at these altitudes. Slippers are useful in the evening. There is seldom any need to dress formally. Sunburn creams and lip salve are useful.

Dress

Maseru

The capital, Maseru, is Lesotho's principal town. The Assembly sits there and it has the official residence of HM The King. It is set in a beautiful landscape, with mountains in the distance, and has a variety of hotels, including the old-established Lancers Inn; the large Lesotho Hilton, with golf, tennis and other sports plus a casino; and the equally massive Holiday Inn. Hotels are not graded, but they are inspected regularly by the government.

Opposite: Swazi mother and child. Photograph COI

Maseru has plenty of shops, though prices tend to be higher than in South Africa, and its speciality is local handicraft products. The Art and Crafts Centre is easily identifiable: it is a thatched building in the shape of a Sotho hat, complete with a looped topknot. Things to buy are beadwork, pottery and the traditional coloured blankets, while not far away are three specialist companies of note. Maluti Skin Products in Mokhomi Road sell sheepskin coats and slippers; the Royal Lesotho Tapestry Weavers not only make fine tapestries, but also carpets and shawls; the Royal Crown Jewellers make modern jewellery in precious metals, ebony and ivory, using Basotho designs.

This reminds us to explain that in most of Africa there is one basic word for the tribe and its language, to which prefixes are added. Thus Sotho is the tribe, the people of which are Basotho and the country Lesotho. The British phonetic variant was Basuto, and in fact Basutoland was only an anglicised way of saying Lesotho.

Information

If you want to know more about this, or about local customs, roads, facilities or anything else, consult the National Tourist Office, Maseru (telephone 2896). Should you be ill there is the Queen Elizabeth Hospital, and various others in the countryside.

Tours

The National Tourist Office organises various excursions from Maseru, notably into the dramatic Maluti mountains.

Near Maseru is the mountain, Thaba Bosiu, once the mountain fortress of Moshoeshoe. Almost beneath it, at Roma, 32 km (20 miles) from Maseru, is the National University of Lesotho. While to the south of Maseru, at Morija, is a museum in which are preserved

Museum

the eighty-million-year-old footprints of dinosaurs, and the shapes of long extinct flora. Morija is also where the first Christian mission was opened.

The Country

As we mentioned earlier, the main attractions of the country are fishing, climbing and riding. Anyone who has an eye for the people round him will find the Basuto villages fascinating, not to mention the magnificent landscapes they are set in. Broadly speaking, Maseru is on a plain between 1,524 m (5,000 ft) and 2,133 m (7,000 ft) above sea level. Moving eastwards the Maluti Mountains bisect the country, then in the far north-east the land reaches its highest levels in the peaks of the Drakensberg, more than 3,352 m (11,000 ft) high.

Hotels

Lesotho's eight or so hotels outside Maseru, mostly mentioned later, are countryfied but comfortable. The best are the Blue Mountain Inn at Teyateyaneng near Maseru and the Orange River Hotel at Moyeni (Quthing) in the south. There are lodges at Qaba, Semonkong, and Marakabei, run by the Fraser Lodge System, PO Box 5, Maseru. You provide food, but all other facilities are supplied, including servants. If you are going camping you will find fresh meat, milk, butter and eggs readily available both in the town and in village stores.

The rivers that rise along the mountainous spine of the country, like the Orange, the Caledon and the Tugela, provide much of South Africa's water. The Orange, named after the Royal House of Orange, winds its way eventually right across to the Atlantic. But at their origin these rivers are perfect highland streams, alive with trout. They were stocked by a few pioneers in the early 1930s and some have never been fished to this day. The best trout fishing is at Semonkong; in the Sehonghong River near Mokhotlong; and in the Tsoelikana River. The largest rainbow trout ever caught in a river in Southern Africa was hooked at Sehlabathebe in the Qacha's Nek district. It weighed over 4 kg (9 lb 5 oz). The trout season is 1st September to 31st May.

Good fishing can also be had at many more accessible spots. Less than 64 km (40 miles) from Maseru on the Mountain Road is the Makhaleng stream, a haunt of rainbow trout. Yellowfish and rainbow trout can also be taken with ease at Senqunyane, on the same road.

The Hotel Mount Maluti at Mohale's Hoek and the Orange River hotel at Quthing make convenient bases for brown and rainbow trout fishing. Mokhotlong is also close to good fishing grounds. The hotel has, unhappily, been burnt down. However, there is a Government rest hut and a mountaineer's chalet on top of the Sani Pass. Ask at the National Tourist Office, Maseru, about these before going. Mokhotlong also has a store, post office and airstrip.

Although most anglers who come to Lesotho go after the trout, the rivers and streams, particularly in the lowlands, sport several other varieties of fish. Barbel, carp, yellowfish and mudfish may be found in the Caledon River, for some distance up the Orange River and in the larger tributaries of both. Catches have included carp up to 11·34 kg (25 lb) in weight and barbel up to 13·61 kg (30 lb). The upper regions of the Orange and its tributaries teem with yellowfish – a small fish with fighting qualities equal to the rainbow trout, but seldom exceeding 2·72 kg (6 lb). A 1·81 kg (4 lb) yellowfish will run 55 m (60 yards) on trout tackle and take 25 minutes to subdue.

Fishing permits may be obtained at most border posts, from the Angling Society of Lesotho, and from Fraser's Store in Maseru.

Climbing, hiking, riding and even skiing draw visitors to many parts of Lesotho and there are excellent safe pools for swimming in the crystal clear highland streams (Lesotho's rivers are free of bilharzia).

Although few organised amenities exist, there are many suitable spots for camping and caravanning. No permits are necessary but

131

it is considered a matter of courtesy for campers to tell the local District Commissioner where they intend to camp.

Expeditions Pony and Land-Rover expeditions into the mountains are run from Maseru by Maluti Treks and Travel (Pty) Ltd, PO Box 295, Maseru (telephone 2554). There are also expeditions up through the Sani Pass in the Drakensberg Mountains into north-east Lesotho run by the Mokhotlong Transport Co, PO Box 12, Himeville, Natal. But the latter start from Natal, not from Maseru. Don't forget that whether going up or down the Sani Pass you cross the South African frontier and need a passport. In planning drives reckon on an average speed of 19 kph (12 mph) and note that most of the tracks are only suitable for four wheel drive vehicles. However, improvements are under way.

Some Suggested Trips

North Hlotse Butha-Buthe and Oxbow In the north Hlotse (Leribe) and the Butha-Buthe area give access to the heart of the mountains. The town of Hlotse was founded in 1876 when the Rev John Widdicombe pitched a tent there on a grant of land from the son of Moshoeshoe. The church dates from 1877 and the fort from 1879. Gordon of Khartoum, the famous British General, once lived here in a small rondavel, which is preserved.

The Mountain View Hotel (PO Box 14) offers swimming, bowls and tennis. Riding can be arranged.

Some eight km (five miles) north of Hlotse on the road to Butha-Buthe there are dinosaur footprints in the bed of the Subeng stream, 400 m downstream of the bridge. They are estimated to be 200 million years old.

Butha-Buthe, where Moshoeshoe established his first mountain stronghold, has the Crocodile Inn (PO Box 72), shops and is the starting point for trips to Oxbow, 68 km (42 miles), set 3,000 m (10,000 ft) up in wild and rugged country. Oxbow is being turned into a modern resort. It already has the New Oxbow Lodge, with facilities for riding, fishing and swimming. Bookings are through Lesotho Hotels Reservation (telephone Maseru 22002). You can ski at Oxbow from June to August. Subsidiary trips may be arranged from Oxbow to the Tsoloane pool, a breeding haven for trout, and to Mont aux Sources, on the brink of the Drakensberg amphitheatre, where there are wide fantastic views over Natal. At the diamond diggings of Letseng-la-Terae a 527 carat stone was found.

Lebihan Falls These falls, among the highest in Africa, descend 192 m (633 ft). Named after a French missionary, they are also called Malutsenyane. Set in magnificent scenery, they can either be reached by a 30 min flight from Maseru followed by 4 km on horseback, or by a 45 km (28 mile) jeep track from Semonkong Lodge (PO Box 5,

Maseru). It is also possible to arrange horseback treks to the falls. Rare spiral aloes grow near them and on the mountain to the west of Semonkong.

This is a lesser waterfall, under 151 m (500 ft) high, but the setting is as wild and beautiful as Malutsenyane. The remoteness of Ketane makes it so difficult to reach that very few non-Basutos have ever seen the falls. You get there by pony, either from Malealea or from Qaba Lodge, which is a five day round trek. *Ketane Falls*

This trip is an easy 46 km (29 miles) from Maseru along the mountain road. Although few Bushmen still live in Lesotho, there are many of their ancient paintings and the ones here are considered the finest in Southern Africa. They can be seen from 0900 to 1700 daily for a small fee. *Ha Baroana Rock Paintings*

Already mentioned, Sehlabathebe is on the Natal border. The name means Plateau of the Shield and the average height is 2,400 m (8,000 ft). Bushman paintings, rare orchids and water-lilies, the lammergeyer bird, and strange rock formations are among its attractions. The easiest access is by air charter. *Sehlabathebe National Park*

Useful facts — LESOTHO

Banks

Barclays Bank International Ltd has branches.

Currency

The Maloti is at par with the South African Rand.

Customs

In the South African Customs area. Few formalities.

Electricity supply

220 volts AC in Maseru. Elsewhere dependent on the generator.

Health Requirements

International smallpox certificates are required. Yellow fever certificate required if you come from an affected area. Lesotho is not a malarial area.

Passports and Visas

All visitors need a passport. You may enter for three months if you are a national of Belgium, Britain, Denmark, Finland, Iceland, Italy,

Liechtenstein, Luxembourg, Netherlands, Norway, San Marino, South Africa, Sweden, Switzerland, USA, Uruguay. Other nationalities need a visa, except Commonwealth citizens.

Public Holidays

New Year's Day (January 1), Moshoeshoe's Day (March 12), National Tree Planting Day (March 21), Good Friday, Easter Monday, King's Birthday (May 2), Ascension Day, Family Day (First Monday in July), Sports Day (First Monday in October), Independence Day (October 4), Christmas Day (December 25), Boxing Day (December 26).

Representation abroad

Lesotho has Embassies/High Commissions in London, Nairobi, New York.

Elsewhere the country is represented by British diplomatic missions.

Time

Two hours ahead of GMT.

Traditional Swazi market

Swaziland

The mystical, strange beauty of Swaziland has never been better described than in Rider Haggard's celebrated books, *King Solomon's Mines* and *Allan Quartermain*. He understood the intrinsic drama of the rugged, mist-shrouded mountains that are the sacred burial grounds of the Swazi kings, and the source of Swazi legends.

This is a small, but excitingly varied, country, poised between the Transvaal, Natal and Mozambique. Geographers would even call it a topographical jumble. Though only 182 km (120 miles) long and 144 km (90 miles) wide, it encompasses highland country between 1,000 and 1,400 m (3,500 and 4,500 ft) above sea level; rolling grasslands of the middleveld; and the arid though fertile bush of the lowveld. At its eastern border the impressive Lubombo escarpment brings the territory to an abrupt halt, where a road winds down to Mozambique. Other main routes into the territory are from Barberton in the Transvaal, from Ermelo in the Transvaal, and from Northern Zululand.

Little is known about Swaziland's early history, although there are definite traces of human occupation in the country from the late palaeolithic period onwards. A composite people of various clans, the Swazi have existed as a distinct tribe only since the beginning of the nineteenth century. The Nkosi-Dlamini, now the ruling clan

History

135

and nucleus of the Swazi nation, formed part of the main body of African migrants who travelled from Central Africa towards Delagoa Bay and then south to Tongaland. They later crossed the Lubombo Mountains into south-east Swaziland. Eventually the whole country, and much of what is now the Transvaal Province of South Africa, came under Swazi control.

There was little contact with Europeans until the 1840s, when both the Boers and English missionaries made contact with the Swazi King. The Boers were keenly interested in the territory, as it blocked their way to a much-sought-after east coast outlet. In 1879 gold was discovered and this led not to a gold rush but to a torrent of fortune hunters seeking concessions from the King for anything and everything – from refreshment bars to clothing shops.

Dual control of the territory by the British and the Boers was tried unsuccessfully, and after much political manoeuvring between the two factions a British Protectorate was established in 1903 at the conclusion of the Boer War.

Swaziland achieved self government in 1966 and Independence in September 1968. It is a monarchy in which H.M. King Sobhuza II, the Ngwenyama (Lion) is the constitutional ruler, advised on traditional matters by his chosen councillors. The Government is presided over by a Prime Minister, and the Parliament consists of a House of Assembly and a Senate. Until 1968 Swaziland was a State protected by Great Britain.

The People
The population is 500,000, of which 95 percent are Swazi, the remaining five percent being mainly of European extraction.

Language
A friendly, mainly pastoral, people, the Swazi are developing as fast as their potentially rich country. SiSwati is their language, but English is spoken in shops, hotels and markets.

Traditional
Ceremonies
There are two major traditional ceremonies, the Incwala kingship ceremony in December–January, and the Reed Dance in June–July. Visitors are allowed to attend the main day of the Incwala and watch men of the Swazi Regiments, panoplied in skin tunics, dance at the Royal Residence at Lobamba, 16 km (10 miles) from the capital of Mbabane. The culmination of the Reed Dance, in which many hundreds of Swazi maidens take part, may also be watched. Cine cameras are not permitted at either ceremony but you may take as many still pictures as you wish.

Climate
In the mountainous area, commonly called the highveld, on the western side of the country, it is pleasantly warm (21°–30°C/70°–85°F) from October to March. In the winter months, however, temperatures drop considerably and early-morning frost is not uncommon. The middleveld, lowveld and Lubombo regions are warmer by several degrees. Rain falls mostly during the hot summer months.

Although Swaziland cannot rival South Africa's Kruger National Park, there are two Wildlife Sanctuaries. The larger is the 17 sq mile Mlilwane, situated 22 km (14 miles) south of Mbabane. It is well stocked with hippo, white rhino, giraffe and many species of antelope. Birdlife is prolific. The Hlane Wildlife Sanctuary, 70 km (44 miles) from Manzini has rhino, giraffe and large herds of wildebeeste. Mlilwane has a rest camp (Bookings PO Box 33 Mbabane, telephone 61037) and there are camping facilities at Hlane. Both charge admission fees.

Wildlife Sanctuaries

Royal Swazi Airways and SAA both operate from Matsapa Airport, eight km (five miles) west of Manzini. As well as these regular daily flights, there are services to Durban, Lusaka, Maputo, Mauritius, Maseru and Nairobi. Charter flights can be arranged with Royal Swazi Airways.

Communications

Air

A passenger bus service from railheads in the Republic is operated by the South African Road Motor Services. These bus journeys are, however, usually long and tiring. An increasing number of firms in South Africa are running luxury bus tours to the territory.

Bus

Internal travel is by road only. The trans-territorial highway runs from Ngwneya on the western border to Lomahasha on the Mozambique frontier. It is partly tarred. Other roads are gravel. The general speed limit is 80 kph (50 mph). Service stations are only open on Saturdays in the mornings and Sundays in the afternoons.

Roads

Car hire firms include Hertz in Mbabane (telephone 42561) and in Matsapa (telephone 52509) and Car Hire Services in Mbabane (telephone 42672).

Car Hire

Hotels are not graded but a list is obtainable from the Swaziland Government Tourist Office, PO Box 451, Mbabane (telephone 42531) as part of their useful *Travellers Companion*. Their office is opposite the Tavern Hotel in Mbabane.

Hotels

Information

The Swazi handicraft markets at Mbabane, Manzini, Pigg's Peak and Nhlangano are well worth a visit. Souvenirs can be bought for a few pence. Grass skirts, mats, and baskets and necklaces made out of colourful seeds are particularly attractive. One amusing gift for people in Europe is a woven grass strainer for the thick Swazi traditional beer.

Markets

If you like to flirt with Lady Luck, the Royal Swazi Spa luxury hotel and casino (PO Box 412, Mbabane) runs roulette, chemin de fer, and blackjack tables in well appointed gaming rooms open every night of the week. Mineral water, from a nearby hot spring, is piped to every bedroom and there is an international standard golf course. The tariff at the Spa, which is in the Ezulwini valley 11 km (seven miles) from Mbabane, is from E 24 (double room). The adjacent Lugogo and Ezulwini Holiday Inns (PO Box 412, Mbabane) have use of the Spa's facilities.

Casino

Mbabane

Swaziland's capital, Mbabane, nestling in the mountains of the highveld, is rapidly changing from a slow colonial-type settlement into a bustling, modern town. Tall new buildings tower over the corrugated iron roofs of their elderly neighbours and the dusty surfaces of the streets are being tarred. The main street is named after Allister Miller, who founded the weekly *Times* of Swaziland, the country's only newspaper, in 1896.

Hotels
The Tavern (PO Box 25), at the western entrance to the town, has a friendly Old English atmosphere. A few hundred yards away, in Allister Miller Street, is the Jabula Inn (PO Box 15) which offers a first class table. On the outskirts of Mbabane, the Highland View Hotel (PO Box 223) has a magnificent view of the Ezulwini valley, though the Swazi Inn (PO Box 121) is the most picturesque hotel. It is three km from the town on the Manzini road. Rates are around E 12 for bed and breakfast, though the Tavern is good value full board.

Shops
There is a range of shops similar to that found in any small town in Europe. Because of transport costs prices are slightly higher than in South Africa. The market is worth a visit for handicrafts. The town has quite a number of restaurants and night life in clubs and discos.

Taxis are available from their stand in Allister Miller Street. There are no taximeters, so agree a price in advance.

For golfers, the Mbabane Club has a beautiful and quite exacting nine-hole course. Other facilities include tennis courts and bowling greens. Temporary membership of the club is available.

Usutu Forest
An interesting and scenically beautiful circular drive of 104 km (65 miles) is from Mbabane to the Usutu Forest, one of the largest man-made forests in the world. The good gravel road crosses the Little Usutu River, goes through the hilly Sipocosini area and then enters the huge, silent forest. Trees by the thousand, mainly pine, cover an area of more than 100,000 acres. At Mhlambanyati, one of the settlements for the Usutu Pulp Company's employees, the gravel turns to tarmac. The road goes on to Bunya, where a huge pulp mill is situated, which exports 136,000 tons of unbleached pulp annually.

After Bunya, the road follows the Great Usutu River into the middleveld. It goes past the new R 600,000 Swaziland Agricultural College and University Centre into the Malkerns valley, an important pineapple and citrus-growing area. Large, juicy pineapples can usually be bought at the roadside for as little as 5c.

A good route back to the capital is by the trans-territorial highway, which links Mbabane and Manzini. It takes you past the Royal Residence at Lobamba, through the Ezulwini valley and up Malagwane hill.

138

As readers will have already realised, the Ezulwini valley is a *Ezulwini Valley* favourite holiday area. It lies between Mbabane and Manzini, has splendid scenery and enjoyable drives, notably in the Pine valley and along the signposted Tea Road, through the tea estates. At the Mantenga Falls, 18 km (11 miles) south of Mbabane is the pleasant Mantenga Falls Hotel (PO Box 15, Ezulwini).

Manzini

Described as the industrial hub of Swaziland, Manzini is 41 km (26 miles) south-east of Mbabane, in the middleveld. Unlike Mbabane, the town is built on much flatter land. It is about the same size as the capital and has similar shopping facilities.

The Manzini Club has a golf course, squash and tennis courts, bowling greens and a swimming bath. Temporary membership is available.

Manzini has two hotels. The George Hotel (PO Box 51) charges *Hotels* from L 8.50 bed only and the Uncle Charlie (PO Box 48) from L 12. There are several restaurants and three night clubs.

The Lowveld

Two of the most interesting areas to visit in the lowveld are the sugar-growing regions of Big Bend, in the south-east, and Mhulme in the north-east. In both areas irrigation has turned the arid bushveld into acres of green sugar cane and this relatively new agricultural industry is now the territory's main single money earner. Besides sugar, citrus is grown at Big Bend and near Mhulme. These two 'oases', with the Lubombo in the background, provide wonderful photographic subjects.

Siteki (Stegi), the largest settlement on the Lubombo, is worth a visit, if only for the magnificent view you get across the lowveld on a clear day. From Siteki you can drive to Goba, in Mozambique, and then on to Maputo. However, a better route is via Nomahasha, at the Mozambique end of the trans-territorial highway. This road is tarred as far as Mpaka, just before the turn-off to Siteki and Big Bend, and the remaining 61 km (38 miles) has a very good gravel surface. But check on it before driving during the rains.

Pigg's Peak

North of Mbabane the road to Pigg's Peak gives you a series of breathtaking mountain views, across a deep valley towards the hills that stretch for many miles into South Africa. This area is one of the most potentially rewarding to explore. Several spectacular waterfalls are near the Peak, namely Phophonyane, 18 km (11 miles) on the Matsamo road, Magonigoni and Nginamadvolo, in a gorge of the Komati river. It's worth asking the District Office in Pigg's Peak for the services of a guide. He could also show you the rock paintings at the Nsangwini Shelter near the Peak, or escort you to the remains of an early gold mining centre. This ghost town, called Forbes Reef, is about 10 km (six miles) along the Motshane road.

The South

In the south of the territory, Hlatikulu, another of the several small settlements in Swaziland, lies on a beautiful mountain range above the Mkondo valley. Grand Valley, a spectacular sight in both winter and summer, is accessible by way of a steep mountain road which leaves the Sitobela road five km (three miles) from Hlatikulu.

Nhlangono, near the Transvaal border 27 km (17 miles) south of Hlatikulu, is the administrative headquarters of the Shiselweni district. Mahamba Gorge, a few miles from the town and reached by a road through the Mohamba Methodist Mission, is a pleasant picnic spot. Nhlangano, formerly called Goedegun, has two hotels, the Robin Inn and the Nhlangano Hotel, with swimming pool and casino.

Sixty-nine km (43 miles) from Nhlangano, on the road back towards Mbabane, is Mankaiana (also on the main route from Piet Retief, in South Africa). At Enqabaneni Mission, a few kilometres from Mankaiana, you can buy beautifully woven shawls and tablecloths and a host of other handicrafts made by the local people. Soon after Enqabaneni the road runs into the Malkerns valley, where it joins the tarred road leading to the national highway.

Useful Facts—SWAZILAND

Banks

Barclays International Bank and the Standard Bank have branches. Bank opening hours are 0830 to 1300 on weekdays and 0830 to 1100 on Saturdays.

Currency

The unit of currency is the Lilangeni. One L is at par with one South African Rand. It is however wise to change Swazi currency back into Rands before leaving.

Customs

In the South African Customs area. Few formalities. The border is manned on both sides and no border posts are open after 2200, many closing earlier. They open at 0800, except Ngwneya, which opens at 0700.

Electricity supply

220 volts AC in Mbabane and Manzini. Elsewhere variable.

Health Requirements

International smallpox and cholera certificates required. Yellow-fever injection advisable.

Passports and Visas

All visitors need a passport. Nationals of the following countries may enter without visas: Britain and the Commonwealth, Belgium, Denmark, Finland, Greece, Iceland, Israel, Italy, Liechtenstein, Luxembourg, Netherlands, Norway, San Marino, South Africa, Sweden, Switzerland, USA, Uruguay. Others need a visa.

Public Holidays

New Year's Day (January 1), Commonwealth Day (March 9), Good Friday, Easter Monday, National Flag Day (April 25), Ascension Day, King's Birthday (July 22), Umhlanga, National Day (September 6), United Nations Day (October 24), Christmas Day (December 25), Boxing Day (December 26), Incwala Day.

Representation abroad

Swaziland has diplomatic missions in London, Maputo, Nairobi, New York and Washington. Visas are obtainable from them. There is an EEC Attaché in Brussels.

Time

Two hours ahead of GMT.

Zimbabwe Ruins

Zimbabwe

It is difficult not to become enthusiastic about Zimbabwe, for the country has practically everything. It's cinemascopic to start with. Outside the towns your field of vision widens perceptibly – and it only takes a 15 minute drive in any direction to be in the wide open veld. There are rolling miles of the veld, strange-shaped trees, acres of wild flower carpets, and startling 'balancing' rock formations. The air – even in the cities – is clean and fresh. Within its 151,000 sq miles are the wonders of the Victoria Falls and Lake Kariba in the north, the dramatic mountainous region of the eastern border, the flat bushveld of the great game reserve at Wankie in the west, and the Great Zimbabwe Ruins and booming lowveld development in the south. The country is bounded by Zambia, Mozambique, South Africa, and Botswana, and lies between the Zambezi and Limpopo rivers.

Broadly, the area round Harare is the richest farmland; there is cattle ranching south of Bulawayo and sugar is grown in the lowveld. There are many small mines, especially in the hills around Sinoia. Copper, emeralds and chrome are produced, while Zimbabwe is the world's third largest exporter of gold.

Climate

The climate is classified as 'temperate'. Actually, summer lasts eight months of the year. Even in winter (May to August), coats and

142

jerseys are generally necessary only at night or in the early morning, and then only on the highveld. Zimbabweans, however, tend to divide the year into two seasons: the rainy season and the dry season. The rains begin usually after the hottest month (October) and continue intermittently until the end of March. Because of the rains the best season for game-viewing and tourism is April to October. Rainfall in the low-lying areas varies from 152–254 mm (6–10 ins) a year, and in the Highlands from 500–1,000 mm (20–40 ins) a year. In some parts more than 1,270 mm (50 ins) are recorded.

The Zimbabwean unit of currency is the dollar ($) of 100c.   *Currency*

The main African languages are Shona and Ndebele. The official   *Languages*
language is English, which is spoken everywhere.

There are 7,100,000 Africans, 223,000 Europeans, 25,900 of mixed   *Population*
race, and 10,900 Asians. Tribally the African population is divided into one quarter Matabele and three quarters Mashona, though there are many smaller groups, including a number of Bushmen.

The history of what is now Zimbabwe is ill-defined up to the middle   *History*
of the nineteenth century. The ruins of Great Zimbabwe point to a well-organised state in the fifteenth century, and Portuguese explorers of the sixteenth century related contacts with a paramount ruler with the title of Monomatapa.

It was the ivory hunters of the mid-nineteenth century, such as Hartley and Selous, who drew the attention of the modern world to the unknown interior north of the Limpopo. However, only the discovery of gold on the South African Witwatersrand prompted settlement and development.

Cecil Rhodes, whose British South Africa Company obtained a concession to exploit the mineral resources of the country from the Matabele king, Lobengula, organised a Pioneer Column in 1890. The armed company effectively annexed Mashonaland and began to settle Europeans on the land. In 1893, deliberately over-reacting to incidents involving Matabele warriors at Fort Victoria, the company attacked Lobengula's capital, Bulawayo, and annexed Matabeleland.

In 1896 the Matabele and Mashona tribes rose in rebellion but were crushed by the settlers. Thus began the European domination of what is now Zimbabwe – then Southern Rhodesia.

The British Government granted internal self-government to the settlers in 1923, and did not concern itself with the political development of the country until the dissolution of the Federation of Rhodesia and Nyasaland in 1963 (of which Southern Rhodesia was a part). Nonetheless the British refused to grant independence to Southern Rhodesia while it was under white control, and this led to the Unilateral Declaration of Independence in 1965. The war which eventually resulted, as black nationalists struggled for universal suffrage, led to a transitional government in 1979. This gave way to an open general election in 1980 which returned the ZANU(PF) party led by Robert Mugabe to power as Prime Minister.

The independent state of Zimbabwe came into being on April 17, 1980. The President is H.E. The Rev Canaan Banana. The Parliament sits in Harare (formerly Salisbury).

Bulawayo is the headquarters of rail communications, and Harare the centre of road and air communications.

Communications

Air

Harare airport, 15 minutes drive from the city with hourly buses (fare $1.20) to and from the Travel Centre, is served by direct flights of Air Zimbabwe from London (Gatwick) and by British Airways from London (Heathrow). Air Zimbabwe and Lufthansa fly from Frankfurt. Other airlines operating from their own countries include Ethiopian, Kenya Airways, South African Airways and Zambia Airways.

Regional air connections link Zimbabwe with South Africa, Botswana, Mozambique, Malawi and Swaziland.

Excursions

Air Zimbabwe operates scheduled services between cities, towns and resorts such as Kariba and the Victoria Falls. There are also various package air holidays which are excellent value, for instance two days at the Victoria Falls for $149. These tours are subject to the ten percent government sales tax.

Air Charter

Chartering an aircraft can be cheaper than going by scheduled flight if you can fill all the seats. Single and twin engined aircraft are available, usually operating out of Charles Prince Airport, 16 km (ten miles) north west of Harare. The principal companies include RUAC, at Harare, Bulawayo and Victoria Falls; Skyline Charters at Harare; Lake Air at Kariba and Airwork at Harare.

Railways

The National Railways of Zimbabwe serve all main towns and cities, but trains are slow. One of the best services for the tourist is the nightly one in both directions between Harare and Bulawayo. First class fare $ 20.40; second $ 14.40. The train leaves at 2000 and arrives the following morning at 0700. The system is connected to South African Railways via Beitbridge and Botswana. Rail travel to Zambia and Mozambique is possible, though the latter is not recommended. It is not possible to Malawi.

Road

Road communications with Botswana, Zambia and South Africa are excellent. At the time of writing it was impractical to attempt driving to Mozambique. Within the country roads are tarmacked between major urban and tourist centres.

Opposite top: Klipspringer in Kruger National Park
Bottom: Kudu bull in Kruger National Park. Photographs SATOUR

144

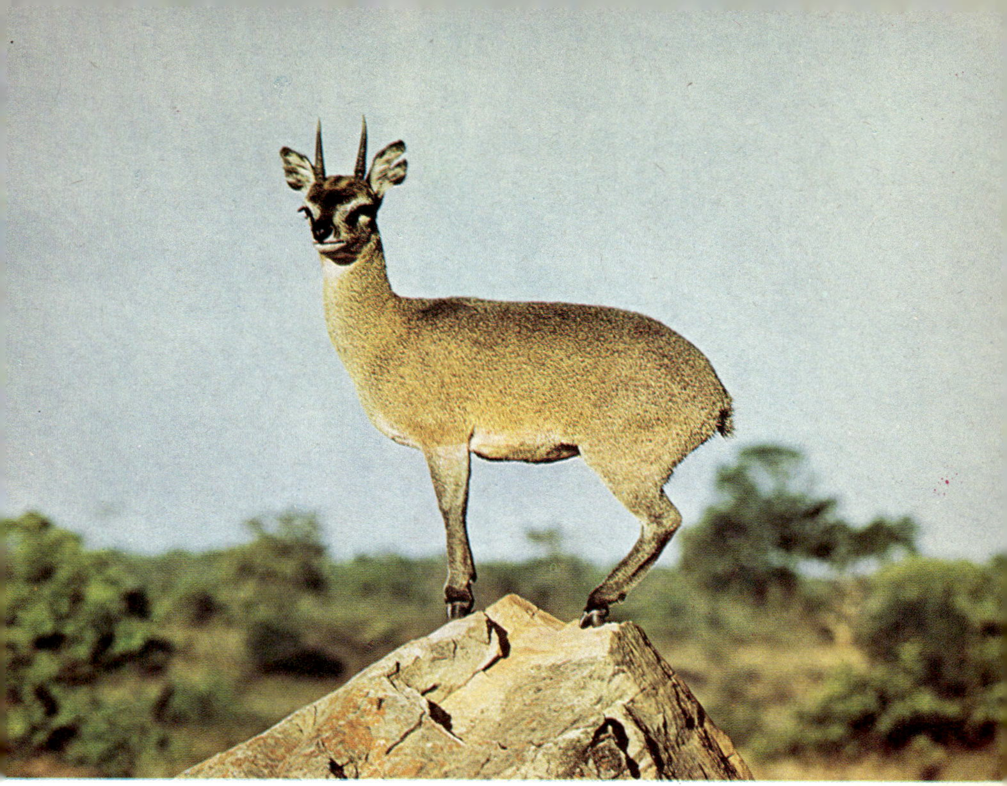

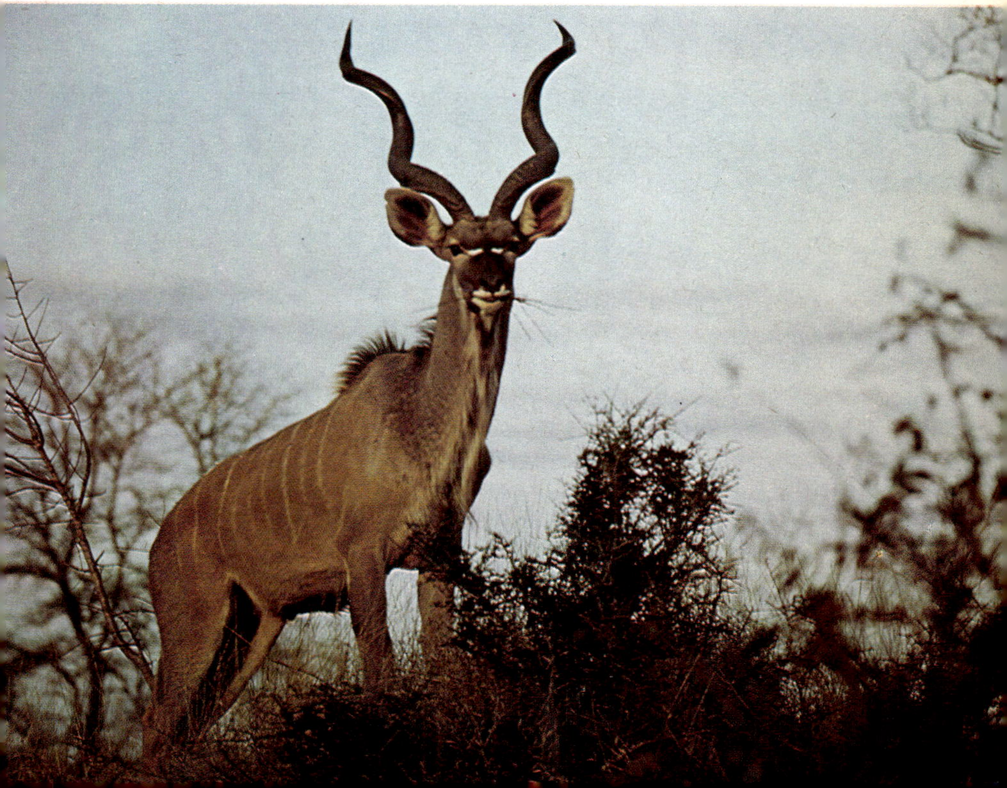

Express Motorways operate luxury coaches linking Harare with the Midlands, Bulawayo and South Africa. There is also a small-bus service between Harare and Umtali. There are public bus services in the major towns of Zimbabwe, but almost without exception, they are worth using only in an emergency. Services are infrequent – in many cases if you miss one bus, it could be well over an hour before the next one leaves.

Bus Services

Self-drive and chauffeur-driven cars are available in Harare, Bulawayo, and most other urban and tourist centres. Avis, Hertz, the local Echo Car Hire (PO Box 3430, Harare) have offices in main centres and at principal airports. Distances in Zimbabwe are not as time-consuming as they first appear. Roads are generally excellent with little traffic. A car journey of 445 km (274 miles) from Harare to Bulawayo (the industrial centre) takes just under five hours.

Car Hire

In Zimbabwe you drive on the left and give way to traffic coming from the road on your right, except where intersections are controlled. There is a general speed limit of 80 kph (50 mph) on nine-foot width tarmac and gravel surfaces, and a general limit of 100 kph (62 mph) on full-width highways, except where otherwise stated. It is advisable in practice to stop at both 'Give Way' and 'Stop' signs. There are parking meters in the cities and main towns. Traffic inspectors patrol constantly during working hours. A parking ticket costs $ 2 if you pay within the stated period.

Driving in Zimbabwe

Motor vehicles may be imported temporarily, provided they are licensed in their home countries and bear the appropriate registration plates and a nationality plaque. The International Certificate for Motor Vehicles (ICMV) is recognised. Vehicles must be insured against third party risks arising in Zimbabwe. Short term policies are obtainable at the border posts at a cost of $ 4.00 for 30 days, and $ 6.00 for 60 days, or $ 8.00 for 90 days. This rate applies to private motor-cars only.

Vehicle Insurance

The AA of Zimbabwe (PO Box 585, Harare) is affiliated to the Alliance Internationale de Tourisme and provides numerous services, including free maps, bulletins and hotel guides.

Automobile Association

For tourist information contact the Zimbabwe Tourist Board, 95 Stanley Avenue, Harare (PO Box 8052, Causeway, Harare, telephone 23150). The Board also has offices in London, Frankfurt, Los Angeles and Johannesburg. It publishes a wide range of free brochures, maps and a guide to hotels. Locally, in Zimbabwe, contact Publicity Associations in towns and cities.

Information

The Zimbabwe Tourist Board inspects and registers hotels suitable for tourists, which are graded from one star to five star. A full list of their amenities and tariffs, is available from the Board.

Hotels

Caravan and camping sites in National Parks are usually spacious and in picturesque surroundings. The tariff is $ 1.50 per site,

Caravan and Camping Sites

Opposite: Elephant in Kruger National Park. Photograph SATOUR

145

nightly. There are many other good municipal and private caravan and camping sites throughout the country.

The People Zimbabweans of all races are friendly and hospitable to visitors. Don't hesitate to ask strangers for help at any time. Ninety-nine times out of a hundred, they'll be delighted. As everywhere in Africa, politics is a good subject to stay off. In conversation it's sure to crop up. All sides tend to be sensitive, so unless you have deep convictions, remain non-committal and polite.

There is no racial discrimination in Zimbabwe; any evidence of it will be received with hostility.

Sport Golf, bowls, tennis, swimming, squash, riding and fishing are widely available. (The tigerfish is a great fighter, other fish are bream, cessa, nkupi and vundu.) In national terms cricket, soccer and rugby football rank high as spectator sports.

National Parks and Game Reserves

'Wild Life Estate' describes the 17,254 sq miles of Zimbabwe set aside as national parks, botanical reserves, historic places, sanctuaries and recreation areas. They total 11 percent of the country's area, running from the huge Wankie National Park to the 5 sq mile Eland Sanctuary near Melsetter. Comprehensive literature is available free from the Department of National Parks and Wildlife, PO Box 8365, Causeway, Harare.

In most game areas you are not allowed out of your car, to leave the roads, nor to exceed 40 kph (25 mph). Game viewing on foot is permitted in some, like the Charara Safari Area and the Mana Pools National Park. Some require permission to enter in writing.

Fishing Fishing is widely available, notably for tigerfish, bream and vundu (similar to barbel). There are limited opportunities for hunting in safari areas (see below). Firearms must be declared on arrival.

Entry charges vary. In the major parks unlimited entry for seven days costs $ 3.00.

Most parks have self-catering accommodation in lodges, cottages or chalets, where bed linen and cooking facilities are provided, at extremely reasonable rates. Thus a cottage sleeping four would be $ 6.75 per night. There are also caravan parks and camping sites. It is advisable to book well in advance through the Central Booking Office, situated in the Travel Centre, Stanley Street, Harare (PO Box 8151, Causeway, Harare, telephone 706077). Pets are not allowed in the parks. You must be in camp by sunset.

The best known of the National Parks are:

146

WANKIE NATIONAL PARK

Over 5,000 sq miles in north-west Zimbabwe some 121 km (173 miles) from the Victoria Falls. Three camps and adjacent luxury safari lodge. Large herds of elephant and buffalo, lion, giraffe, kudu, wildebeest and many other species. Open all year.

ZAMBEZI AND VICTORIA FALLS NATIONAL PARKS

The world's second greatest waterfalls are adjacent to the 230 sq mile Zambezi National Park, with elephant and sable antelope. Fishing. Hotels and camps.

MATUSADONA NATIONAL PARK

On the southern shore of Lake Kariba, elephant, buffalo, kudu, impala and waterbuck are common. Fishing.

MANA POOLS NATIONAL PARK

847 sq miles along the Zambezi river. Elephant, rhino, buffalo, prolific bird life. Camps. Open 1st May to 31st October.

RHODES MATOPOS NATIONAL PARK

1,668 sq miles south of Bulawayo, including game park, fishing, rock paintings and Cecil Rhodes' grave. Camp. Open all year.

Safari Areas

Hunting

Hunting is permitted in safari areas controlled by the Department of National Parks, and on land controlled by the Ministry of Internal Affairs and the Zimbabwe Forestry Commission. There are also thousands of square miles of private land available for hunting, as the national policy on wild life preservation is to encourage land owners to regard it as a valuable natural resource.

Registered professional hunters lease concessions in safari areas and on private land. These hunters are licensed by the Zimbabwean Government and can provide all facilities, including transport to and within hunting areas, comfortable accommodation, good food, trackers and skinners, and even weapons. Most are members of the Zimbabwean Professional Hunters' Association, which is affiliated to the International Professional Hunters' Association. A full list is available from the Zimbabwe Tourist Board.

Harare

The capital of Zimbabwe, set 1,478 m (4,850 ft) above sea level, is a clean, well-laid out and modern city, where blue skies and

147

flowering trees soften the lines of the high rise blocks, which soar beside old colonial buildings. In Cecil Square, site of the first pioneer encampment on September 12, 1890, and still the city's focal point, the jacaranda trees create a beautiful blaze of mauve from October to February. The tree gives its name to the annual Jacaranda Festival in early October, when there is a programme of cultural and sporting events. Other flowering trees, scarlet flame trees and flamboyants, line the avenues north of the city.

Roughly speaking, Harare's north–south roads are numbered. First Street is the principal shopping thoroughfare. The east–west roads are mainly avenues.

Museum The Queen Victoria Museum is at the civic centre and has an excellent wild life section depicting natural scenes, while archaeological and historical galleries illustrate the history of man in Zimbabwe from the earliest times. Opening times are 1000 to 1700, Monday to Saturday and 1430 to 1700 Sundays. There is an admission charge.

National Gallery The National Gallery is a modern art centre, with a permanent collection and a workshop school of African art, which has received wide acclaim and offers some work for sale.

Theatre Theatre companies, both visiting professional and local semi-professional ones, stage shows throughout the year. There is a regular ballet season and celebrity musicians include Harare on the Southern African circuit. For details see the local newspapers.

Curios Curios – including copper ornaments, soapstone carvings and skins – are available from numerous stores. Often, however, the curios are mass-produced for the tourist. If you plan to tour Zimbabwe, or unless you see something you especially like, wait and buy direct from African sellers on the roadsides, and at places like the Victoria Falls.

Gemstones Tumble polished and cut Zimbabwe gemstones are on sale in Harare at fairly moderate prices. You can buy them in unusual necklaces, bracelets and brooches. Local Sandawana emeralds are notable for retaining brilliant colour even in very small stones.

Hotels Hotel rooms are at a premium in Harare and advance booking is essential. There are 20 registered hotels, plus many unregistered hotels and boarding houses. Unquestionably the best known is Meikles Hotel (four star) on Cecil Square, established here in the heart of the city since 1915, though totally rebuilt with conference facilities and four restaurants. Other four star hotels are the new 200 room Monomotapa and the Jameson. Their rooms are around $ 33 per night single. Recommended three star hotels are the Ambassador and the Park Lane, while the Oasis (two star) is good. Nor should you ignore suburban hotels, since they are not far out and tariffs are lower. Such are the Feathers, George, Beverley Rocks and Red Fox, all two star. Rates at these would be about $ 10 single, bed and breakfast.

148

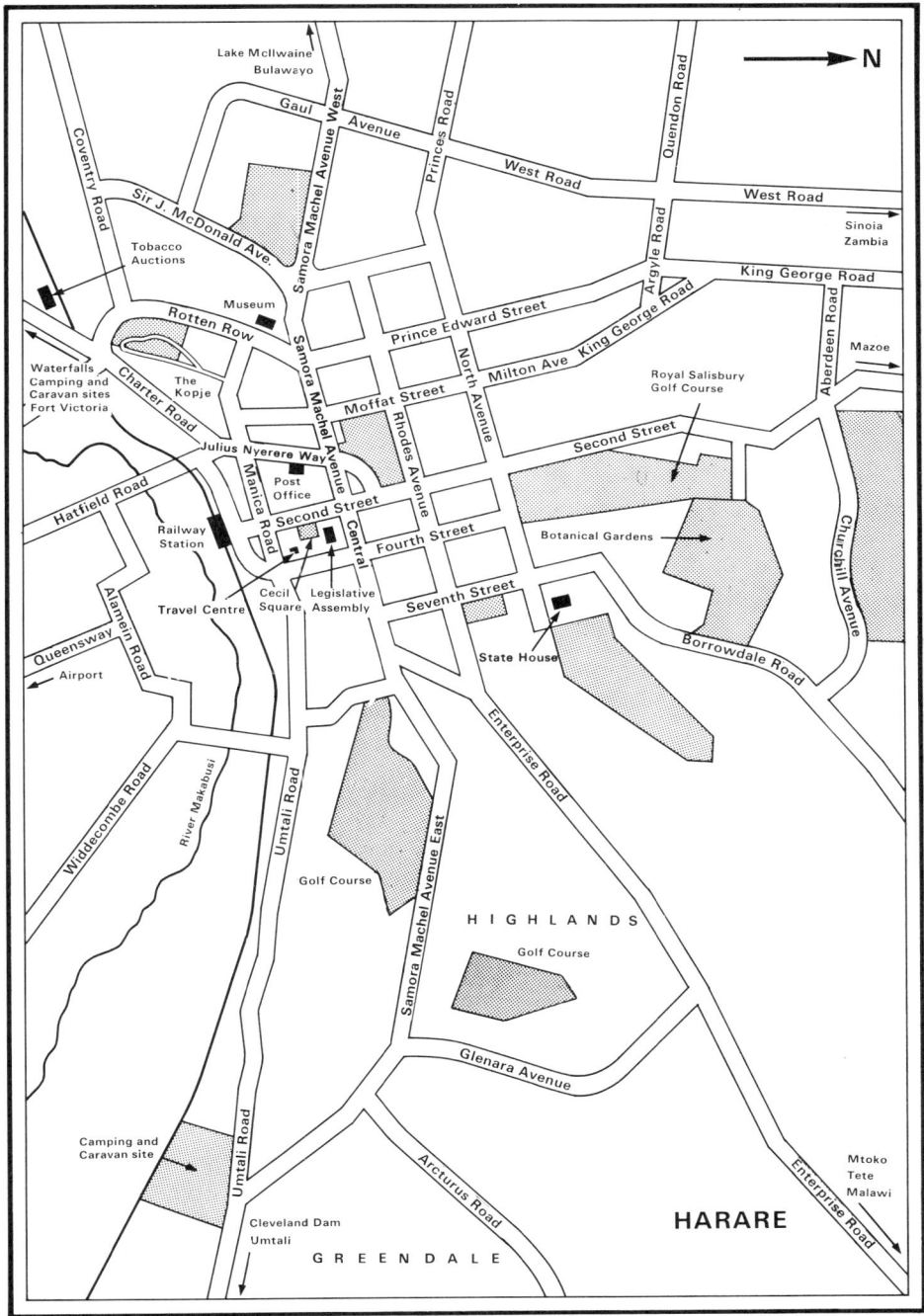

N

Lake McIlwaine
Bulawayo

Gaul Avenue

Princes Road

Quendon Road

West Road

West Road

Sinoia
Zambia

Coventry Road

Sir J. McDonald Ave.

Samora Machel Avenue West

Argyle Road

King George Road

Aberdeen Road

Mazoe

Tobacco
Auctions

Museum

Prince Edward Street

North Avenue

Milton Ave

King George Road

Rotten Row

The Kopje

Charter Road

Moffat Street

Rhodes Avenue

Second Street

Royal Salisbury
Golf Course

Churchill Avenue

Waterfalls
Camping and
Caravan sites
Fort Victoria

Julius Nyerere Way

Manica Road

Post
Office

Second Street

Central

Fourth Street

Botanical Gardens

Hatfield Road

Railway
Station

Cecil
Square

Legislative
Assembly

Seventh Street

Borrowdale Road

Travel Centre

State House

Alamein Road

Queensway

Airport

Widdecombe Road

River Makabusi

Umtali Road

Samora Machel Avenue East

Enterprise Road

Golf Course

HIGHLANDS

Golf Course

Glenara Avenue

Camping and
Caravan site

Cleveland Dam
Umtali

Umtali Road

Arcturus Road

Enterprise Road

Mtoko
Tete
Malawi

HARARE

GREENDALE

Restaurants	The visitor is well served for restaurants in the city. Standards of cuisine and decor are high and prices are reasonable, from $ 7 to $ 20 per head. Beefsteak is almost a national dish and will be found on most menus. Recommended restaurants are: The Howff (slightly out of town, but worth the trip), Chez Roger (French cuisine at the 7 Arts Centre, Avondale), Bagatelle at Meikles Hotel (expensive but ideal for a special occasion), La Fontaine (also at Meikles Hotel but less pricey), Tiffany's at the Jameson Hotel (à la carte and a superb table d'hôte menu at very reasonable cost), and the Ten Thousand Horsemen at the Monomatapa Hotel. Exotic tastes are catered for at the Bali Hai at the Monomatapa (Polynesian and Indonesian), Bamboo Inn (Chinese), Acropolis (Greek – but be prepared to queue), Guido's (Italian), King's (Portuguese), Bombay Duck (curries – plain, but cheap).

Nightclubs   Many restaurants provide music for dancing; these include The Causerie disco at Meikles, and the Ten Thousand Horsemen, while there are a selection of nightclubs serving meals. The best are the Archipelago, Time and Place (disco scene), and Samanthas.

Sport   The city has five golf courses, including the Royal Salisbury, close to town. Bowls, tennis and squash are also available to visitors.

Car hire has already been mentioned. Regular tours of Harare and surrounding areas are offered by the United Touring Company at the Travel Centre, Speke Avenue/Third Street, PO Box 2914, Harare (telephone 793701).

The Country around Harare

This part of Zimbabwe is mostly fairly flat, though sprinkled with rock topped *kopjes*, or small hills. It is typical of the great Central African plateau. You should take a trip to Salisbury Kopje, from which you get a panoramic view of the city. Skipper Hoste Drive leads out to it.

Fourteen km (nine miles) out of Harare on the Bulawayo road, the Snake Park adjoins the Salisbury Motel. Snakes from the non-poisonous to the deadly are kept at safe distance either in glass cases or in a central pit surrounded by a moat and concrete walls.

Larvon Bird Garden   Also on the Bulawayo road is the Larvon Bird Garden where there are 230 indigenous species of bird life housed in extremely well-tended aviaries and enclosures. All the birds are magnificent specimens, in beautiful condition, and range from the small Heughlin's Robin to majestic eagles, huge vultures and the African ostrich.

Lake McIlwaine   Thirty five km (22 miles) towards Bulawayo is Harare's playground, Lake McIlwaine, where you will find yachting, water skiing and fishing. The Hunyan Hills Hotel is on the northern shore, as are tea rooms. Arrangements can be made to take parties of up to 40 persons by motor launch to the Bushman paintings, where one of the finest examples of wall paintings in Zimbabwe can be seen. The lake is part of the 61 sq km (23 sq mile) Robert McIlwaine Recreational Park, including a small game park, part of which can be traversed on foot. There are duiker, steenbuck, reedbuck, oribi, zebra, eland and the whole area is ideal for bird watching: 200 species have been recorded in a single weekend. For enquiries on accommodation, camping and fishing in the Park write to the Warden, Private Bag 962, Norton.

A word at this point about swimming in African dams, lakes and rivers. Bear in mind the dangers of bilharzia infection. You will see grim signs about it. Bilharzia is caused by a microscopic organism in the water which enters the body through cuts or abrasions. It can be fatal if left untreated for a number of years – but then so can appendicitis.

Forty km (25 miles) north-east of Harare is Ewanrigg, a 283 ha botanical garden of aloes, cycads and cacti, regarded as unique in Southern and Central Africa. It's a very good place for a picnic and a beautiful sight all the year round. The best time to go, however, is in June–August when the aloes are in full flower. The cycad is a rare, palm-like, pre-historic plant. *Ewanrigg Botanical Garden*

Another 40 km (25 mile) journey, this time north of Harare, brings you through attractive hills to the rich Mazoe Valley, fed by streams and by the Mazoe Dam. You will see rolling acres of citrus trees on the Mazoe Estates, founded more than 70 years ago. The area is another recommended picnic spot. *Mazoe Valley*

Mermaids Pool is on a river 40 km (25 miles) from Harare, with a huge natural granite slide into the pool. The water is treated and filtered, and the pool is regularly drained and cleaned. There is accommodation and a restaurant. *Mermaids Pool*

If you are spending a few days in Harare, do not miss the opportunity of visiting Domboshawa, the Balancing Rocks and the beautiful Sinoia Caves.

Domboshawa is about 32 km (20 miles) north-east of the city, on the Borrowdale road. Fine views are obtained from the top of a large granite hill from which the area takes its name. A cave on the eastern slopes contains many Bushman paintings. *Domboshawa*

The Balancing Rocks never fail to fascinate people. They are giant boulders, weathered over centuries that perch seemingly precariously on top of each other. Take the Widdicombe road for 11 km (seven miles) until just before the Epworth Mission. The rocks are a short distance off the road, on your left. Some bear ancient paintings. *Balancing Rocks*

The Sinoia Caves are about 128 km (80 miles) from Harare on the Kariba road. It is an easy hour and a half drive. You pass through *Sinoia Caves*

Sinoia and six km (four miles) further on fork right to the **Caves Reserve**. The caves are not very big but they are breathtaking. The focal point is The Sleeping Pool, actually a limestone cavern, the roof of which has collapsed, giving the appearance of a natural shaft. The water is 45 m (150 ft) below the roof and the light gives it a magnificent deep blue colour. Divers have proved the pool to be at least 91 m (300 ft) deep. The main entrance to the caves takes one down an inclined passage, or one can venture down steps that reach it through the Dark Cave. In the 1880s the caves were used as retreat by the Mashona Chief Chinoyi. Today there is a hotel and restaurant by them.

The Victoria Falls and the Wankie National Park

This western corner of Zimbabwe contains some of the most breathtaking sights in all Africa, while running up the border with Zambia is one of the biggest artificial lakes in the world, Kariba.

Flying from Harare you could first visit the Falls, then go to Wankie and up to Kariba. Or, perhaps better, take the lake ferry on a fascinating 24 hour journey from Mlibizi up to Kariba. The ferry leaves Kariba once a week at 0800 on Monday, returning from Mlibizi next day (see below).

The Victoria Falls are one of the greatest natural wonders of the world and second only to Niagara in size. They are created by the Zambezi river, the only major African river to flow eastwards into the Indian Ocean, plunging from its flood plain in Zambia into a natural fault, eroded into its present shape over hundreds of thousands of years. This rent in the earth is from 70 to 108 m deep and 1,700 m – a mile – wide.

David Livingstone was the first white man to see this mighty cataract, having walked to investigate the clouds of spray which are visible from 20 miles away. He wrote in his daily journal, in November 1855, 'scenes so lovely must have been gazed upon by angels in their flight'. Local Africans call the falls 'Mosi-oa-Tunya' or 'the smoke that thunders'. They do so with reason. The clouds of spray rise 500 m into the sky and the falling water creates a continuous rumbling roar. In October, at the end of the dry season, nearly four million gallons a minute pour over. At the height of the flood, in April, twenty five times as much descends and you can only glimpse the falls every few seconds as the spray parts. So the best time for seeing them is before or after low water in November.

The crest of the Falls is divided into five sections. Devil's Cataract is closest to the Zimbabwe bank and overlooked by Livingstone's statue. The water runs deepest here at a speed of more than 160 kph (100 mph). The falls are always a little frightening, but the adventurous can descend the Chain Assisted Path to a point one third of the way down the side of the gorge. A huge baobab, almost 20 m (67 ft) in circumference and known as the Big Tree, is reached by a path heading from Livingstone's statue.

Opposite the Falls is a second cliff, acting as a superb vantage point. Tropical vegetation, constantly soaked in spray, has caused this part to be named The Rain Forest. Do not forget your raincoat and stout, flat-heeled shoes. The Rain Forest continues for three-quarters of the length of the Falls until cleaved by the Zambezi River continuing its way through the Boiling Pot, beneath Danger Point. You will find these dramatic names fully justified.

Rain Forest

Separated from Devil's Cataract by Cataract Island are the 731 m (800 yds) Main Falls. East of these are Livingstone Island and the crescent shaped Horseshoe Falls. Then comes the highest of the cataracts, Rainbow Falls, which plunge from a height of 108 m (355 ft) and are the next widest to Main Falls. A depression in the lip of the Falls, known as The Armchair occurs before the last section which is the 101 m (333 ft) Eastern Cataract.

Main Falls

The Victoria Falls is the perfect place for a holiday of two or three days. Take the 19 km (12 mile) launch trip up the Zambezi to Kandahar Island, have a picnic lunch on the shore, and if you are in luck see elephant and hippo. Or try an air trip over the Falls, known as 'The Flight of Angels'. Tours in micro-buses of the Falls area are operated by the United Touring Company, picking up tourists from the hotels. These also visit the craft village, curio shops and the crocodile ranch. Transport to and from the launch sites is also available.

Kandahar Island

Touring

At the Craft Village craftsmen work in stone, wood and bone. There is also a recreated Matabele village, depicting tribal life as it existed at the turn of the century.

Craft Village

A number of excellent curio shops sell indigenous work in wood, ivory, stone, copper and bone. The local leatherwork is also of a high standard, and gemstone jewellery is reasonably priced. In the shops haggling is frowned upon, but the wayside curio-seller will expect to have his first price refused. By being good-natured, bargains are available.

Curio shops

A visit to the nearby Crocodile Ranch is worthwhile. Here, over 2,000 live reptiles are reared, from those only 50 cm in length to adults 4·5 m long. Articles in crocodile skin may be purchased at a small museum and shop on the site.

Crocodile Ranch

Displays of tribal dancing are held nightly at a·replica of a tribal village within the grounds of the Victoria Falls Hotel.

Tribal dancing

A night at the local casino can be fun. Roulette, blackjack, and chemin de fer are the principal games, with a bank of fruit machines for the less adventurous. If one wishes to export one's winnings this must be declared to the croupier before play begins, and chips be purchased with foreign currency.

Casino

There are four hotels at the Victoria Falls, all with air-conditioned rooms and swimming pools. The most famous is the Victoria Falls

Hotels

Hotel. It is within sight of the spray rising above the Falls and is a graceful example of spacious colonial architecture. Others are the four star Makasa Sun, the three star A'Zambezi (on the banks of the river) and the two star Victoria Falls Motel. There are also chalets and national park lodges, and caravanning and camping facilities.

Sporting facilities

The Elephant Hills Country Club, overlooking the Zambezi River, has sporting facilities available to all visitors. These include squash, tennis, bowls and a 6,000 m golf course designed by Gary Player. Look out for hippo and crocodile in the water hazards! Clubs, racquets and balls are available on hire at the Club.

Livingstone

The Falls are, of course, right on the border of Zambia and close to the point where four countries meet – the other two being Namibia (South West Africa) and Botswana. It is well worth seeing something of the Zambian side, especially Livingstone, which is only a few miles away. Equally you are not far from Botswana's Chobe Reserve (see page 124), though there can be delays at the frontiers.

Zambezi National Park

Do not miss touring the Zambezi National Park, which spreads along the Zambezi River and covers 221 sq miles. There are almost 128 km (80 miles) of scenic and game viewing roads in the park, including the Zambezi Drive. This takes you to one of the few accessible stretches of the Upper Zambezi. Along it are 13 designated stopping places for fishing (particularly bream and the fighting tiger fish) and picnicking. Fishing permits are not required. The Zambezi is one of the loveliest rivers in Africa, and you will have a chance of seeing elephant, hippo and crocodile, as well as numerous species of birds.

You can also take the Chamabonda Drive, which lies in the southern half of the park and is reached from a turn-off on the Victoria Falls/Bulawayo road. In the beautiful bush country, you have outstanding opportunities to see elephant, buffalo, eland, kudu, waterbuck, impala, bushbuck, zebra and giraffe, as well as some of the finest and largest herds of sable antelope in Africa today. Lions, leopard and cheetah are occasionally seen. The drive is normally open May to November.

Access to the Falls and the Zambezi is easy. Air Zimbabwe operates scheduled services daily, there are rail connections and the 440 km (275 miles) road from Bulawayo is tarred. Flights stop at the airfield in the Wankie National Park, which lies west of the road to Bulawayo, after passing the coal mining town of Wankie. Thoughts of industrial output will rapidly disappear, however, as you approach the Park.

Wankie National Park

Zimbabwe's greatest National Park, rivalling Zambia's Luangwa Valley as one of the finest elephant sanctuaries, is situated 121 km (76 miles) from Victoria Falls and 278 km (174 miles) from Bulawayo. Within the Park are three camps – Main, Simnatella and

Robins – from which networks of game viewing roads connect with a central road system (speed limit 40 kph/25 mph). The most visited part of Wankie's 5,645 sq miles is in the north and east, where game congregates in the dry season. Wankie is basically an extension of the Kalahari, its vegetation being scrub and sparse woodland, though including teak trees.

Wankie's wildlife includes 107 species of animals, from the elephant to the shrew, and 401 recorded species of birds. A game count in November 1980 indicated an elephant population of 19,800, while among other game are buffalo, impala and numerous antelope, zebra, giraffe, wildebeest and lion, the latter being more frequently seen in the northern areas, near Robins Camp. Game-viewing platforms have been erected at some of the principal waterholes and provide an excellent, safe vantage point for photography. The elephant is a member of a family group *Elephant* whose behaviour it is particularly fascinating to watch as each takes its turn at the water-hole, waiting until a previous herd has left before drinking and wallowing to cover their skins with mud as a protection against biting insects. Even crocodile will vacate the water when a large herd arrives.

Accommodation within the Park is in serviced cottages and lodges, very cheaply priced. Main Camp, near the airfield, has a shop selling basic foods. At the time of writing the restaurant was closed. Simnatella, built on a plateau overlooking the plains has accommodation but at present no shop. Robins, in the north west near the Botswana border, is open only from May to October. Petrol is only available at Main Camp, or at the Safari Lodge (see below). For details of camping and caravan sites and for bookings *Camps* write to Central Booking Office, PO Box 8151, Causeway, Harare. Entry fee to the Park is $ 3 per adult, valid one week.

Just outside the national park boundary, near the National Park *Safari Lodge* airport, is the luxury Wankie Safari Lodge (three star. Bookings Zimbabwe Sun Hotels, PO Box 8221, Causeway). This well designed, 105 room, hotel has its private 100 sq mile game reserve and overlooks a *vlei*, or swampy waterhole which attracts many animals. The hotel runs game viewing drives and has its own bush camp, where you can stay aloft in a tree house/bedroom, savouring the excitement of the African night.

The National Park airport has daily Air Zimbabwe flights from Harare, Kariba and Victoria Falls (connecting to Bulawayo). Trains from Bulawayo and Victoria Falls stop at Dett, but during the night, so you must arrange transport in advance. Game viewing tours and airport transfers are arranged by UTC, using special safari vehicles.

Hunting is permitted in the Matetsi area north of Wankie between *Kazuma Pan* May and September, within which lies the inaccessible 120 sq mile *National Park* Kazuma Pan National Park. The natural pans here flood seasonally, attracting gemsbok, oribi and cheetah, plus a large variety of waterfowl. Game viewing on foot is allowed, but you must obtain entry permission from the game warden at Victoria Falls. There are no facilities in the park.

Kariba and the Zambezi Valley

Kariba Dam

Lake Kariba is many things: a 1,930 sq mile expanse of blue, island studded water, fringed by mountains; a year-round source of water for an abundant animal and bird life; a playground for water sport enthusiasts; and home of the most challenging freshwater fishing in Africa. Yet it was never intended to be any of these things, for the damming of the Zambezi River by the slender 128 m (420 ft) curving concrete wall, completed in 1961, was undertaken to provide hydro-electric power for the industries of Zimbabwe and Zambia.

Batonka Tribe

Until 1960 the remote Zambezi Valley was the home of the Batonka people, whose primitive huts may still be seen in certain parts of the Kariba area. The Batonkas held that the river spirit, Nyaminyami, would never allow the completion of the dam, and many refused to leave their villages until they were forced to by the rising waters. They still believe he waits, in the depths of the lake, to free the river from its bondage. When the great gates in the dam wall are opened, each discharging 1·5 million litres of water a second, it is easy to imagine a primitive and hostile force at work.

Operation Noah

Humans were not the only ones displaced by the lake as it grew. Animals were marooned on hilltops that overnight became islands, and which often disappeared altogether. To rescue them, Operation Noah was organised in 1959/60 and thousands of animals, from elephants to snakes, were saved in an operation that caught the imagination of the world.

Kariba Township

Casino

At Kariba township, which is built on steep hills 370 m (1,215 ft) above the Lake, hotels and harbours have been created, providing sophisticated tourist amenities. Among the five hotels are the two star Lake View and down on the lakeshore, the two star Cutty Sark and the Caribbea Bay Resort. The Resort is designed as a Sardinian style village, and accommodation is in self-contained casitas, all of which are air-conditioned, with a restaurant, shop, marina, swimming pools, and caravan and camping site. The Kariba Casino is situated here.

Indeed, the town has become a considerable holiday centre, helped by a good road from Harare and daily scheduled flights (going on to Victoria Falls). The best time to visit Kariba is between April and September, the dry winter months. The hottest months – and they really are steaming – are October and November. Take salt tablets if you visit Kariba during the rainy season, and malaria pills whenever you go.

Sightseeing

A day of sightseeing could include a visit to the dam wall, to the crocodile farm, and a tour of the township with its many

156

viewpoints over the lake and its unique church of St. Barbara, which is built in the shape of a coffer dam and which commemorates the workers who lost their lives in the construction of the dam and power station. For the technical, the Kariba dam is a double-curvature concrete arch, with a maximum height of 36 m (420 ft) and a crest length of 617 m (2,025 ft). It carries a 12 m (40 ft) wide road, and contains about 1,275,000 cu yards of concrete. There are six flood gates, each 9·14 m (30 ft) high by 9·45 m (31 ft) wide. The capacity of the lake when full is 40,837,500 million gallons, and the length from tip to tip is about 281 km (175 miles).

Everyone who visits Kariba should embark on the lake, for it is only from this vantage point that the character of this inland sea can be appreciated. You can hire sailing dinghies and power boats from a number of operators, learn to waterski, or join regular cruises. Some cruises skirt the shoreline where, particularly in the late afternoons, animals come to drink or wallow in the shallows.

Boating facilities

The adventurous visitor after an unusual 'in the wilds' game viewing trip should try Mana Pools, a wildlife paradise in the Zambezi Valley east of Kariba, via Makuti. This National Park occupies 2,196 sq km (848 sq miles) along the river and is not widely visited and is only open May 1 to October 31. You must get prior permission from the Warden, Private Bag 2061, Karoia. There is a camp site. It's advisable to obtain clear directions on the route from Makuti, past Marangora, a distance of 101 km (63 miles). This said, the effort is worth it.

Mana Pools

The area is one of the most prolific game areas in Zimbabwe. You will see large numbers of elephant, and herds of buffalo of up to 700 head. Also watch for lion, leopard, rhino, warthog, wild dogs, zebra, sable and so on. Mana Pools and the Zambezi River are renowned for their fishing. Water may be drawn from the river, but keep a sharp look out for crocodiles. Don't forget to boil your water and take normal anti-malarial precautions. Also take an insecticidal spray with you to guard against tsetse fly bites.

Westwards from Kariba, the lake shores are largely untouched wilderness, where safari companies provide facilities to enjoy the solitude and scenic splendour of these remote areas with their superb gameviewing and fishing.

Along the southern shore, extending west from the dramatic Sanyati Gorge, lies the wildlife heritage of the Matusadona National Park. The reserve covers 521 sq miles, one third of which is provided with bush roads. Its shoreline and the heavily wooded and well watered plain form a habitat for many species of game, large and small, while water birds roost in the whitened branches of drowned trees. Special boats take one game viewing here and it is a unique experience. You can always go out in the bush on foot from camps at Muwu on Elephant Point and Ume, on the mouth of the Ume river.

Matusadona National Park

157

Island Resorts   An exciting alternative is to stay at the island resorts of Spurwing or Fothergill, a few kilometres offshore from the Matusadona National Park. Accommodation is in thatched huts, but full hotel meals and bar services are available. The operators provide game viewing cruises along the wooded shorelines, while buffalo and other animals swim to the islands themselves. The islands are served by boat services from Kariba, or by float plane.

The most luxurious safari camp on the lake is west of Matusadona in the Bumi Hills, where Club Bumi offers an all-inclusive package for $ 90 a day, where you can stay on fully equipped houseboats as an alternative to the luxurious lodge. Bookings through Zimbabwe Sun Hotels, Harare, who organise the flight from Kariba.

Float plane   Lake Air operates a float plane charter service from Kariba to the island resorts and to the western end of Lake Kariba, where there are minor resorts at Binga and Milibisi, best known for their fishing. Lake Air (PO Box 102, Kariba) offer excursion returns down here and to the Victoria Falls, landing on the Zambezi for an

Car Ferry   overnight stop. However the most useful service is the weekly *Sea Horse* car ferry from Kariba to Mlibizi, which enables motorists to make the circuit round to the Falls and Wankie, cutting out 1,250 km (781 miles) driving, since there is no direct Kariba to Wankie road. It is run by Kariba Ferries on Mondays. Single fare is $ 40.

Bulawayo and the Matopos National Park

Travelling further in to Zimbabwe from the Falls and Wankie, you reach Bulawayo, the industrial centre. This is in Matabeleland, former stronghold of the Matabele people where they were led by Mzilikazi and Lobengula. Bulawayo used to be Chief Lobengula's kraal, and its name means 'Place of Slaughter'. Now it is a city of 200,000 people, and the Zimbabwe Trade Fair is held here for 10 days in early April. It is an ideal base for visiting the south of the country.

Museums   Bulawayo's National Museum illustrates the history and mineral wealth of Zimbabwe, and the wildlife section includes the second largest mounted elephant in the world. The Railways Museum, on Prospect Avenue and First Street, Raylton, displays old steam locomotives and railway memorabilia.

State House, a delightful white porticoed building nearly five km (three miles) out is on the site of Lobengula's royal kraal, of which there is a model in the rondavel in the garden, where Rhodes lived before the house was built. The Snake Park and Aviary are in Hillside Road.

Craft Centre   Contemporary ceramic sculpture and pottery is made and sold at the Mzilikazi Arts and Craft Centre (mornings only).

The shopping district centres on Main Street around the junction with Eighth Avenue. The Jairos Jiri Craft shop, famous for Africana, is on the corner of Grey Street and Selbourne Avenue. *Shopping*

The city has nine registered hotels, and many more unregistered establishments and boarding houses. The two three star hotels are the Bulawayo Sun Hotel and the Holiday Inn. Others recommended are the two star Selborne, New Royal, Grey's Inn and Cecil. All are situated in the city centre. *Hotels*

The choice of restaurants is fairly wide, particularly for steak houses. These include Friar Tuck's, The Calabash and The Cavern. For *cuisine* which is a little more *haute* try Maison Nic; the Italian food at the Capri is consistently good, and the *aficianado* of Spanish food will enjoy the Granada. *Restaurants*

For a taxi ring Bulawayo 60221 or 60704. Yorks Car Hire on Grey Street (telephone 63382) hire out drive yourself cars, as do Avis (telephone 82447) and Hertz (telephone 61402). The Railway Travel Bureau is at 87 Abercorn Street. A daily coach runs to Fort Victoria (see below). Local buses start from the City Hall on Eighth Street. There are several travel agents in the city. *Transport*

Bulawayo is in flat, sparsely wooded cattle ranching country. To the east, off the Gwelo road, in the direction of Fort Victoria, are three interesting sets of ruins, at Dhlo Dhlo (96 km/60 miles), Regina and Naletale, the latter having the finest ancient decorative walling yet found in Zimbabwe. Twenty-two km (14 miles) south-west of Bulawayo, at Khami, are even more extensive remains, with relics displayed in a site museum. Lobengula used the main hill here for rain making. The ruins are far older of course and very like those at Zimbabwe. They consist of a series of terraces and passages supported by massive granite walls, some of them overlooking Khami Dam and Gorge. Building in stone began in this area over 500 years ago, while some relics found at the site are over 100,000 years old. *Khami Ruins*

The main attraction near Bulawayo, however, is the Rhodes Matopos National Park, where the hills rise dramatically out of the flat landscape. *The Rhodes Matopos National Park*

There is a stark, dramatic splendour in these massive granite hills. When Rhodes reached the boulder-strewn crest he exclaimed: 'The peacefulness of it all . . . the chaotic grandeur of it . . . I call this one of the views of the world'. The hill was in fact called Malindidzimu, a place sacred to the Matabele as being the home of benevolent spirits. It is now known as 'World's View'. When Rhodes was buried there, the firing party, in deference to Matabele beliefs, did not discharge their rifles. In addition to Rhodes' grave and the impressive granite monument commemorating the slaughter of Major Allan Wilson and his Shangani Patrol, the hilltop is also the burial place of Sir Leander Starr Jameson,

Rhodes' friend and lieutenant, and Sir Charles Coglan, who was the first Minister of the colony.

The Rhodes Matopos National Park combines some of the finest examples of Zimbabwe's prehistoric rock art, a game park covering 2,500 acres, and many facilities for recreation and relaxation. Ask for directions to the rock paintings, which are to be found in easily accessible caves, such as *Pomongwe* (small melon), *Bambata* (to caress) and *Nswatugi* (place of jumping). Among the wildlife are wildebeest, zebra, warthog, ostrich and rhino of both the black and the rare white species, four of which were brought from Natal in 1966. The curious balancing rock formations are the haunt of the little dassie or rock rabbit, and the agile klipspringer. In the rock's more inaccessible heights are the nests of the rare black eagle.

Fishing

For the fisherman, numerous dams have been built in picturesque settings within the park, and some of these provide excellent bass and bream fishing, as well as facilities for boating and picnicking. Licences to fish in the park are obtainable from the Park Warden, Private Bag K 5142, Bulawayo, from the Rhodes Matopos Hotel and from certain sports-goods shops in Bulawayo. Chalet accommodation and camping sites in the Park can be booked through the Warden.

Chipangali Wild Life Orphanage

Situated 23 km (14 miles) south of Bulawayo, the Chipangali provides a home for orphaned, sick or abandoned wild animals. There are lion, leopard, cheetah; many species of antelope; bush pig and warthog, and a large collection of reptiles and birds. The Orphanage is open daily except Mondays, and on all public holidays except Christmas Day.

Fort Victoria, Zimbabwe and Lake Kyle

Fort Victoria is Zimbabwe's oldest town and a minor tourist centre. Within easy distance of it are the fascinating and eerie Zimbabwe Ruins, Lake Kyle, two extensive National Parks, two game reserves and rolling miles of granite hills and deep ravines. It came into existence because the Pioneer column in 1890 kept well south to avoid the hostile Matabele tribes on the march to Mashonaland, making its way east of the normal trail through Bulawayo on to the Mashonaland plateau through Providential Pass, which drops down to the present site of Fort Victoria. Even today the town has kept some of the atmosphere of these pioneering days. From the

Bell Tower

bell tower in the Old Fort, the 'curfew' is tolled nightly at nine o'clock. A small pioneer museum is in another tower.

During World War II many Italian prisoners of war were interned in the area, and the artists among them decorated the Roman Catholic Church just outside the town, giving it a richly coloured style not often found in Zimbabwe.

Fort Victoria has the two star Chevron Hotel and the Flamboyant Motel, but has declined as a tourist centre because the principal attraction in the locality is now Zimbabwe, where the Zimbabwe Ruins hotel has been renovated. The Glenlivet Hotel (one star) is 45 km (28 miles) away at Lake Kyle: see below.

The Zimbabwe Ruins are 29 km (18 miles) from Fort Victoria and were first revealed to the outside world in 1868 when a hunter, Adam Renders, stumbled upon this mysterious, deserted city. No-one knows what happened to the people who built Zimbabwe. Archaeologists believe it is African in origin and flourished from AD 1200 to 1450, being the largest of some 150 sites in the country.

Zimbabwe Ruins

The earliest ruins are to be found on what is called the Acropolis, a high hill where intricate dry-stone walls seem to cling precariously to the steep granite slopes, incorporating huge boulders in their course. Some of the most interesting archaeological finds were made in this complex of ruins. From this lofty vantage point the visitor may look down on the Valley of Ruins where a number of individual ruins are dominated by the Temple, or Great Enclosure, with its walls over 10 m (33 ft) high and 106 m (350 ft) wide.

Acropolis

The most striking feature within the Temple ruin is the Conical Tower which is 10 m (33 ft) high with a base circumference of 17 m (56 ft). The purpose of this magnificent example of dry-stone masonry has defied explanation, although many scientific observers believe it was associated with fertility rites. A drawing of it is at the start of this chapter.

Near the ruins is a reconstruction of a Karanga village, which illustrates the way of life of the local people at the time of the discovery of Zimbabwe. Huts and artefacts have been painstakingly re-created, and a potter may be seen at work making pots by the ancient African method – without the aid of a potter's wheel. A popular figure here in the village is the witchdoctor, who will 'throw the bones' and tell one's fortune.

Kyle National Park is near Zimbabwe on the south-eastern edge of the highveld. Centred on Lake Kyle the park offers the visitor beautiful scenery, boating and fishing. The park is best known, however, for its 69 sq miles of game reserve situated on the lake's northern shore, where pony trails and walks are organised. There are over 30 rare white, or square-lipped rhino in this reserve, plus a great variety of antelope including the very rare oribi, Lichtenstein's hartebeeste, and nyala. The Park is open the whole year round, although in extremely wet conditions some of the roads may be closed. Camping and caravanning facilities and lodge accommodation are available. Contact the Warden, Private Bag 9136, Fort Victoria.

Kyle National Park

You should also visit Mushandike Sanctuary, 38 km (24 miles) from Fort Victoria, which provides excellent fishing and boating in lovely surroundings. Sable, kudu, waterbuck and smaller antelope can be seen. It has furnished accommodation in two camps. Enquiries to the Warden, Mushandike Park, Private Bag 9036, Fort Victoria.

Mushandike Sanctuary

The Eastern Highlands

The Eastern Highlands lie along Zimbabwe's eastern border with Mozambique. They extend for about 350 km (219 miles) from Inyanga in the north to the Chimanimani Mountains in the south. Mid-way along the mountain chain is the small city of Umtali and the Vumba Mountains area. The highlands are for the motorist, as they are not served by Air Zimbabwe, and the National Railways of Zimbabwe and the coach services connect only Harare with Umtali.

Inyanga

Inyanga has the distinction of being the location of Zimbabwe's highest mountain, Mount Inyangani, 2,790 m (9,154 ft). It is here that the rare aloe *(a. inyangensis)* is to be found growing on its highest peaks, and the dwarf msasa forests which clothe many westward-facing slopes are a botanical curiosity. The elevation of this area is generally high, but the country is open and accessible, and contains spectacular waterfalls and walks along winding footpaths through fragrant pine forests.

No part of Zimbabwe is as rich in drives of scenic beauty as Inyanga, but you should go a short way off the beaten track and look at the vast complex of forts, pits, enclosures and terraces built near the present town. They cover some 129 sq km (50 sq miles) and what tribe of people originally built them from the Iron Age onwards is a mystery. One of the most curious things about Inyanga and Zimbabwe is that no African tribes of modern Zimbabwe know how to construct in the same way, nor is there any folk memory of how the ruins were made. Possibly the original inhabitants were driven out or exterminated by the migration of Bantu tribes from the north in the eighteenth century.

National Park

There is a strong local historical association with Cecil Rhodes, for he purchased an enormous estate, which on his death formed the nucleus of the Inyanga National Park. One hotel incorporates his old homestead within its structure. This hotel, Rhodes Inyanga, is set in an elevated position above Rhodes Dam. There is a wide choice of hotels in the Inyanga area adjacent to the Park, the best being the Troutbeck Inn (three star) and excellent caravan and camping facilities. There are abundant trout streams in the Park and five stocked dams have been created. Licenses are available from the Park offices.

Fishing

Umtali

The city of Umtali is set halfway along the line of the Eastern Highlands, where the roads from Melsetter, Harare and Inyanga meet. Situated among steep, wooded hills, and attractively laid out with wide, tree-lined streets, it lays a strong claim to be Zimbabwe's most beautiful town. It has a modern civic centre and extensive parks.

Museum

A history of this part of the Eastern Highlands is graphically shown in the local museum, which also has a transport gallery showing examples of horse-drawn carriages and early locomotives.

162

Recommended hotels in Umtali are the three star Wise Owl Motel and the Manica Hotel. Both have *à la carte* restaurants. Other hotels in the city are the two star Christmas Pass Hotel and Aloe Park Motel, and the one star Impala Arms.

Thirteen km (eight miles) from Umtali is La Rochelle, the beautiful *La Rochelle* home of the late Sir Stephen and Lady Courtauld. Here 14 ha (35 acres) of gardens include rare orchids, unusual trees and ornamental shrubs. The grounds display a variety of formal gardens and careful landscaping. There are also numerous water gardens, waterfalls and fountains – all within the setting of the forested Penhalonga Valley.

A few kilometres outside Umtali the road to the Vumba mountains *Vumba* begins its scenic climb, winding through steep mountains and rolling farmland. At each turn new vistas over the surrounding countryside are revealed, and viewpoints have been created at appropriate locations.

Twenty-nine km (18 miles) from Umtali is the Vumba Botanical *Botanical* Garden, beyond the dense Bunga Forest. Here there are 30 ha (74 *Garden* acres) of landscaped flower gardens set within a larger area of 'natural' woodland on the eastern slopes of the mountains. Indigenous and exotic flora provide year-round colour and the hydrangeas, azaleas and fuchsias here are numbered in their thousands.

The name Vumba means 'mist', and the sight from one's hotel of the mountain peaks appearing through morning clouds gives the area a fairyland quality.

There are three hotels in the Vumba Mountains: the White Horse *Hotels* Inn (only eight rooms, so there is individual service) and Leopard Rock Hotel (built like a Scottish country house), both two star, and the English Mountain Lodge Hotel (one star). All have swimming pools and extensive views.

Driving south from Umtali one may take the scenic road through *Chimanimani* Cashel to the village of Melsetter and the rugged splendours of the *Mountains* Chimanimani Mountains, the peaks of which, rising to over 2,500 m (8,200 ft), dominate the eastern horizon. This is a place for the ardent hiker and climber, for access to the mountains is by foot only, but they should always be treated with respect as the region is subject to sudden storms and mists. Three hours' hard walk from the foot of the mountains takes you to the mountain hut accommodation, provided by National Parks, where there are separate dormitories for men and women with bunk beds and sleeping bags with linen available.

The only hotel in Melsetter is the Melsetter Hotel (two star) facing the Chimanimani Mountains. A golf course is less than a km (half a mile) away and there is trout fishing high up in the mountains. Bridal Veil Falls, just behind Melsetter village, is a favourite picnic *Bridal Veil* spot. A delicate curtain of mountain water plunges into a large *Falls* pool.

Chirinda Forest An hour's drive south of the Mountains brings the visitor to the green tea estates of Gazaland, and the Chirinda Forest Botanical Reserve which is one of the last remaining areas of the great tropical forest which, in primeval time, covered the whole of this part of Africa. Inside the cool peace of the forest you will see rich bird life and magnificent age-old trees. In spring, the forest is particularly beautiful. The common ironwood trees bloom white pea-like flowers.

The stopping place for this area is Chipinga, where the Chipinga Hotel (one star) is a true 'local', frequented by farmers.

Useful Facts—ZIMBABWE

Banks

The following banks are represented: Barclays International Bank, Grindlays Bank Limited, Rhobank Limited, Standard Bank Limited. Banks are open Monday, Tuesday, Thursday and Friday: 0830 to 1400 (some country branches close at 1300 on these days); Wednesday 0830 to 1200; Saturday 0830 to 1100.

Currency Regulations

Visitors may bring up to $ 20 in Zimbabwe banknotes and any amount in foreign banknotes, but are advised to register the amount of foreign banknotes with Customs at entry, as otherwise they will be allowed to re-export only $ 20 in Zimbabwe banknotes and the equivalent of $ 20 in foreign banknotes. These provisions do not apply to travellers' cheques. At the time of writing the Zimbabwe dollar was worth 70p sterling or US $ 1.54.

Customs

A visitor may import, for his own use, used clothing, and used personal effects, including used binoculars, typewriters, radios, tape-recorders, dictaphones, cameras, camping and sports equipment. Consumable stores are liable for duty, but an allowance is made for goods in use. You may bring in free of duty $ 50 of goods, but alcohol is limited to five litres per adult of which only two litres may be spirits.

The importation of citrus, tomato and banana fruit or plants is forbidden. For clearance on other fruit and plants write to the Ministry of Agriculture, Private Postbag 7701, Causeway, Harare.

Visitors wishing to import firearms and ammunition must declare their weapons at the border post, produce their permit for their country of residence, and complete a form which allows them to bring the weapon into the country for a limited period.

Diplomatic Representation

Representatives of the following countries have offices in Harare: Algeria, Australia, Belgium, Bulgaria, Canada, China, Cuba,

Denmark, Egypt, France, Ghana, Germany (Democratic Republic), Germany (Federal Republic), Greece, Holy See, India, Italy, Japan, Kenya, Korea (Democratic Peoples Republic), Libya, Malawi, Mozambique, Nigeria, Holland, Pakistan, Portugal, Romania, Sweden, Switzerland, Tanzania, Togo, United States of America, United Kingdom, Yugoslavia, Zaire, Zambia.

Health Requirements

With the exception of children under one year of age, all travellers arriving in Zimbabwe from infected areas are required to possess valid vaccination certificates against smallpox and yellow fever.

Passports and Visas

All visitors require valid passports. The nationals of the following countries do not need visas:
1. British subjects being 'Citizen of the United Kingdom and Colonies';
2. Nationals of: Andorra, Australia, Austria, Bahamas, Bangladesh, Barbados, Belgium, Botswana, Brunei, Canada, Cyprus, Denmark, Dominica, Fiji, France (including French Departments and Territories), Guadeloupe, French Guinea, Martinique, Reunion, St. Pierre & Miquelon, French Polynesia, New Hebrides, New Caledonia, Crozet Archipelago, Kerguelen Islands, St. Paul, Nouvelle Amsterdam and Terre Adelie, Gambia, Ghana, Greece, Grenada, Guyana, Iceland, India, Ireland, Italy, Jamaica, Kenya, Kiribati, Lesotho, Liechtenstein, Luxembourg, Malawi, Malaysia, Maldive Islands, Malta, Mauritius, Monaco, Nauru, Nepal, Netherlands, New Zealand, Nigeria, Norway, Pakistan, Papua New Guinea, Portugal, Saint Lucia (W. Ind.), Samoa (Western), San Marino, Seychelles, Sri Lanka, , Swaziland, Sweden, Switzerland, Tanzania, Tonga, Trinidad & Tobago, Tuvalu, Uganda, United States of America, Zambia.

Nationals of the following countries must make prior application for entry visas to the Chief Immigration Officer, Private Bag 7717, Causeway, Harare, from whom the prescribed forms of application can be obtained: Afghanistan, Albania, Algeria, Angola, Bhutan, Bulgaria, Burma, Cape Verde Islands, China (Peoples Republic), Cuba, Czechoslovakia, Ethiopia, Germany (East-Democratic Republic), Guinea Bissau, Hungary, Iran, Iraq, Kampuchea, Korea (North-Democratic Peoples Republic), Laos, Lebanon, Libya, Mongolia, Mozambique, Philippines, Poland, Romania, Somalia, Sudan, Syria, Tibet, USSR, Vietnam (Soc. Rep.), Yemen (Arab Rep.), Yemen (Peoples Dem. Rep.), Yugoslavia.

Nationals of other countries may be granted entry visas on arrival, provided they are in possession of a return ticket to their country of domicile and have sufficient funds to cover their stay in this country.

Postal Rates

Internal – letters not over 20 g, 5c.
Airmail – Europe, Great Britain and N. Ireland, Gibraltar, Ireland, Malta, 17c per 10 g.
Aerogrammes – 9c to any destination.

Public Holidays

Public Holidays, when banks, shops and Government offices close are: New Year's Day (January 1), Good Friday, Independence Day (April 18), Easter Saturday, Easter Monday, Workers' Day (May 1), Africa Day (May 25), Heroes' Day (August 11), Heroes' Day (August 12), Christmas Day (December 25), Boxing Day (December 26).

Sales Tax

Sales tax of ten percent is payable on all purchases of goods and services within Zimbabwe. This includes hotel accommodation, airline and train tickets. Some shops and hotels build this ten percent into their price; ascertain this point before purchase or signing of register.

Shopping Hours

Shops are generally open from 0800 until 1700.

Time

Time is two hours ahead of GMT.

Regional Air Services and Excursions in Southern Africa

Jan Smuts airport, Johannesburg, is the focal point of flights in Southern Africa and is served by many international airlines, as well as all the local carriers.

The dominant airline is South African Airways, operating some 570 flights per week linking major centres in the Republic and in Namibia both with Johannesburg and with Botswana, Lesotho, Malawi, Mauritius, Mozambique, Reunion, the Transkei, Swaziland, Zambia and Zimbabwe, where points served direct include the Victoria Falls. SAA's fleet includes 13 wide body Boeing 747's, six Airbus A300s and 30 other jets, mostly Boeing 727s and 737s. The airline has a computerised reservation system (SATAMARS) which also handles car hire and hotel bookings.

SAA services work in association with those of Air Botswana, LAM, Air Malawi, Lesotho Airways, Royal Swazi Air, Zambia Airways and

Air Zimbabwe. Relevant services to neighbouring territories are detailed in SAA timetables. There are also feeder services operated by Comair, Namib Air, Theron Airways and other firms, linking minor centres with major airports.

Excursion Fares

Concession and excursion fares are available from all points on the SAA international network, APEX fares from Europe being notably good value. Cheap flights from Luxembourg to Johannesburg are operated by Luxavia Airways, 11 Grant Buildings, London WC2. 01-839 5221. There are useful excursion savings on fares within the Republic, but tickets must be purchased there.

Air Zimbabwe runs a cheap coach air service between Harare (Salisbury) and Johannesburg. Within Zimbabwe the airline offers various excursions, including a one day excursion to Kariba, all inclusive, at $58. There is a Tuesday to Thursday tour of Kariba and Victoria Falls at an all inclusive cost of $183 and for $299 the airline offers a six day Harare–Kariba–Wankie–Victoria Falls–Bulawayo–Harare tour.

Some Coach Tours in South Africa

South African Railways offer a series of coach tours which include food and accommodation and are excellent value for money. Four of the best are:

A five day tour from Johannesburg to the Eastern Transvaal and Kruger National Park, departing Tuesdays. This includes three nights in rest camps in the Park. The cost is R 259 per person.

A six day trip via the Kruger National Park, Swaziland and Hluhluwe Game Reserve to Durban, departing Mondays. This includes two nights in Kruger and two nights in Hluhluwe. The price is R 369 per person. The same trip can be made from Durban departing Sundays.

An eight day trip from Cape Town to Johannesburg, or vice versa, via the Garden Route, Republic of Transkei and Drakensberg areas. The cost is R 466. There are also shorter Garden Route tours from Cape Town.

A seven day trip to Walvis Bay and Etosha National Park, departing Wednesdays from Windhoek. You stay at Okaukuejo and at the historic Namutoni Fort. The cost is R 377 per person.

A greater variety of tours, including similar routes are run by Grosvenor Tours and Safaris (PO Box 6932, Johannesburg) and Springbok Atlas Safaris (PO Box 115, Cape Town). These range from a two day Garden Route coach tour (R 240) to an 18 day tour of Namibia (R 560). By contrast Afro Ventures (PO Box 10848, Johannesburg) run more adventurous camping and hotel safaris, usually in Land Rovers, to the Cape, Namibia and Botswana.

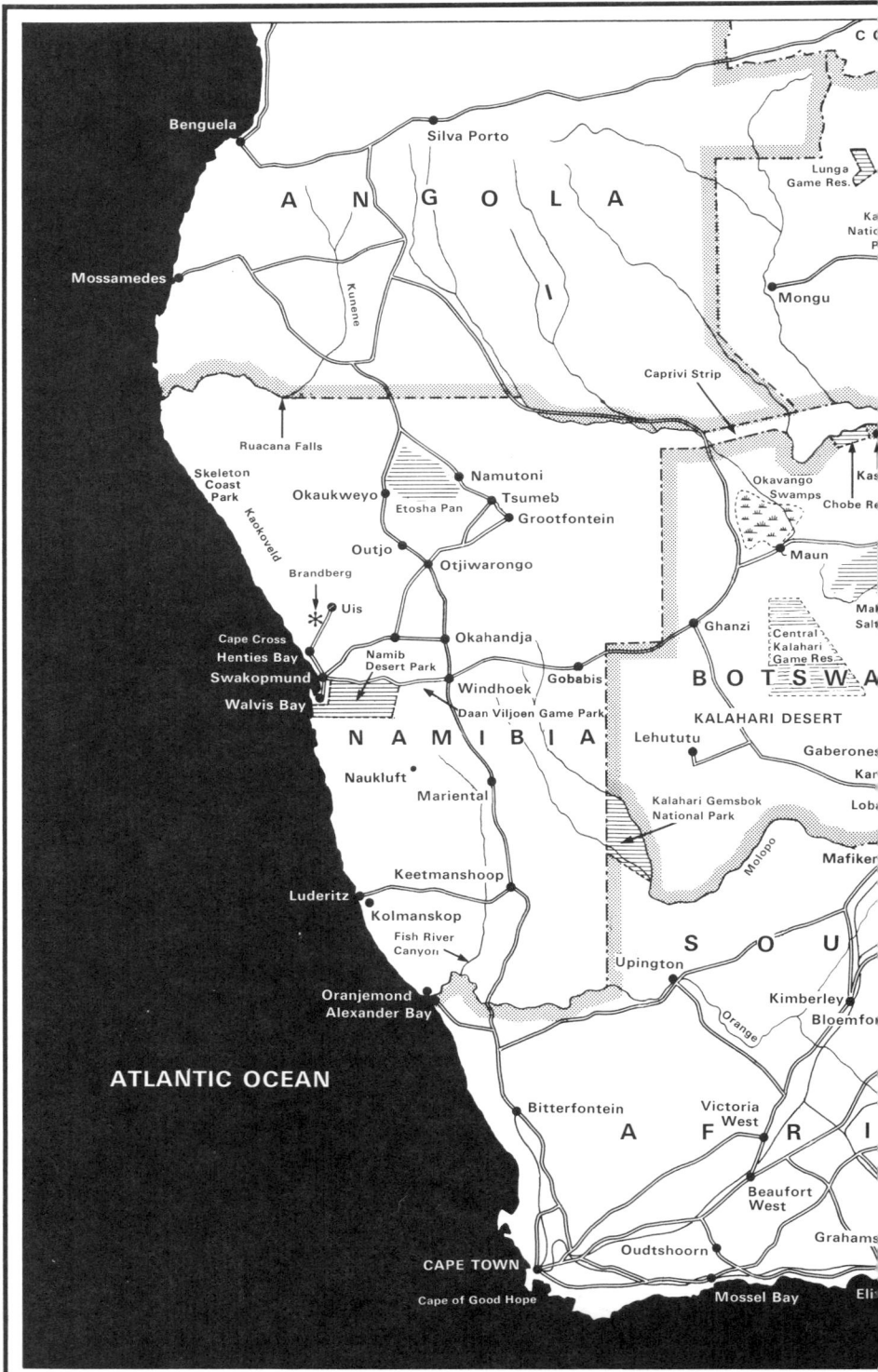

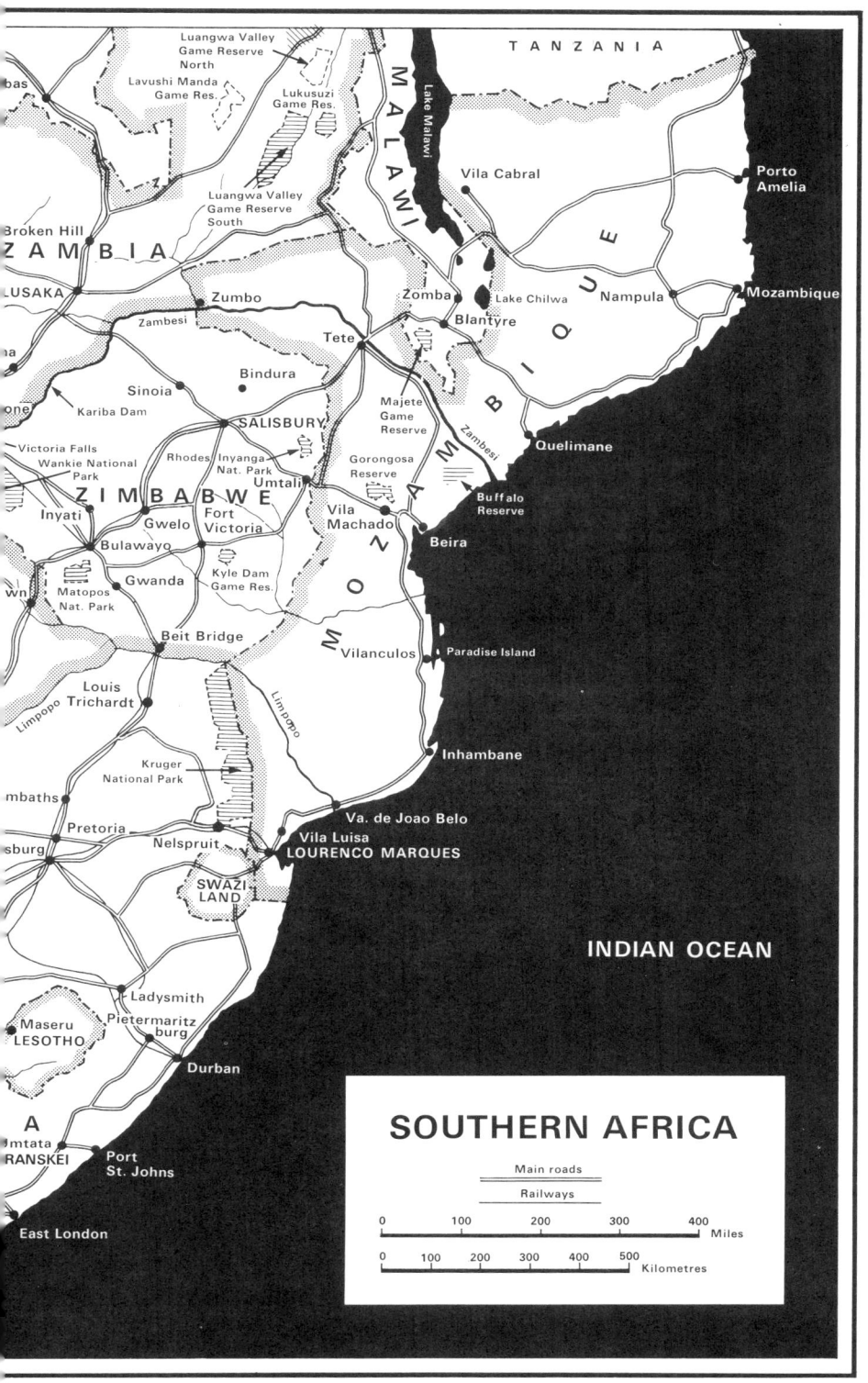

SOUTHERN AFRICA

Main roads

Railways

| 0 | 100 | 200 | 300 | 400 |
Miles

| 0 | 100 | 200 | 300 | 400 | 500 |
Kilometres

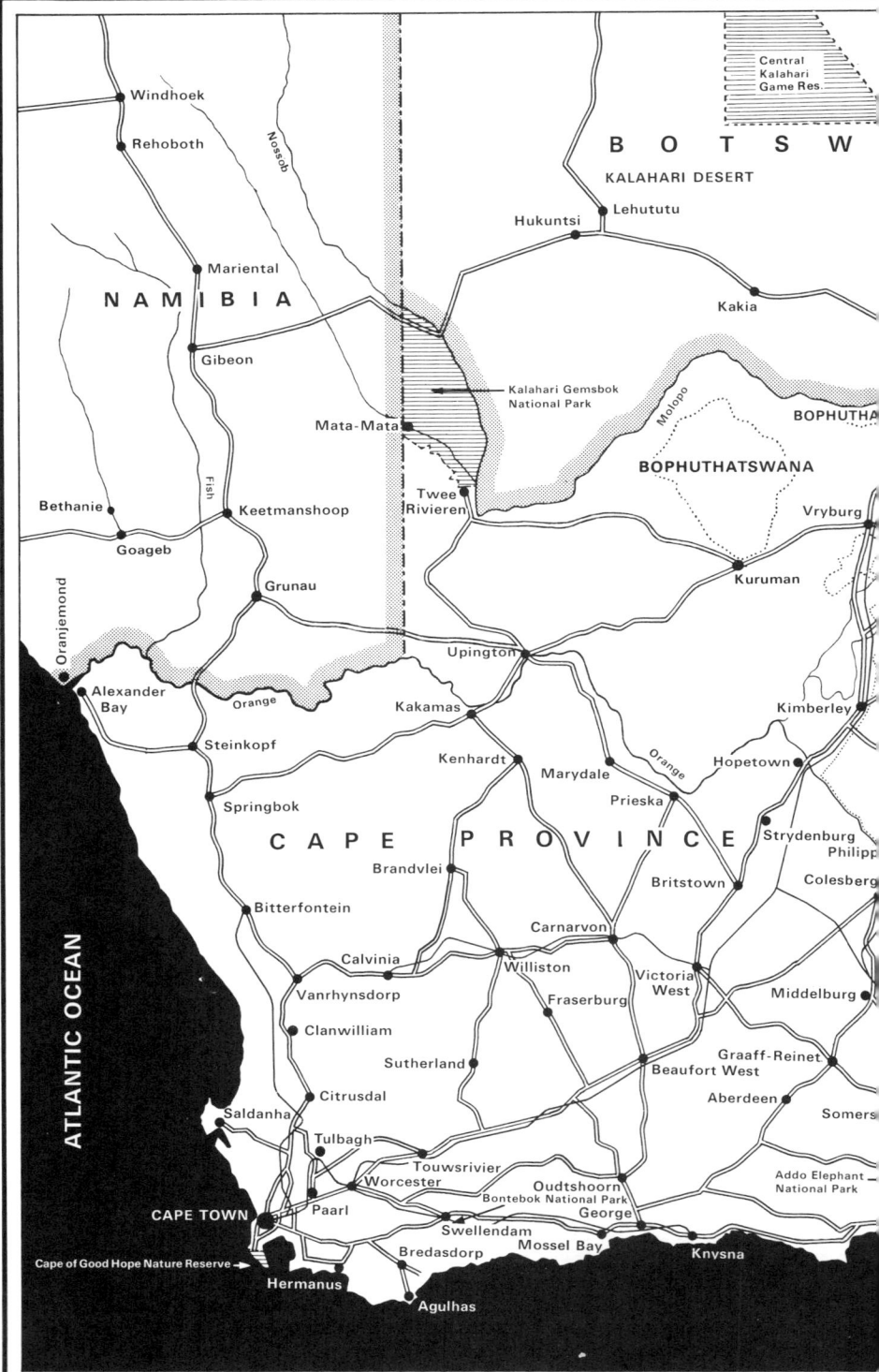

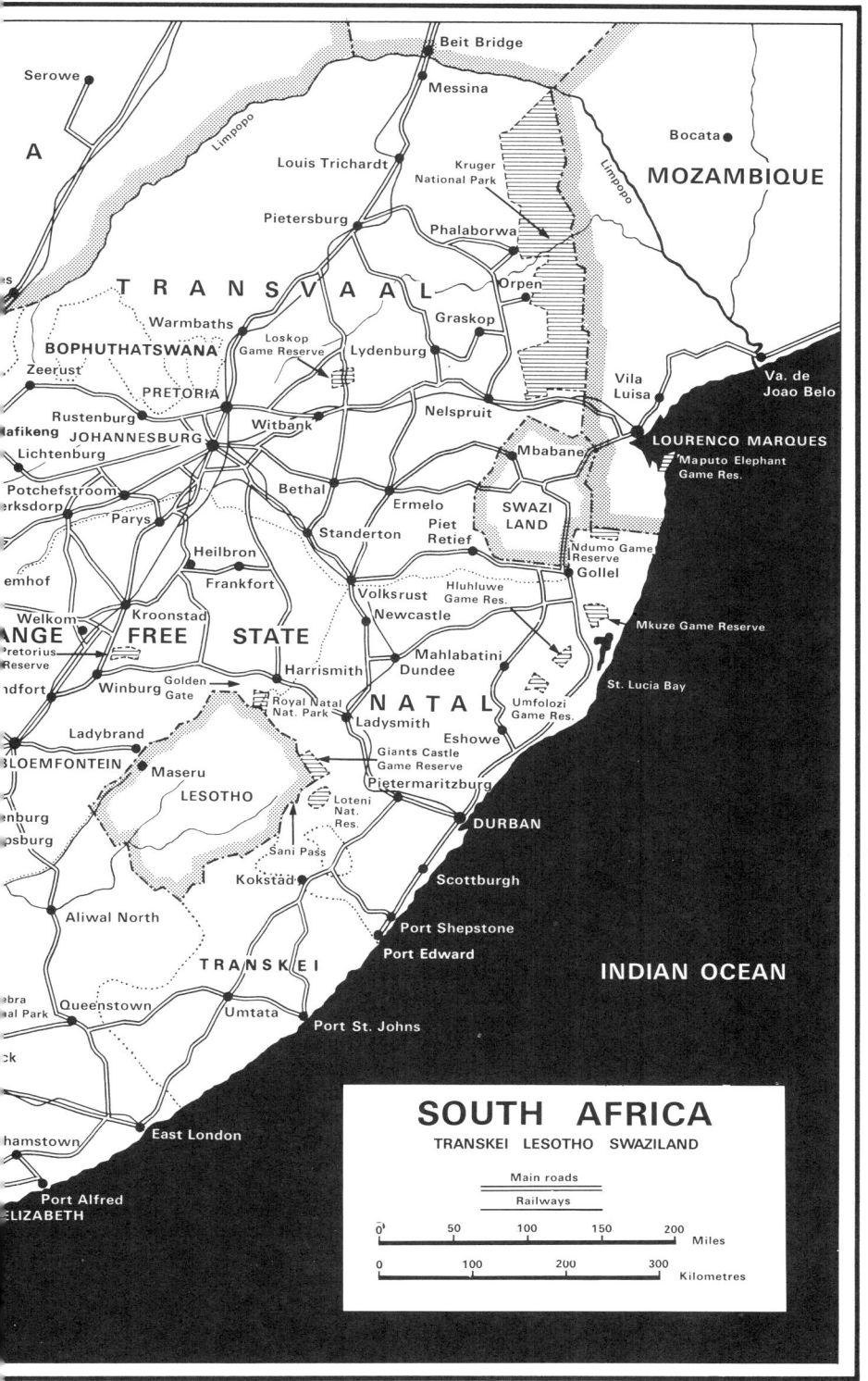

Serowe

A

Limpopo

Beit Bridge

Messina

Bocata

MOZAMBIQUE

Louis Trichardt

Kruger
National Park

Limpopo

Pietersburg

Phalaborwa

Va. de
Joao Belo

T R A N S V A A L

Orpen

Warmbaths

Graskop

Zeerust

Loskop
Game Reserve

Lydenburg

BOPHUTHATSWANA

PRETORIA

Nelspruit

Vila
Luisa

LOURENCO MARQUES

Rustenburg

afikeng

JOHANNESBURG

Witbank

Maputo Elephant
Game Res.

Lichtenburg

Mbabane

Bethal

Potchefstroom
rksdorp

Ermelo

SWAZI
LAND

Parys

Standerton

Piet
Retief

Ndumo Game
Reserve

emhof

Heilbron

Frankfort

Volksrust

Gollel

Hluhluwe
Game Res.

Welkom

Kroonstad

Newcastle

Mkuze Game Reserve

ANGE
retorius
Reserve

FREE   STATE

Harrismith

Mahlabatini
Dundee

St. Lucia Bay

dfort

Winburg

Golden
Gate

Royal Natal
Nat. Park

N A T A L

Umfolozi
Game Res.

Ladybrand

Ladysmith

Giants Castle
Game Reserve

Eshowe

BLOEMFONTEIN

Maseru

Pietermaritzburg

nburg
psburg

LESOTHO

Loteni
Nat.
Res.

DURBAN

Sani Pass

Kokstad

Scottburgh

Aliwal North

Port Shepstone

T R A N S K E I

Port Edward

INDIAN OCEAN

abra
al Park

Queenstown

Umtata

ck

Port St. Johns

hamstown

East London

Port Alfred
ELIZABETH

SOUTH   AFRICA

TRANSKEI LESOTHO SWAZILAND

Main roads

Railways

0	50	100	150	200

Miles

0	100	200	300

Kilometres

Index

174